RELIGION IN PSYCHODYNAMIC PERSPECTIVE

RELIGION IN PSYCHODYNAMIC PERSPECTIVE

The Contributions of Paul W. Pruyser

EDITED BY

H. Newton Malony
Bernard Spilka

New York Oxford
OXFORD UNIVERSITY PRESS
1991

Oxford University Press

Oxford New York Toronto
Delhi Bombay Calcutta Madras Karachi
Petaling Jaya Singapore Hong Kong Tokyo
Nairobi Dar es Salaam Cape Town
Melbourne Auckland

and associated companies in
Berlin Ibadan

Published by Oxford University Press, Inc.
200 Madison Avenue, New York, NY 10016

Library of Congress Cataloging-in-Publication Data
Pruyser, Paul W.
Religion in psychodynamic perspective: the contributions of
Paul W. Pruyser / edited by H. Newton Malony, Bernard Spilka.
p. cm.
Includes bibliographical references and index.
ISBN 0-19-506234-5
1. Christianity—Psychology. 2. Psychoanalysis and religion.
I. Malony, H. Newton. II. Spilka, Bernard, 1926- . III. Title.
BR110.P74 1991
200'.1'9—dc20 90-47084 CIP

2 4 6 8 9 7 5 3 1

Printed in the United States of America
on acid-free paper

To Jansje Martha Pruyser

Preface

This book brings together several of the seminal writings of Paul W. Pruyser.

At the time of his death on April 9, 1987, Pruyser was the Director of The Interdisciplinary Studies Program and Emeritus Henry March Pfeiffer Professor of Research and Education in Psychiatry at the Menninger Foundation in Topeka, Kansas. Coming to Kansas in 1954 as a senior psychologist at Topeka State Hospital, Pruyser joined the staff at Menninger's two years later.

An able clinical psychologist and a notable psychologist of religion, he was able to lecture on such widely divergent topics as the localization of brain dysfunction as well as the psychological dynamics of St. Augustine. The *Bulletin of the Menninger Clinic* stated his creativity well: "Paul was an inspired and inspiring teacher; his enthusiasm for teaching comes through in his prolific writing" (1987, p. 416). He wrote five books, 27 book chapters, and more than 80 journal articles. One memorial tribute declared, "Paul was a psychologist in the broadest sense; like William James, whom he greatly admired, he was fascinated by all perspectives on the human psyche and he was equally conversant with the brain and with the spirit" (1987, p. 417).

Among his books are three that assured his place among the best known of this century's psychologists of religion. They were *A Dynamic Psychology of Religion* (1968), *Between Belief and Unbelief* (1974), and *The Minister as Diagnostician* (1976). These, in addition to such essays as those reprinted here, have made Paul Pruyser a prime spokesperson for understanding religion through sympathetic psychoanalytic eyes.

Pruyser involved himself with religion—personally and professionally. For many years he was a member and elder at the First

Presbyterian Church in Topeka. Serving on denominational and National Council of Churches committees, Pruyser was at one time president of the Society for the Scientific Study of Religion. Also, he was on the editorial boards of both *The Journal for the Scientific Study of Religion* and *Pastoral Psychology*. He was an adjunct lecturer in the Department of Religious Studies at the University of Kansas. Two high honors were given Pruyser by his colleagues, the Bier Award, by Division 36 of the American Psychological Association, and the Distinguished Contributions Award, by the American Association of Pastoral Counselors.

Paul Pruyser was our friend and colleague. Both of us spent time with him at the Menninger Foundation. We admired and were stimulated by his thinking. We are among the many who retain his influence in our work.

It was our conviction that Pruyser's contributions be made even more visible that led us to bring this selection of his essays together. In our belief they are seminal anchor points for understanding his approach. We offer them to students of religion and psychology certain that they will evoke the same type of thought and creativity that they have stimulated in us. Our introductory and summary essays will, we hope, assist readers in contextualizing and evaluating the essays.

Pasadena H.N.M.
Denver B.S.
September 1990

Contents

RELIGION IN PSYCHODYNAMIC PERSPECTIVE

1

An Appreciation of Paul Pruyser

reality as a whole cannot be fully defined
and is always individually edited

Though written at a time of great trial in his life, Paul Pruyser penned these words to describe not only his plight in "maintaining hope in adversity," but a fundamental fact of human existence.[1] This was a basic characteristic of the man. His life was an exercise in discovering primary truths, and he lived these realities with little concern for the niceties of convention.

"He was a rebel." Thus Jansje Pruyser opened our interview about her late husband. Indeed he was a rebel, but not one who was strident, noisy, or bellicose. Paul Pruyser brought a combination of intellect and charm to every topic of personal concern. He had the rare knack of propounding controversial and iconoclastic ideas in a manner that might elicit disagreement but never hostility. Insofar as "rebel" connotes "radical," he was a true radical, the kind who knew not to deviate in trivial, inconsequential ways, but to strike to the heart of the matter and take a stand on what really counted. He was therefore not one to contemplate the superficial, but searched instead for the essence of what it meant to be human. This led him to psychology and the practice of psychoanalysis, for both allowed him to look within the individual. Concurrently, there was another issue, the fact that people always exist in relationship, not only to others, but to a still largely undefined cosmos. But where can a person turn when the necessity is to locate oneself in the scheme of things? Pruyser chose religion, for its perspective centers on the relationship of men and women to ever larger contexts—to self, to others, and to the universe with its potential for the real and the ideal. Religion was united with clinical psychology, and the combination made Paul Pruyser one of the foremost psychologists of religion of the twentieth century.

Pruyser: The Man

How did Paul Pruyser become the person he was? Fortunately, to find the answer to this question we had three sources, his widow, Jansje Pruyser, his writings, and our own knowledge of him. First, Mrs. Pruyser was kind enough to spend time being interviewed, and we gained much insight into her husband through that interview. This magnificent woman cannot be treated as in that old canard "behind every great man there is a woman," for she shines in her own right. She was his companion—emotionally and intellectually—in the fullest sense. Second, Paul's writings contain many allusions to his personal life, his feelings, and his aspirations as he wove these ideas into his technical books and papers. Finally, our own personal and professional relationships with Paul Pruyser spanned the last 31 years of his life.

But what kind of a man was he? Where did he come from, and what contributed to his greatness? Though we enter the realms of theory and speculation here, our purpose is not to date the significant times in his life, but rather to identify some of the factors that influenced him.

The Significance of Father Loss

Self-Determination. Paul Pruyser was extremely young when his father died, and the lack of a strong socializing father figure was probably a significant influence in his willingness to stand against authority and convention. In more than a passing sense, as a young child he became the powerful father, the "man" in and over the world.

He tells us that, as a child, he played with the prayerful phrase "Our Father who art in heaven," and distinguished it from the early teaching that his own father was in heaven. Claiming on the level of reality to distinguish between the two referents, he notes an imaginative paralleling of the "fathers."[2] An analytic perspective could analogize from the loss of the father in the real world to the subsequent denial of an anthropomorphized deity. With this failure of attachment and rejection of the latter may come recognition, as William James noted, of how people need and "use their Gods." Divine power as an aspect of one's inner, subjective, autistic world, becomes a human construction, and a necessary legitimation for existential dominion and control vanishes. It is an inevitable step from such a revelation to the hope that Paul Pruyser expressed to students at a conservative Presbyterian college that they encounter failure so that "Such situations will help you find your essence"[3] (p. 480). This was a challenge to confront reality without fantasy and unnecessary dependency. These concerns were central components of his lifelong adventure, for in the last analysis, he knew he had to rely on himself.

Valuing Old Age. Much of the self-descriptive character of Pruyser's writing reveals a search for meaning in the loss of his father. An excellent example of this quest is found in one of his final papers, "Creativity in aging persons."[4] Although it has a personal quality, this is not an egocentric production, but rather a work that focuses on an important but neglected topic. Still, on a number of levels we see the man reflected in the words he chose. First, to put him in proper perspective, we need to dispel a popular myth, namely, the too widely accepted image of age as a time of total decline rather than a period of potential growth and development. Creativity and intellectual fruitfulness are considered characteristics of the young; Paul Pruyser repudiated this view, and for good reason. When he died, he was not young, and he was concerned both professionally and personally with age. He was not "the exception that proves the rules," but as correct logic would have it, his own works offer all the evidence necessary to relegate this myth to the oblivion it merits. Paul Pruyser was growing to the moment he died, and this is evidenced in his work on aging and creativity.

A second consideration is that Paul accepted the psychoanalytic view that creativity is related to the loss of "parents or siblings . . . in early childhood"[4] (p. 425). One can thus view his accomplishments as "both memorializing a lost person or relative and then finding, or rather making, a symbolic restitution for that loss" (p. 426). In his own words, here is the death of his father.

While recognizing the negative aspects of aging, Pruyser makes his readers aware of the unique contributions that the elderly can make. Among the positive prospects he saw for aging, so many of which characterize him, one stands out—the assertion that "aging gives *a new freedom for revealing one's innermost thoughts*"[5] (p. 116). For him, "candor for speaking without inhibitions" (p. 116) was open honesty, with an element of challenge, if not demand, to those who may have been the objects of his insights. One had to grow regardless of age, and as Paul continued to develop, he would not tolerate stagnation in those with whom he interacted.

Becoming an Individual

Achieving identity and individuality requires strong internal controls, and such were developed within a loving and supportive home atmosphere cultivated by Paul's mother, to whom he was strongly devoted. Three brothers, and a close extended family round out this picture of a household in which he could develop his potential. This was also a home steeped in the Dutch Reformed tradition; he was educated early in a Dutch Calvinist school, where he encountered a rigid and restricting atmosphere that contrasted markedly with that of his home. The God-of-the-school constituted authority to be questioned, and Paul saw himself forced into a perspectival choice by the sharpness of this home–school divergence. Therefore, by the time he reached adolescence, he had explicitly rejected the ritual, rules, and imagery of the reformed tradition.

An iconoclastic pattern was developing that would continue for the rest of his life. He was not going to accept blindly the dictates and strictures of any authority. This was further evidenced during the Nazi occupation of Holland when he became a member of the Dutch underground. It was here that he met Jansje Fontijn, his future wife, a woman much like himself, ready to challenge conformist doctrine and institutional power. They also shared a common understanding and appreciation of art, nature, and reality that is found in too few relationships.

The Role of Religion

Creating a Personal Faith

Even though Paul Pruyser refused to accept the Dutch Reformed religious tradition, he did not deny the significance of faith and preferred to cultivate a personal system that was both intellectually and experientially satisfying. This system did not have to exist outside a formal religious framework, hence there was never any simplistic rejection of the institutional church. In fact, for many years he was an active member of the Presbyterian Church. Nevertheless, for the last 15 years of his life he did not attend services. It was clear from early in his life, however, that religion would have to touch deep personal chords in his personality, and these were usually aesthetic, moral, and intellectual. Many of these elements were united in his understanding of worship, and one may ask if they also express a dream of how he might have wanted to relate to his own father.[2]

> The hand of God, much talked about in school, was closer to my mother's tender-and-firm hand than to the threatening and often slapping extremities of my teachers. Small wonder then, that I have always found the highlight of worship the benevolently outstretched hands of a fulsome pastoral blessing, and that one of my dearest pictures is Rembrandt's etching of the father blessing the prodigal son on his return home. (p. 363)

In addition, religion clearly exercised Paul's intelligence and sensitivities. He conceived of spiritual transcendence and mystery as stimulants to thought, action, and enlightenment.

The Need for a Realistic Religion

The symbolic playfulness with which Paul treated religion as a child was an ever-present aspect of his adult life. His imagination and emotions were constantly aroused by spiritual forms, but most of all by what he regarded as the potential in religion for growth. At the same time, he was alert to the aspects of formal and personal faith that counter the ability and motivation of people to cope realistically with the world.[6]

Despite clear differences between his own position and that of the Dutch Reformed tradition, Paul Pruyser was eventually confirmed in the church, but, because of his resistance to conformity, this occurred later than for his siblings. In part, he probably took this step to please his mother. He was still not going to be "one of the flock," but instead, a voice of protest against the easy religious answer regardless of its source. Whether the latter were scripture, church doctrine, or one who wore the badge of ecclesiastical authority, nothing was "sacred" except the freedom to challenge and search for new answers. He sought a "healthy religion . . . a search demanding the greatest curiosity, the full use of all human functions, talents, and gifts, and the belief that the search, long and arduous as it may be, holds a promise"[6] (p. 348). In keeping with this viewpoint, and probably to search for this "promise," during early adolescence he enjoyed attending catechism class, but primarily for the intellectual stimulation. From the established perspective, his approach was likely to connote "rebelliousness."

One noteworthy incident reveals Paul's drive to understand religion with a totally open mind. While in graduate school, he did translations from German for a Presbyterian minister. Never willing to let an opportunity for informed debate pass, he argued with the minister. At one point, his opponent, unexpectedly but apparently correctly, accused Pruyser of hubris. He recognized the validity of the accusation and he and his wife then joined that minister's congregation.

Realistic Religion: A Problem in Reason and Feeling

Jansje Pruyser put it well when she said, "He had to explain, explain up to the point of the 'leap of faith.'" This is a pivotal assertion for it opens the door to Paul Pruyser's innermost thoughts; it reveals something of his personal struggle with reason and feeling. In his system, both had their place and their limits, and resolving this conflict explains the energy he put into understanding religion. His examination of religion was an avenue to self-comprehension. D. W. Winnicott's system describes Paul's rational approach to faith, for he sought a middle ground between the inner world of total subjectivity (feeling) and the outer sphere of objective reality (reason). As much as he distinctly rejected the autistic realm of religion, it is difficult to know to what degree religion as illusion in his personal life included spiritual referents in the objective world. Such referents were undoubtedly there, but they remained undefined. They could also have been part of the inner secret religion to which Clark refers[7] as the ideas and images that people always keep to themselves, no matter how close they may be to other people.

Like most psychoanalytic thinkers, Paul Pruyser's epistemology looked to the inner life and essentially avoided analysis and denotation of the constituents of the "real" world. When it came to transcendent possibilities, he was consistent in his writings and refused to succumb to fantasy. He would not claim as knowledge that which was obviously belief.

We suspect that Paul was writing about himself when he said, "in some intellectuals with critical and analytical minds their engagement in psychology of religion is a substitute for, or a once-removed form of engagement in religious thought"[8] (p. 175). In his writings the line between psychological and theological thought is often blurred. Recognizing this, he suggested "that the disciplines of psychology and religion can function vis-à-vis one another in the first place as ancillary sciences"[8] (p. 176). Though questions can be raised about the meaning of science, this stance is at the core of much modern theology, particularly that denoted as stressing process.[9]

Connotations of Personal Faith

In a paper[1] that he frankly termed self-descriptive and a "statement of personal belief,"[10] Paul Pruyser identified with the position of his namesake, the apostle Paul, whose "only certainty is that the Creator who presided over his birth and his life will also be present at his death—and it is just this *presence* of God in mankind's life and death that makes all the difference" (p. 473). At that time, Paul was battling cancer and was concerned, as he put it, with the "meaning of reality." This involved "a passionate mental action, a choice, a commitment, in which one draws upon a philosophy of life, a religion" (p. 470). This emphasis may have been accentuated by his illness, but the "meaning of reality" as inner reality was always his interest. In what he termed "perspectival integrity,"[8] such meaning resulted in the integration of his psychology with what we venture to call "his theology."

Paul Pruyser could not accept the illusionary religion of most people, but he did accept one view of Freud that "illusions need not be necessarily false—that is to say, unrealizable or in contradiction to reality"[11] (p. 164). Though Paul Pruyser strongly identified with this position, he firmly rejected "Freud's pejorative application of the term *illusion* to religion" (p. 164), particularly because it was premised on Freud's personal antipathy to religion, and on Freud's positivism. Nevertheless, Paul accepted religion as illusionistic in the Winnicottian sense, as part of that "third world" between the realms of internal fantasy and external reality.

For Pruyser, Winnicott's system left the door open to an independent, objective reality that could be termed *religious*. This has been alluded to in a number of his works. One may ask if it is part of his self-avowed identification with the concept of "hoping" as opposed to "wishing," when he accepts the view that the former "is based on a belief that there is *some benevolent disposition toward oneself somewhere in the universe, conveyed by a caring person*[1] (p. 467). But even this may be too strong an expression. He was quite averse to defining the elements of a spiritual domain. More appropriate may be the imagery he used to close his 1968 *A Dynamic Psychology of Religion.*[12] Here he offered the metaphor of a screen, which necessarily possesses two sides. On one side are the wishes, dreams, and projections of people; on the other side he placed ultimate reality and the divine referents and symbols of humanity. Here was Paul Pruyser's "leap of faith."

To heighten his reader's appreciation of what he had in mind, he was not going to admit any semblance of anthropomorphism into this faith, and he was quite willing to shock those who hold such images. Relative to a religion of maturity found in some of his aging friends, and one with which he explicitly identified, he spoke of a "religiousness [that for some people] may become atheistic in the sense that they no longer feel impelled to pay homage to a quasi-human God in worship and prayer"[8] (pp. 178–179). His substitute was "a more abstract principle of cosmic creativity, ethical value, or ultimate truth"[8] (p. 178). This is the deity of much of modern theology; this is also the talk of reason, not of feeling, and Paul Pruyser made many concessions to feeling that tempered his commitment to the abstract faith that reason demands.

Searching for Experiential Religion

Paul Pruyser saw ritual as an avenue to religious experience, and when he was active in the church, he partook of the sacraments. But even here he objected to the cheapening of established symbolism. He wanted wine, not grape juice; real bread, not tiny pieces. Reason gave way to feeling and the memories of childhood seasoning.

Authentic religious experience was actively sought through aesthetic and intellectual avenues. His "Lessons from Art Theory for the Psychology of Religion"[13] is not only a brilliant paralleling of art and religion through a Winnicottian analysis, but also a discussion that freely, if not enthusiastically, employs experiential language. He offers his own point of view when he claims that "both [music and art] strike us as awesome in their manner of confronting us, blissful in the momentary happiness they produce, tantalizing in demanding our recognition, assent, or belief"[13] (p. 2). The connection is further personalized when he asserts, "I cannot shed the associations between religion and art which beset my stream of consciousness" (p. 3). The remainder of the paper continues this play of emotional expression versus reason.

The Importance of Music. Music, as part of public worship services was extremely important to Paul, and he distinguished unambiguously between the various kinds of music one heard in church. Disapproving of what he felt were shallow musical forms that appealed solely to neurotic wishes and "pacific libidinal fantasies"[6] (p. 334), he demanded that which could only be called "creatively real." Under this rubric one found the ageless works of Bach and other great classical composers, who have often expressed their artistic needs in religious themes.

Authentic religious expression via music was not, however, restricted to the classical realm, but included folk productions. We remember the enthusiasm Paul manifested when a powerful old Welsh hymn was used in a religious service. In an ensuing discussion of Erikson's *Young Man Luther*—a discussion that might have been stimulated by this music—Pruyser lamented the fact that Luther's rigorously structured personality did not allow him to have intense religious experiences. The impression was created that he, like Luther, aspired to such experience.

Intellectual Experience. The search for religious expression probably extended to all aspects of Paul Pruyser's life, not the least of which was his love of learning. One may ask if such motivation spurred him to use his knowledge of Greek and Latin to translate Erasmus from the Latin and read the Bible in Greek. His writings abound with poetry, citations from philosophy, theology, history, and what might be termed the arts and humanities in general. Though, he was less inclined to mention the sciences, it was clear that reading and learning were themselves experiential forms of great personal importance.

A Place for Tradition. Although they were not married in the church, when their children were young, Paul and Jansje Pruyser prayed at table and engaged in Bible reading in their home. Old Testament stories were employed to teach values, and Paul delighted in transforming these into dramas that elicited great emotion from both his children and his grandchildren. On one occasion, his audience was so moved that tears rolled down the cheeks of his young listeners.

Though he preferred private prayer over public prayer, he did engage in formal prayer during his last stay in the hospital. Jansje Pruyser felt that "His writing and his whole being was almost praying." She further asserted that her husband's writing was "poetry," and there is some evidence that he did write poetry.[14] More common was his ability to turn a phrase and make prose poetical. As avid readers of his works, we know the exhilaration such poetic expression can arouse. The thrill of writing was undoubtedly another exercise in his quest for experience and personal expression.

The Contributions of Paul Pruyser

Paul Pruyser was a prolific writer. Author, coauthor, or editor of eight books, 27 book chapters, over 80 papers, and 150 book reviews, plus innumerable book notes, he influenced vast numbers of scholars. His contributions, however, were not restricted to the written word. He was also a popular lecturer, and his audiences were invariably awed by his scholarship. It was a privilege to be a part of such an audience and to listen to what he had to say. He was a man of ideas, and his creativity and ingenuity were always abundantly evident.

When we characterize Paul Pruyser as a psychology scholar, this is not to say that he was a researcher in the sense that modern psychology uses this term. He opposed the positivistic stance underlying mainstream psychology and adopted a posture that might be called "humanistic psychoanalysis." His intent was praxis, but his strength was first in theory. Though his clinical skills permitted him to translate his ideas to the realm of application, they usually remained on a plane above the level of practice. We believe that future researchers will find ways of systematically operationalizing the concepts he advanced.

At present, the scientific character of psychoanalysis remains controversial.[15] Paul would have taken a stand supporting psychoanalysis as science, but he himself was much more a clinician and humanistic theoretician than a rigorous scientist. In addition, the position that psychoanalysis is a science has been questioned by the dominant contemporary version of the philosophy of science.[16,17] Given conceptions like those advanced by Paul Pruyser, the door must remain open for psychoanalysis to evidence its public nature, its reproducibility, and its validity. Though it will take time, psychologists of religion will undoubtedly attempt to find ways to transform his ideas into objective empirical data.

The Plan of the Book

In this book, we offer a small but representative collection of Paul Pruyser's major work. Eventually, we expect that his books and papers, like the work of William James, will be brought together as "collected works." His 1968 *Dynamic Psychology of Religion* is already a classic in the psychology of religion, and *Between Belief and Unbelief* (1974) will undoubtedly soon follow. Likewise, *The Play of the Imagination* (1983) is gathering a following in psychoanalytic circles. The books can be read over and over again, and with each reading new insights evolve. Pruyser was not simply a scholar for his own time but a thinker whose contributions will be relevant for psychoanalysis, the psychology of religion, and clinical psychology for many years to come.

With the present collection, we have sought to demonstrate the range and depth of Paul Pruyser's thinking. Here we see how he viewed (1) contemporary religion and religious beliefs, (2) some of the functions of religion relative to praxis and theology, (3) what method in the study of religion meant to him, (4) his central interest in the origins of religion, and finally (5) his ideas on what the future of the psychology of religion should be.

Opening with a very significant paper titled "A Psychological View of Religion in the 1970s,"[18] it is apparent that, although this was written as the 1970s opened, the message was not an agenda for that decade but for, as he broadly stated, "man's religious quest in the future" (p. 77). There are no time limits to his evaluations and prognostications, and they are as relevant for the 1990s as they were 20 years ago. Drawing material from Freud and a number of modern theologians, Pruyser indicates why religion will continue to be with us into the indefinite future.

His second message is a harsh one, namely that much of the force of current religion comes from the persistence of irrationality in both our culture and our individual lives. Among the effects of irrationality that he decried is the sponsorship of a consoling faith as opposed to a challenging one. Finally, as gospel, he brings religion to bear on "real world" problems of humanity's place in nature, the issues of equality, authority, privacy, intimacy, death and dying, and one of his own intimate concerns, the investigation of experiential religion. This initial paper shows the grand scope of Paul Pruyser's aspirations and vision.

"The Seamy Side of Current Religious Beliefs"[6] is a starkly blunt critique of what institutional religion can do to reduce human potential. This approach permitted Pruyser to introduce his concepts of neurotic and healthy religion, and with the latter he offered a framework that sounds remarkably like the goals of process, liberation, and feminist theologies.

"Narcissism in Contemporary Religion" further specifies some of the elements in the above paper, but does so through a psychoanalytic and theological focus on narcissistic and anti-narcissistic components in modern religion. In it Pruyser explores theological and institutional supports for self-love plus motifs that attempt to put humanity "in its place" relative to God and the temptation for self-aggrandizement, glorification, and separation. The social order is coordinated with contemporary religion to show how both mutually reinforce self-centeredness. This paper is a special tribute to Pruyser's scholarship.

Relatively speaking, the foregoing papers are concerned with abstract issues that have important repercussions in everyday life. They are representative of the majority of Pruyser's writings and illustrate very well the breadth of his knowledge and his intellectual strength. At the same time, as a clinician, he was oriented toward application and practice. Most of his writings on such topics integrated pastoral and clinical psychology. Of particular note is the book *The Minister as Diagnostician: Personal Problems in Pastoral Perspective.*[19] The paper "Religion in the Psychiatric Hospital: A Reassessment," which is presented here as Chapter 5, is an example of this genre. Aware that clinical personnel in the psychiatric hospital invariably ignore the religious aspect of the person, Pruyser showed how inappropriate this is, for such information may be significant in diagnosis. He further recognized the importance of the multidisciplinary mental health team for meeting the various needs of patients. Where traditional teams might include a nurse, social worker, psychiatrist, psychologist, and possibly other therapists, Pruyser points out the vital roles a chaplain might play for patients. Nevertheless he advocates a team in which any member can deal with any topic, and this includes religion. In the last analysis, this paper is not an appeal for professional identity, perspective, or integrity, but rather for patient-centering.

"Anxiety and Guilt in the Atonement"[20] is a fascinating exercise in theological psychology. Initially, one may get the not so far-fetched impression that Paul Pruyser was a frustrated theologian masquerading as a psychologist. His grasp of history and theology relative to atonement is breathtaking. While explaining what he calls the ransom, satisfaction, and moral influence theories of the atonement, he integrates them with the functional roles of ego, superego, and id. Never satisfied, he then criticizes himself so that readers will cautiously consider the generalizations he makes. He thus demands awareness of the complexity of the issues with which he deals. The basic theme is that theology and psychology are inseparable, and that their intertwined natures may be understood via a phenomenological approach. If anything, this paper is a call for creative thinking when one attempts to comprehend the subtle nuances of religion–psychology associations.

Shifting from the functions of religion in the personality, Pruyser reveals how theology and religion have practical import. Though the emphasis is now on praxis—the use of knowledge and skills—Pruyser could never abandon theory, which to him, was always primary. In his "Assessment of the Patient's Religious Attitudes in the Psychiatric Case Study,"[21] the issue of the role of religion in diagnosis, and, by implication, in treatment, continues the theme from "Religion in the Psychiatric Hospital." Now the problem is much more fully developed as Paul Pruyser analyzes in depth the reasons mental health professionals avoid dealing with the patient's faith. Among those offered, he presents an original analysis of transference and countertransference factors in this process.

Religion is analyzed in depth relative to a variety of ways in which it may be expressed, and these are viewed as coping devices, both normal and abnormal, on the part of the individual. The editors know of no other source where religious psychopathology is detailed in such a clear and succinct manner as one finds in this paper. A brief, but insightful treatment of the new religions concludes the paper.

"Psychoanalytic Method in the Study of Religious Meanings"[22] is a wonderfully well written treatise on the use of the free-association method. Through personal examples that give us much insight into himself, Pruyser shows us how this approach yields information. What is probably of greatest significance is the framework within which this psychoanalytic technique is placed. Here we are treated to the meanings of a variety of viewpoints—holistic, dynamic, adaptive, and developmental. Never one to be reckless, he elaborates on the lack of data available and the need for norms, and he points the way to how such information may be gained. This paper may use the word "method" in its title, but it is no exposition of procedure per se, but rather of praxis in theoretical perspective.

Turning from methodological considerations to the dynamics of religion, we are introduced to Paul Pruyser's treatment of Winnicott's theoretical framework. First, in "Psychological roots and branches of belief,"[23] we are given not only a psychoanalytic view of the concept of belief, but an approach with more than a passing nod to philosophy. The definitions of belief and their association with personal identity touch on Hume, Kant, and the phenomenologists. Ranging far and wide in his examples, Pruyser stressed the functionality of religion for the individual. A discussion of illusionistic thinking à la Winnicott offers entree into the way beliefs are developed and relate to the inner autistic realm and the external reality of coping with life. This should be a core paper for psychoanalytically oriented scholars.

"Forms and Functions of the Imagination in Religion"[2] will undoubtedly acquire the status of a "classic" in the psychology of religion. In it, Pruyser claimed to "combine two of my major intellectual preoccupations, namely, the nature of creativity and the nature of illusionistic thought" (p. 354). Much is borrowed from his book *The Play of the Imagination*,[11] but in his work nothing is ever exactly the same. The writing is tighter, new illustrations are introduced, and what has been said previously is read as fresh, innovative ideas. This is primarily an adaptation of Winnicott's ideas to the psychology of religion, and with superb organization, illusionary thinking is detailed by both personal example and impersonal theory. Though the association of illusion with the inner world is discussed, greater emphasis is placed on the relationship of the illusionary transitional sphere with external reality. Paul Pruyser was not one to allow his readers an opportunity to forget the final power of life in the "real world."

The last paper in this collection, "Where Do We Go From Here? Scenarios for the Psychology of Religion," in a sense, brings us back to the opening work on "A Psychological View of Religion in the 1970s." Both show the breadth of Pruyser's vision for the psychology of religion. Sixteen years separates the two offerings, yet they are complementary. The later effort has the benefit of all the thinking and writing that intervened. It shows a different organizational rigor that shifts from the earlier work's stress on religion per se to the state of the psychology of religion, or rather, "psychologies of religion." Many creative questions are posed regarding conceptualization of the discipline. Areas for research are carved out, and these possess an integrative quality that applies not only to the psychology of religion but also to other burgeoning fields in psychology, such as the domain of aging, and what might broadly be termed "social cognition." As could be expected, Pruyser brings the views of "outsiders" like Erwin Goodenough and Bernard Lonergan to bear on the psychology of religion. More doors are opened for thinkers in the field.

Finally, we have the pleasure of commenting further on this extraordinary scholar. He was a man of many ideas; a visionary of truly great intellectual, aesthetic, and moral proportions. In the last analysis, he was a brilliant comet in our psychological firmament, or as Santayana would say, "a lyric cry in the midst of the wilderness." We were privileged to know Paul Pruyser, and we hope that this collection will be intellectually enlightening and that it will also convey the richness of his mind and his feeling for humanity and the world of ideas.

Notes

1. In Maintaining Hope in Diversity. *Bulletin of the Menninger Clinic*, 1987, *51*, 463–474, p. 465.
2. Pruyser, P. W. Forms and functions of the imagination in religion. *Bulletin of the Menninger Clinic, 49*, 353–370, 1985.
3. Pruyser, P. W. Now what? *Bulletin of the Menninger Clinic, 51*, 475–480, 1987.
4. Pruyser, P. W. Creativity in aging persons. *Bulletin of the Menninger Clinic, 51*, 425–435, 1987.
5. Pruyser, P. W. Aging: downward, upward, or forward? *Pastoral Psychology, 24*, 102–118, 1975.
6. Pruyser, P. W. The seamy side of current religious beliefs. *Bulletin of the Menninger Clinic, 41*, 329–348, 1977.
7. Clark, W. H. *The Psychology of Religion*. New York: Macmillan, 1958.
8. Pruyser, P. W. Where do we go from here? Scenarios for the psychology of religion. *Journal for the Scientific Study of Religion, 26*, 173–181, 1987.
9. Spilka, B., Bridges, R. A. Theology and psychological theory: Psychological implications of some modern theologies. *Journal of Psychology and Theology, 17*, 343–351, 1989.
10. Pruyser, P. W. (12 February) Letter to B. Spilka, 1987.
11. Pruyser, P. W. *The Play of the Imagination*. New York: International Universities Press, 1983.
12. Pruyser, P. W. *A Dynamic Psychology of Religion*. New York: Harper & Row, 1968.
13. Pruyser, P. W. Lessons from art theory for the psychology of religion. *Journal for the Scientific Study of Religion, 15*, 1–14, 1976.
14. Pruyser, P. W. An author's alphabet. *Bulletin of the Menninger Clinic, 51*, 500–504, 1987.
15. Rubinstein, B. B. *Psychoanalysis and Contemporary Science*. Vol. II, New York: Macmillan, 1973.

16. Appel, K. E. Psychoanalysis and scientific thought. in J. H. Masserman (ed.), *Science and Psychoanalysis. Vol. 1: Integrative Studies.* New York: Grune & Stratton, 1958.
17. Hook, S. (ed.) *Psychoanalysis, Scientific Method,and Philosophy.* New York: New York University Press, 1959.
18. Pruyser, P. W. A psychological view of religion in the 1970s. *Bulletin of the Menninger Clinic, 35*, 77–97, 1971.
19. Pruyser, P. W. *The Minister as Diagnostician*. Philadelphia: Westminster, 1976.
20. Pruyser, P. W. Anxiety, guilt, and shame in the atonement. *Theology Today, 21*, 15–33, 1964.
21. Pruyser, P. W. Assessment of the patient's religious attitudes in the psychiatric case study. *Bulletin of the Menninger Clinic, 35*, 272–291, 1971.
22. Pruyser, P. W. Psychoanalytic method in the study of religious meanings. *Psychohistory Review, 6*, 45–50, 1978.
23. Pruyser, P. W. Psychological roots and branches of belief. *Pastoral Psychology, 28*, 8–20, 1979.

I

INTRODUCTION

2

A Psychological View of Religion in the 1970s

Despite Pope's bit about fools rushing in where angels fear to tread, looking into the future should not come under a special taboo. Preconstructing the future is as important as reconstructing the past and should be just as respectable. The manager makes his five- or ten-year plans; the scientist makes his predictions; the husband takes out life insurance; the housewife makes budgets; the prophet foretells; the trusting soul hopes. All of these expectations can be right or wrong, as time will tell. But so can be all the world's history books, the biographies of significant people, the reflections we have about our fathers and grandfathers and family trees. And, as clinicians know, we can be very wrong about the past by the selective memories and screen memories that each of us entertains about his own personal life. The look forward is no more prone to error than the look backward—both can be guided by secondary process thought or thwarted by primary process manifestations.

And so I shall address myself to man's religious quest in the future with a few constraints but without inhibitions. One constraint is that I will confine myself to the near future, say, the next decade. A second constraint is that I will handle time in the way Augustine proposed, namely, by assuming the coexistence of three qualities of time in the present: "A time present of things past; a time present of things present; and a time present of things future."[2] Thirdly, I shall try to remain in my area of expertise, which

Reprinted with the permission of the *Bulletin of the Menninger Clinic*, 1971, *53*(2), pp. 77–97.

is psychology, well knowing that religion has social, anthropological, philosophical, and various other dimensions as well.

My presentation will be in three parts. I shall first argue that religion will continue to influence the minds of men; I shall then look at manifestations of the irrational which influence religion or are intertwined with it; and third, I shall sketch new trends and forces that are likely to influence religion in a creative direction.

Psychological Reasons for the Continuity of Religion

To start with the most blatant point, I am comfortable in asserting that religion is here to stay, and we have no reason to expect any decline in religious activity. I am not making this claim on historical grounds, although these may be persuasive enough, but on the basis of psychodynamic realities. I am saying it in the first place on the grounds which Freud advanced about the psychological functions of religion and religiosity. One is that the irrational is ineradicable; it is our phylogenetic heritage and our ontogenetic burden. The irrational also permeates the social system whose institutions, mores, values, and language structures provide opportunity for reinforcing the potency of irrationality in the individual.

A second point that Freud made has to do with each man's tendency to claim omnipotence for himself, and the chronic difficulty he has in relinquishing this claim. Freud defined animism as the state in which omnipotence of thought is expressed in magic rituals. He defined religion as a state in which one cedes some omnipotence to his gods while retaining a portion of it for himself in order to influence these gods in his favor. He went on to describe science and reason as a state in which omnipotence is overcome, with resignation to the overpowering forces of nature and necessity. But he still recognized in that condition a remnant of omnipotent thinking in the belief that the mind has the power to cope with reality. It is interesting to note that this psychodynamic observation about the omnipotence of thought which individuals assume for themselves also lies at the heart of some definitions of religion by religionists. I quote one of its modern formulations, recently given by the church historian Sidney Mead: " . . . no man is God. This is what I understand to be the functional meaning of 'God' in human experience. Whatever 'God' may be—if indeed being is applicable to 'God'—a concept of the infinite seems to me necessary if we are to state the all-important fact about man: that he is finite."[3]

Freud described a third and very potent factor which seems to guarantee the continuation of religion: the fact that religion is so gratifying. It promises so much, so persuasively, despite the demands it makes. For this very reason, religion cannot be seen as a sublimation: it stands by itself as a perennial form of wish fulfillment and need gratification. Religion, according to Freud, is not strict enough in demanding renunciation of infantile wishes; on the contrary, it condones them by symbolic satisfactions. It consoles man all too well in his sadness over having to grow up to an inevitable death. If anyone would dismiss Freud's insistence on renunciation as too stoical, he would inadvertently buttress Freud's argument, for it derives from the observation that religion is a very popular thing which most people engage in most of their lives and nearly all people during some time in their lives.

I have thus far cited only Freud's strictly psychological observations. If his anthropological and historical constructs from *Totem and Taboo* and *Moses and Monotheism* are taken into account,[4] another motive for religion is advanced: the dynamics of corporate and personal guiltfeelings and their expiation or mitigation. This is a very circular dynamic factor in the sense that religion, to the extent that it is one way of coping with the problem of guilt, tends to articulate and institutionalize itself in such a way that it entails secondary and tertiary chains of guiltfeelings and expiations. For instance, mere belief in God is not enough; one must also have faith in and loyalty to him and live up to his ordinances. One must also be loyal to the religious group and its demands. This makes religion a costly therapy for those who had naively hoped to be rid of guilt through religion in one fell swoop.

Finally, Freud did not peg religion to the presence of any special religious feeling or disposition in man. He anchored it in man's general feeling of helplessness in the face of the overpowering forces of nature, of which death is the most radical demonstration that no one can escape. And he anchored it also in man's feeling of helplessness and frustration in the face of the demands and structure of culture, which dispenses its gratifications unevenly, so that some men are dispossessed or oppressed. Building further on this thesis, I would hold that religion is, psychologically, something like a rescue operation, whatever other functions it may have or whatever it may be in essence. It is born from situations in which someone cries "Help!" The Salvation Army and the so-called evangelical groups know this, and the Psalmist gave it poetic expression in words that can move hearts of stone.

There are others whose work does postulate a special feeling or disposition to account for religion. Schleiermacher[5] did this with his "feeling of utter dependency" to which religion is the only and necessary answer. In a more sophisticated vein, Otto[6] spoke of man as having "a talent for numinous experience" and singled out the category of the Holy as a persistent dimension of life, just as independent and irreducible as the categories of Beauty and Justice. I side with this thesis, not only because it is so experiential, but also because of its methodological implications: on the questions of origin and development of religion, it lets religion come from religion, as art comes from art, and as ethics comes from ethics. Each category of experience has thus an inner consistency and specific dynamics.

Another group of arguments for the continuity of religion, particularly prominent today, is of a cognitive-linguistic order. These arguments involve the notions of symbolism and language games. Tillich[7] may be seen as an exponent of the symbol theory. For him, a culture is organized around symbols, i.e., very complex and highly value-laden cognitive structures which at once reveal and conceal, and which participate in the otherwise not quite graspable reality to which they point. Religious ideas and acts, the actualities of creed and cult, are just such symbols. The life blood of symbols comes from the hidden order of reality as well as man's need for cognitive grasp. The language game notion, developed mostly by British linguistic philosophers, adds to the symbol theory the idea that special aspects of life as lived require special words and rhetorics in which to take hold of their experiential peculiarities. Thus, religion can be seen as a special rhetoric, a serious game of words and phrases and syntax that one chooses to play when relevant, just as one may choose to play the language game of romantic love, of science, of poetry, or of art at other times. Both theories have the virtue that they can encompass developmental and historical observations. For instance, they enhance the likelihood of seeing that many erstwhile symbols have become mere signs or platitudinous emblems and that new symbols may be in the making without everybody knowing it. Or they help us perceive that certain religious phrases have become cheap little word-tokens, whereas new manners of speaking may be invented by creative individuals without guarantee of wide circulation for all of them.

And so, religion is born from religion and gives birth to religion. It fulfills persistent human needs. It addresses itself to perennial human themes. It revolves around symbols. It is a rhetoric. It gives satisfactions, albeit not without imposing new frustrations. Moreover, religion is so manifest, so concretized, so omnipresent, so patently real in its works and its trappings that anyone wishing to discard it or evade it or escape from it will have a hard time doing so. The religious circle, to speak with Tillich,[7] is so large that efforts at stepping out of it are likely to result only in finding relocations within it. Historically, and in the life histories of individuals, religion shows excesses and shortages, progressions and regressions, infantile and mature forms. The questions are: What can we say about activities in the religious circle during the next decade? What may be the tenor or forms of religious quest?

Preponderance of the Irrational

There is abundant evidence that irrationality will not only continue but is increasingly coming to the surface in proportion to reason. The signs of the zodiac are no longer an antique rarity; they are listed in contemporary dictionaries with the same prestige that adheres to tables of weights and measures, letters of alphabets, and monetary units used around the world, as if to suggest that they are an unquestioned part of the fabric of life. Horoscopes are a boon to any newspaper entrepreneur. Used as ornaments, the astral signs now produce income to anyone who has anything packaged to sell. Supernaturalism is again fashionable, not only among self-declared witches who are having a fitful renaissance a little over a hundred years after the last known witch-trial in the Western world, but also among millions of magazine readers who watch the witches' doings with fascination and vicarious satisfaction. Superpatriots are as vocal as ever in pairing God and country, and the God they mean to boost is typically some steady, strict, and disciplinarian, white-collar or blue-collar, father-God who has more affinity with pronouncements of the Federal Bureau of Investigation than with those of the National Council of Churches, and who is a far cry from the alleged "God of our fathers." The Supreme Court's school-prayer decision is still bitterly fought, not by the leaders of the major church establishments who have in fact welcomed the decision, but by individuals who insist on magical and ritualistic approaches to averting the loss of moral fibre which they see all around them. And unidentified flying objects have their devotees in organized clubs, whose members alert one another to fearsome electronic *Walpurgisnachts* in which modern incubi once more visit the earth.

Sadly enough, irrational phenomena are not confined to the lunatic fringe. In a recent speech, Robert Ebert,[8] Dean of the Harvard Medical School, called attention to widespread antiscientific attitudes in intellectually well-endowed people, the vehemence of which cannot be explained by the legitimate and limited fears which rational people may have of some of the undesirable consequences of certain scientific applications, such as the war industry. I would like to call attention to the aggressively ahistorical or antihistorical attitude of large numbers of students in higher education. While attention to the here and now and a dedication to current realities is in itself welcome, and certainly better than the kind of otherworldliness which lets this world go by, the new attitude seems to be based on impatience with time per se and reluctance to participate in processes that take time. It is paired with the feeling that the past has no instructional value and no accrued knowledge, so that one jumps into the future by seriatim short-lived impulses rather than planning for it by considered steps. To call such an attitude existential is only condoning it through euphemistic labeling. Much irrationality also adheres to the hue and cry for revolution in the sense that many would-be revolutionaries refuse to be instructed by the past about the all-important difference between successful and unsuccessful revolutions, and an assessment of their aftermath. It seems to me that when such attitudes prevail their irrationality will tend to stimulate two possible effects. On the one hand, it may produce homemade pieties and quasi-religiosity notable for displacement of numinosity from traditional gods to new objects. On the other hand it may, within the life of organized religion, promote inarticulateness, vagueness and incoherence because historical reflection and rational assessment are discarded in favor of private musings, whims, and fitful feelings.

Within organized religion, the penchant for supernaturalism takes a subtle form, full of technicalities. Much has been written about increasing polarization of attitudes within the churches, most often in regard to such large dimensions as the priestly versus the prophetic, the secular versus the sacred, and individual salvation versus corporate melioration. Stepping into the language game of the churches themselves, I think there is another polarization; namely, between those whose major devotion is to God and those whose major loyalty is to Jesus, taking both in the technical Christian sense as the first and second persons of the Trinity. The first group deals with the differences between the creator and the created. The latter group tends to take the incarnation seriously, and fosters the mechanism of identification; it emphasizes Jesus' concrete manhood and social commitments, his ethical activism, and the ambiguity of his having been both victor and victim. What I am trying to say is that, in reality, few people are trinitarians. Despite their creeds they pick and choose with distinct preferences. By and large, they either opt for a supernatural God about whom so little is known from naturalistic sources that he is indeed largely a compound of projections, or they opt for the better known, historical, more natural and more fully documented Jesus, puzzling as he may be, who had the capacity to confront people with existential human realities. Considering the widespread hostility of church members toward the God-is-dead theologians (whose arguments they have not been trained to understand in the first place), the unpopularity of Bonhoeffer among the majority of churchmen (his works are far more popular in the so-called secular campus culture), and the declining financial support for churches which have made efforts to take their cues for action from Bonhoeffer's "man for others," the supernaturalists seem as strong as ever, if not gaining ground.

Let no one confuse my use of the term supernaturalism with that fashionable existential word or that old theological term, transcendence. When I speak of supernaturalism I mean a stark, diehard, old-fashioned, more or less neo-Platonic or idealistic belief that ultimate reality is "out there" in the sky or beyond it, with a concomitant denigration of the world in which we live and the stuff we are made of, and with much freedom to fashion the assumed supernatural entities according to our tastes. Although Jesus too has at times been Platonized beyond recognition, I hold that according to the early documents and later creeds, and in the parlance of those Church members who opt for his manhood, he was far more empirical, far more structured and concrete, and had much greater delineation than any pie-in-the-sky god. But he was or is transcendent precisely in his unassailable character, in the consistency of his love theme, and in the radical application of his principle of nonviolence. Two great ethical leaders of man in our century saw him so: Gandhi and King. This kind of transcendence is not a matter of being a notch higher on an ontological ladder in some philosopher's book, but a mark of authenticity, of superiority in the courage to be. And the remarkable result of this transcendence is that by its power to confront people with its reality it leaves little room for dreaming, and less room for projection than does the blank screen of the sky behind which gods have their hiding places.

I wish I could say finer things, but I fear that bleak days lie ahead, both for the state of religion itself and for the role religion may have to play, through the persistence of primitive human longings and wishes, in the service of the politics of retaliation, vengeance, violence, and oppression so rampant throughout today's and tomorrow's world. Billy Graham's crusades and his words, which are both hortatory and fatherly-consoling, continue to attract large crowds. The President now has worship services in the White House, not with any congregation but with private guests, as at a party. The Vice-President lashes out at the National Council of Churches in the name of a good old-fashioned Word of a good old-fashioned God who has been tamed to subscribe to an alleged code of civil morality. The military industries have just allocated a huge fund for launching a public relations campaign through which they hope to improve their popular image. As the antipode of St. Francis, Eric Hoffer continues his hate campaign against nature and ridicules whole peoples who trail behind the fittest in the struggle for survival. Marcuse's élitism does not seem to scare his youthful readers. The military continues to maintain its tax-paid chaplains. Fathers Philip and Daniel Berrigan are in prison, and quite a few other courageous men live under the threat of imprisonment. Large networks of radio stations continue well-financed pious hate campaigns in the name of an entrenched, chauvinistic religiosity against those who would define religion more as a search than as a find. The Vatican has retrenched into an authoritarian position after the *aggiornamento* days of the late Pope John, whose *Pacem in Terris* seems to have been forgotten. The New Dutch Catechism has recently been supplemented by a much needed White Book that documents the immense power intrigue directed to its withdrawal from circulation. In Brazil the people are being tortured by their leaders. The recent movie, "Z", so frightening in its portrayal of the corruption that power brings, ends on a rather nihilistic note which is just not frightening enough, so that it actually teaches people to bear with it and manage a grin or two. But in that film, the generals and the police chiefs play god, while the right-wing speechmakers enhance their omnipotence by invoking god, just as Freud said the pious would. And while Freud may have had some kind of tunnel vision in seeing mostly the seamy side of religion, we need his observational acumen more than ever, for that seamy side is rather large and very strong.

Within the large religious circle, but between the subcirclets of denominationalism, lies the noteworthy phenomenon of system switching. Especially popular today are attempts made by many young men and women, brought up in Western religious lore, to espouse Eastern religious concepts and practices. Without for a moment denying the legitimacy and enrichment potential of serious efforts made by some people in that direction, my impression is that many others are less than serious in these pursuits and engage in a kind of faddism, whereby they end up being just as illiterate and inarticulate about their alleged newfound faith as they were about their old one. For instance, the precepts of Zen-Buddhism are widely misunderstood by those who have read a book or two about it as a diversion from regular college courses, and many readers have no inkling of the great demands it makes in self-discipline and assiduous training. Similarly, if mysticism is practiced as pill-induced instant mysticism without schooling, discipline, hard work, regular study, and self-abnegation, its benefits are of a very different order from those gained by the classical mystics in either the Western or the Eastern tradition. Shoddy religion remains shoddy religion, Eastern or Western, and the tree still has to be proven by its fruit.

All these signs from the world of politics and the world of religion point in one direction. There seems to be far more interest in consolation, quiescence, and immediate gratification of childish wishes for security, warmth, and stability than in searching for religious innovations or for creative new applications of religion to the exigencies of the modern world. There is more hankering after a consoling religion than espousal of a disturbing faith. To put it again in Freud's language, the primitive penchant for omnipotence of thought is very manifest. The homemade gods are tightly kept on the leash of all those pieties which were meant to tame and influence them. In fact, the dog metaphor could be amplified by an old observation of Karl Menninger[9] who noted that dogs and other pets represent symbolically the psychic values of a totem, sometimes a phallus. Dogs are in that sense extensions of our own body image.

The continuous power of the irrational also plays havoc with otherwise welcome attempts at self-renewal within organized church life. Let me make a few, almost random, observations. Recently I read an article in a major Protestant denominational family magazine[10] which summed up the results of research into the possible causes of declining enrollments in church schools. While the research findings led to some interesting conjectures which I do not wish to minimize, not a word was said about a major possible cause of dwindling attendance, namely, sheer boredom in students whose curiosity is constantly thwarted by the forces of tradition in content material and teaching methods. Apparently one does not say such things because the blinders which church officers wear within the system do not allow them even to see boredom as a possibility.

Far worse is the profound self-defeat inherent in the style and structure of religious education in most church schools, particularly Protestant ones. In a recent speech to specialists in religious education I found myself summarizing my critique in the following terse phrases: (1) Everything in church education is so contrived and presented as to convey to the would-be learner that he is not to take the offered instruction seriously. (2) There is a deep-seated dynamic resistance to learning in many affiliated church members which keeps the defeatist contrivances intact because these same church members benefit psychologically from them. What is this dynamic resistance? It is, as Freud noted, based on the fear of having to doubt the validity of one's religious precepts, of unveiling the motives which impel him to religious practices. And so we have many classes without enforced attendance, without tests of knowledge, without grades, without clearcut beginning and ending of courses, but only a tedious, ongoing grind that offends all learning principles.

A few more critical observations must be made which show persistent ambiguities within organized religion. Churches still resist paying local taxes, and by that posture they seem to indicate that they would rather see their cities bleed than break away from a tradition that no longer fits the exigencies of the modern world. Clergymen are still being judged by congregations in terms of their goodness of fit with the civil image of the parish; they are generally grossly underpaid, and the courageous ones among them are made the butt of jokes and vilification, despite the fact that they are also described as Reverend or Father. Though women far outnumber men in church membership and worship attendance, women have a very hard time being heard in the councils of religion. There are few social institutions with fiercer male dominance and discrimination against women than the churches. Though many believers talk of liturgical renewal and praise abstractly the idea of celebration, most of them are at a loss to indicate what they would celebrate and how the forms of celebration may be made commensurate with their object, let alone how celebration can evolve from the spirit of the celebrating subjects. Sensitivity training under any name is often being advocated as a congregational cure-all without the slightest concern for the goals it should enable people to attain, the limitations it has, and the dangers it entails. Lastly, there is that magnificent word "dialogue" which is on everybody's tongue while there is so sadly little disposition to it in the hearts of many churchmen. I described these situations earlier as ambiguous; now I add that they signal a profound ambivalence of feelings in the believers who themselves constantly hold the tenets of their own religion at bay. Indeed, omnipotence has not been fully ceded to the gods, and the affairs of the church are obviously not left to divine providence.

Promising New Themes in the Religious Quest

I have painted a bleak picture. I have said that religion is here to stay for the miserable reasons that forged its being. I have pointed to the persistence of irrationality and its increased visibility in our time. I have exposed the seamy side of religion, shown how large it is, and how many ominous signs at present combine to keep it strong. I have hinted at the defeatism and impotence inherent in some furtive attempts at self-renewal of religion. Is there anything else in the "present of things present" that should correct our picture of the "present of things future"? I have said nothing about religion as a way in which man's "talent for the numinous" is exercised for making existential discoveries, for the melioration not of man's lot but of his heart and mind, for giving form and content to our sense of wonder and our capacity for admiration, for broadening our view of reality so that we are open to the immense universe in which we have our being. Is there any hope that the religious quest may bring forth new answers to old problems, give new vistas to curious seekers, or approximate more closely the transformation of man from a sad into a happy creature? Yes, I think there is hope, and I shall try to sketch some of its grounds.

From a dozen trends I would single out as most important the reassessment of man's place in nature forced upon us by the gruesome effects of his spoliation of the earth. Most of us are still in shock over the discovery of what man has wrought, but already some better minds are pointing out that at the root of our predicament lies a religious problem, or more precisely, a theological misconstruction. It is that man has assumed dominion over creation, instead of fulfilling his duties of stewardship toward, and loving partnership with it. If the critical difference between dominion and stewardship is grasped, we may rediscover the happy Christianity of Saint Francis who saw brothers and sisters in birds, asses, wolves, and the celestial bodies, rejecting all arrogance. Religion should and can make the most of our condition of shock and use it to reeducate us to a fundamental transformation of our self-image in the chain of being.

The ecological theme should also be used to confront men and women with the narcissistic element in the complex of motives for self-propagation. The Biblical adhortation, "be fruitful and multiply," may have been constructive in an agrarian society with a high infant mortality rate, but it is becoming destructive in today's world. To take this text out of context and to turn it into an everlasting moral injunction is a pernicious form of fundamentalism—pernicious not only because of its disastrous consequences, but also because it fails to come to grips with the moral issue involved in self-reduplication. The issue is no longer whether *I* can survive in *my* offspring, whether *my* family or tribe or nation can survive, but whether mankind can survive. The solution of this issue will require, among other things, an entirely new theology of propagation and a new ethic of reproduction based upon a fresh assessment of the relations between the individual and the species, and the role of man in the whole order of creation.

A second trend to which I attach great importance is the reassessment now taking place of the relations between men and women. Though the noisier part of the Women's Liberation Movement appears to be largely secular, and is driven by very heterogeneous motives, religious convictions about the equality of men and women may be an important source of energy for its thrust. Right now, the Movement is rightfully indicting organized religion for its tenacious upholding of male dominance patterns in ecclesiastical structures, which stands in flagrant contrast to the human values which Christianity proclaims. Well-trained and professionally qualified women stand ready to assume ecclesiastical functions formerly held solely by men, and they are no longer willing to hide their lights under a bushel. Though they will have to overcome considerable resistance, they will undoubtedly assume leadership roles in religion, and it will be fascinating to see whether their ministries, pastorates, or priesthoods will give new shapes or special contents to the traditional religious quest of the Judeo-Christian mainstream in the Western world. There is already an effort to purge liturgical texts and ceremonial formulas of archaic patriarchal remnants, as in marriage ceremonies; to undo the misogynic heritage, and to discourage the use of Biblical proof texts which put women back into the place they had two thousand years ago in Hebrew or Hellenistic culture.

I believe that egalitarian relations between gender will affect the religious quest in several ways. Under the influence of vocal feminine leadership, religion will probably become more concerned with practical issues and is bound to become more activistic in the political and cultural arenas, if only because women represent a very large and underdeployed reservoir of energy. It is likely also that forms and instances of male hubris will be exposed which may have a salutary effect on the control of hubris in general. Women may be better than men in those ministries and pastorates which mobilize the laity to fulfill tasks and duties evolving from their creed; they may have real talent for the so-called enabling ministries which the clergy currently considers desirable but for which it seems temperamentally unfit. Contrary to an earlier speculation of

Jung, I predict that with increased ecclesiastical and theological leadership by women, Mariology will decline rather than flourish. In fact, it is already declining if attendance at novenas is taken as a measure. For much of its earlier growth over several centuries in Catholicism is attributable to male fantasies demanding a separation between spiritual and carnal women. Furthermore, articulate women are bound to give the declining fathers, divine or human, a new lease on life.

A third trend of importance for the religious quest now and in the near future is the increasing interest in attitudes toward death and dying. The controversy over the funeral industry a few years ago, and psychological studies on grief led to fresh observations about prevailing hospital practices. Now we see a willingness of educators in medical schools, and in geriatric and psychiatric training programs, to help health professionals come to terms with their feelings toward the dying patient. An awareness is growing that institutions and professionals have fostered the use of the denial mechanism regarding death, instead of promoting the realism that enables people to be reconciled with the inevitable. There is also some realization that the so-called triumphs of medicine which allow the forestalling of death at the cost of prolonged illness may be a mixed blessing, and that they should be subject to psychological and social critique.

Thanatology is the title of a journal through which these new interests in death and dying are being stimulated, and the very fact that we now have a word for this concern may help us rediscover the classical position which held that dying well is a part of living, if not the crown of a life worth living. On this point, Stoicism and Christianity have always met, albeit Christianity stands for elaborating the point by the role of hope. But then again, the idea of hoping is now being looked at critically by psychiatrists, psychologists, and theologians who have found, by and large, that much which passes for hope is in fact a rather blatant search for immature wish-fulfillment. Now that hoping, promising, and dying have become respectable research domains I expect that the religious quest in the next decade will be less preoccupied with speculations about the otherworldly shape of things to come in a hereafter and have more to say about the qualities of living including the process of dying.

In the meantime, there is a sobering lesson for demythologizers in a recent study[11,12] of attitudes toward death and dying conducted by Hempel which shows that large segments of the population, young and old, lustily continue to think in terms of a three-story universe and engage as heartily as ever in fantasies about pearly gates and welcoming committees at heavenly doors. I always thought with Freud that the voice of reason is soft, but persistent, but now I am more impressed by the persistence of unreason and its loudness. Jaspers may have been right in his debate with Bultmann[13] when he pointed to man's insatiable need for myth.

A fourth trend of significance is the narrowing of gaps between clergy and laity. This involves many details. I have mentioned the desire of many clergymen and laymen that pastoral leadership assume an enabling character: the enabling of laymen to perform tasks and functions formerly vested in the clergy's role. Arguments for the abolition of the celibacy rule for ordained priests can also be seen as an attempt to bridge the gap between clergy and laity, if it were only that it makes the priest who is free to marry appear more natural, more human, more laic in the original sense of the word, namely, more "one of the people." This can also be said of the desire of many clergymen to engage in a secular occupation in addition to their ministerial calling. Liturgical renewal, in demanding a more active congregational participation in worship, also assumes greater egalitarianism between clergymen and laymen. All these are signs of increasing democratization of institutional religion, with the important corollary that obedience to religious leaders, once a basic ingredient of the religious life and a virtue in itself, is on the decline.

Obedience to clergy and other religious authorities is likely to decline further, given the enormous discrepancies between top-level ecclesiastical rules and the demands of life as lived by millions of believers in regard to such practices as birth control, abortion, interfaith marriage, and premarital sexual intercourse. People who follow their personal ethics or the demands of their reality situation on these issues are apparently willing to, and psychologically capable of, putting up with a slightly uneasy conscience. We may thus infer that their guiltfeelings, if any, are weak, probably not so much because their values are corroded or their consciences lax, but because of a hope or conviction that the Church will eventually come around to their point. In other words, they see their church as a changing institution which will stand or fall by its relevance to life as lived.

It seems to me that Mitscherlich's book, *Society without the*

Father,[14] fosters a deeper understanding of these changes and prepares us for their inevitability. It throws light on the question of obedience which is so important to religion. Mitscherlich notes the gradual decline of patriarchalism and paternalism as Western culture has moved from an agrarian to an industrial form. The authority of the father becomes less, as does the contextual authority of tradition and institutions which gave to fathers and father-substitutes their strong roles and prescribed to the sons a subordinate posture. If the father-son relationship has indeed changed as significantly as Mitscherlich suggests, man will have to take back from the divine father-image and its ecclesiastical derivatives certain projections traditionally backed by experience and reinforced by the culture, but now no longer experiential. This, by the way, is one psychological reason for current constructions of theologies of the death of God.

If we no longer project the image of the agrarian head of household and provider onto our gods, what do we project? It would be too trite to suggest that the new projection is the image of the corporation manager who uses democratic, participatory management techniques. Father-son and father-daughter relations are too intimate and too emotional for any mere manager's image to be viable. Fathers will still be fatherly, and if they are no longer tribal heads, judges, or mouth-feeders, they will be needed as friends, advisors, instructors, advocates, and concerned emotional supporters who rejoice in the joys and suffer in the pains of their children. In a word, they are terribly important participants in the thoughts and feelings of their offspring. This image of friend and participant, with the capacity for intimacy may well be one of the newer projections the next generation will make onto the divine object. And it may be a healthy supplement to the authoritarian image with its demand for obedience. Such an image could also contain the element of a divine encourager, who invites the sons and daughters to come of age and take as much responsibility as possible for themselves. Indeed, Nouwen[15] speaks of religion as "a source of creative autonomy."

Along with a friendly and easily approachable God to whom one pays homage spontaneously because one can genuinely like Him rather than to do so only upon His stern command, there may come a rediscovery of the values of privacy and intimacy, with renewed respect for what Kierkegaard called the solitary individual.

In an age in which group experiences, group techniques, group actions, group values, and group confrontations are played to the hilt, when a book by Mary McCarthy with as unqualified a title as *The Group* quickly becomes a best seller, when churches are increasingly taking cues for their own work from the secular preoccupation with groups, and when two concepts as different as "group" and "dialogue" threaten to be merged into one panacea, the value of the individual will have to be rediscovered. What is difficult about this is that the individual will practically have to rediscover himself, for no one else will help him do it. In the prevalent culture, everybody else already too glibly thinks of a man only in terms of his good or bad "group membership," i.e., his capacity to assume the roles he is expected to play.

I do not wish to polarize the notions of the individual and the group. I merely want to see the balance between these two redressed so we may develop and deploy all the rich potentialities of human life. But my point is difficult to make in the present climate, which is so saturated with group phenomena and group language that original thoughts of great minds sometimes become sadly misrepresented. For instance, when Buber developed his thoughts on the difference between I-Thou and I-It relations, he was well aware of privacy and intimacy as the conditions for personal encounter, and he was Kierkegaardian enough to have a deep respect for the ultimate solitariness of each person. He also knew that dialogue belongs to the sphere of face-to-face privacy and cannot be a public display of words between two speakers each leafing through his own notes in front of an audience.

Personhood is not the same as being at ease in any and all groups. Personhood is not indiscriminate use of such tokens of intimacy as touching, smiling, and gabbing about one's feelings. Personhood requires reserve based on acceptance of one's own solitariness and reverence for the solitariness of others. Personhood is coming to terms with one's contingency, reassessing all that has thus far passed for love of others, and scrutinizing the facets of one's narcissism, all of which will be brought to the final test in one's own forthcoming demise, which is surely the most solitary moment of life. These considerations may furnish us with another projection fragment for a future image of God: one in which a divine solitariness, a divine singleness and a divine concern with individuals are celebrated so as to make companionship with such a divine being possible despite the vast differences in scale and the radical difference between the contingent and the non-contingent. This possibility is far removed from the historical Platonic conception of God as a lover of souls, as well as the pietistic tradition of anxiety about one's personal salvation. It is, rather, a tentative formulation of religious awareness going down to the roots of the courage to be.

There is another danger in groups which tends to be overlooked by its vocal advocates. It is that the groups which one is asked to experience are too small and too selective: they leave out too much of mankind and turn too many outsiders into potential enemies. We have seen this danger amply demonstrated in religion: believers set themselves off from and up against non-believers; members of faith groups oppose those of other faiths; denominations bicker with denominations, and sects find only a handful of friends in a vast world full of dangerous enemies. In *Group Psychology and the Analysis of the Ego*, Freud noted how much the love which group members bestow on each other is offset by hatred which they bestow on members of out-groups. We all know how difficult it has been, and still is, for the ecumenical movement, even within Christianity alone, to gain a hearing. If I may be autobiographical for a moment, I must say that I have come to feel increasingly ill at ease with the parish or the local church, primarily because it is too small and therefore too homogeneous, too cliquish, too clannish, too "groupy." The handshakes and smiles exchanged at the end of a worship service tend to become a bourgeois gesture of social recognition, a way of saying "You're one of us." Worse, they may become intrusive or oppressive. For me, worshipping with the same local group over the years has lost its savor. Right now I would prefer being caught up as a completely anonymous individual in a mass of strangers with whom I could engage in common worship precisely because their common humanity can be assumed more easily when their superficial distinctions are kept unknown. I am saying these things with the empathic hunch that I may be speaking also for many others, especially young adults, who describe themselves as alienated but who are searching for a more personal posture in life, religious in a sincere and honest vein, one which they find so hard to achieve within the established units and structures of organized religion. At issue are the boundaries between the personal and the social world, the balance between privacy and publicness, the ratio of solitariness to gregariousness.

Religion must pay heed to those problems, and I think it is at this moment in a very good position to do so because it is at a critical juncture in its course. It has been felt for some time that religion has lost its hold on the masses of people, that it is antithetical to reason and science, and that mankind would outgrow its need for mythological thinking. When positivism reigned, myth and faith were bad words. In the meantime, they have gained a new prestige. Now the paradoxical situation has been reached in which an increasing interest in religion and an anguished search for faith are matched by a declining interest in church affiliation. The paradox is buried in that loaded question: *Where* is the Church? For some, this question may mean: Why isn't the Church leading in solving the social crises of our time? For others it may mean: Shouldn't the Church help in population control? For still others the question is answered by the assertion: wherever there is charity and meliorative action among men, there is the real Church. This could be the NAACP, the ACLU, a local mental health association, an Alcoholics Anonymous chapter, or a group of war protesters. In other words, the old distinction between the sacred and the secular has given way to a more sophisticated distinction between the Church as a functional action group of witnessing men of faith and the Church as a structure that holds like-minded believers together in ceremonial engagements. Moreover, education about religion is again becoming a respectable function of universities, at the same time that church school enrollment is reported to be at a low ebb. There is much experimentation with religion in the large circles of the unchurched while at the same time there is very little experimentation going on within the religious establishment.

When there is indeed as much tension between the felt religious needs of man and the forms of religion offered by the contemporary Church as I have assumed, the verdict of history and the conjectures of dynamic psychology join in predicting that the needs of man will prevail and find satisfaction either through inventing new forms or putting new grafts on the old stems. Pope John's word *aggiornamento* means "updating," the relinquishing of old forms and hollow pieties for promising new ventures of faith, for creative religious thinking, and for celebrations that help people realize whatever happiness lies hidden in a contingent life. Maybe that happiness consists in the courage to be—the courage to be in a finite way, with that image of the infinite which instructs a man that he is not God.

Finally, I must point to a scientific avant-garde which not only holds promise for understanding religion, but is already fostering an intriguing cooperation between men of science and men of faith, or perhaps I should say between the posture of science and the posture of faith. It is the burgeoning experimental work on so-called altered states of consciousness, which raises the whole question of the relations between the outside and the inside world in a new vocabulary, with new concepts and with far better tools than the classical theologians and yesterday's positivistic scientists had. Using the work of my esteemed colleagues Murphy and Spohn[16] as a reference point, a vision is shaping up in which human consciousness stands on the bridge between an immensely complex "outer world" and an equally complex "inner world" constantly looking both ways, perpetually trying to integrate both directions, and refusing to be trapped into a forced choice position of loyalty to the one and disloyalty to the other. Reality is immense in both directions: the infinitely large and the infinitely small, the intimately private and the patently public. We all edit this immense reality by breaking it up into various kinds of reality, levels of reality, or manageable little words. It seems to me that religion, among other things, has the task and the opportunity of telling each one of us that we have edited reality too narrowly, too partially, too comfortably, and that our worlds and our gods are far too small. We need contact with all of reality, not all at once to be sure, but in an ever-enlarging series of ever-larger visions and ever-deeper loyalties.

* * *

I have sought to speak in all respects after Dr. Leo Bartemeier's heart, and I now hope that he finds I have succeeded. In trying to rise to the challenge of my difficult topic, I have tried to honor a man who is a man of science, an activistic helper of mankind, a patient and pensive observer of human follies, an admirer of everything creative in man, and a man of faith. Like many of his great psychiatric forebears he has been intrigued for a lifetime by the function of faith in reason and the function of reason in faith. Like Freud, he has always been curious about the fascinating details of religion and its intricate phenomenology. Like Janet he has always asked himself how he, a man of faith, could also be an articulate man of reason. And like Zilboorg he has affirmed himself as a man of faith, faith in a universe that is ultimately benevolent, ultimately personal, ultimately beautiful, and ultimately reasonable.

Notes

1. On September 11–13, 1970 at the Seton Psychiatric Institute in Baltimore, Maryland, a symposium "Future of Man: Psychiatry Tomorrow" was held honoring the 75th birthday of Dr. Leo H. Bartemeier. Dr. Pruyser was the speaker at the reception and dinner September 11 and this paper is an edited version of that speech originally entitled "The Future of Man: His Religious Quest."
2. Augustinus, A. *Confessions and Enchiridion*, tr. & ed. by A. C. Outler. Philadelphia: Westminster, 1955, p. 259.
3. Mead, S. E. In Quest of America's Religion. *Christian Century* 87: 752–56, June 17, 1970.
4. For the diverse works by Freud on religion, see my book *A Dynamic Psychology of Religion* and my chapter "Sigmund Freud and His Legacy: Psychoanalytic Psychology of Religion," *Beyond the Classics*, (1973) edited by Charles Glock and Philip Hammond. (New York: Harpers, 243–290).
5. Schleiermacher, F. E. D. *The Christian Faith*, tr. & ed. by H. R. Mackintosh and J. S. Stewart. Edinburgh: Clark, 1928.
6. Otto, R. *Das Heilige*. München: Becksche Verlags-Buchhandlung, 1936.
7. Tillich, P. *Systematic Theology*, Vol. 1. Chicago: University of Chicago, 1959.
8. Ebert, R. H. *Medicine and Psychiatry in a Time of Change*. Third William C. Menninger Memorial Lecture. Topeka: Menninger Foundation, 1970.
9. Menninger, K. Totemic Aspects of Contemporary Attitudes Toward Animals. In *Psychoanalysis and Culture*, G. B. Wilbur and Warner Muensterberger, eds. New York: International Universities, 1951.
10. Chapman, W. E. Why are Church School Enrollments Declining? *Presbyterian Life*, July 1, 1970, pp. 16–17.
11. Hempl, D. J. The Conceptual Shape of Death. Unpublished graduation paper, Menninger School of Psychiatry, 1969.

12. ______. Adolescent Conceptions of Death. Unpublished graduation paper, Career Training Program in Child Psychiatry, Menninger School of Psychiatry, 1970.
13. Jaspers, K., and Bultmann, R. K. *Myth and Christianity*. New York: Noonday Press, 1958.
14. Mitscherlich, A. *Society without the Father*, tr. by Eric Mosbacher. New York: Harcourt, Brace & World, 1969.
15. Nouwen, H. *Intimacy—Pastoral Psychological Essays*. Notre Dame, Ind.: Fides, 1969.
16. Murphy, G. and Spohn, H. E. *Encounter with Reality*. Boston: Houghton Mifflin, 1968.

II

CONTEMPORARY RELIGIOUS BELIEFS

3

The Seamy Side of Current Religious Beliefs

When Freud[3] pulled together his clinical experience with obsessional patients and his observations about religion, he ventured "to regard obsessional neurosis as a pathological counterpart of the formation of a religion" (p. 126) and coined the famous [or notorious] epigram describing "neurosis as an individual religiosity and religion as a universal obsessional neurosis." (pp. 126–27) Though the phrase proved to be offensive to believers and elicited much protest, the objections tended to be partisan: While defending their own religion against Freud's onslaught, many believers were ready to concede that Freud might well be right in regard to tenets and practices found in other religious groups or in ancient and so-called primitive religions. Such partisan attitudes—judging one's own religion as "healthy" and other religions as "sick"—seem sharpened today. Much current religious debate includes a conspicuous amount of acrimony, vilification, and backbiting. Among religious groups there is much contention about tenets and practices, litigation about forced methods of indoctrination, and accusations of brainwashing, followed by attempts at counterpurging their alleged victims. The immense psychological power of religion seems to have sprung into the public eye lately, with religion's propensity for thought control being increasingly recognized.

I find this present cantankerous time ideal for exploring in detail the pertinence of Freud's epigrammatic judgment about religion. I have always found his statement pungent as well as catty, acute

Reprinted with the permission of the *Bulletin of the Menninger Clinic*, 1977, *41*(4), pp. 329–348.

and blunt, insightful and beclouding. The negative no less than the positive feelings which the statement elicits are an indication that it strikes several nerves. The statement's immediate plausibility is increased by its producing an alerting response. In my own case, it prompts the immediate profession "Hear, hear!" even though this reaction is sooner or later followed by qualifying afterthoughts. The question that suggests itself is: If we could adequately formulate the salient features of neurotic behavior and contrast them with healthy behavior, would we find clues for a reasoned assessment of neurotic versus healthy religion? This question undercuts the propensity for using *neurosis* and *neurotic* as euphemistic words of condemnation, disagreement, or opprobrium and lifts them out of their present vulgarization.

Psychoanalysis itself would raise a first caveat to the question I have formulated by pointing out that mental health and neurosis cannot be used as categorical rubrics with clear-cut boundaries. They are only loosely conceivable zones on a continuum, for there is much evidence of a "psychopathology of everyday life" as well as of sound coping and adaptation in neurotic lives. Psychoanalysis enters a second caveat in pointing out that neurosis is not a well-defined medical entity but, rather, is a psychological condition of diminished well-being and personal efficiency, born from certain types of intrapsychic and interpersonal conflict handled by compromise formations. These fated compromises impose a tax on the individual's share of the average expectable human happiness. Neurotic behaviors and many psychic mechanisms are part of the general human condition *in a state of culture*; and the culture itself, through its institutions, teems with neurotic features that have become corporate prescriptions and proscriptions. Therefore, even an otherwise healthy person is up against the neurotic features of his culture which he must sort out, if he can, from the culture's unmitigated goods and necessities. At any rate, he is asked to take into account in his adaptive response to his culture the multitude of messages coming his way from its various institutions, among which is religion or, more precisely, a bewildering multitude of religions.

Sources and Functions of Religion

Mindful of these provisos in the psychoanalytic view of neurosis and their implications for religion, I[4] wrote an article on religion in the 1970s which I began by marshaling the psychological reasons for the continuance of religion. Unlike other observers, I foresaw no quantitative decline of religion; and I asserted that, precisely on the grounds laid out by psychoanalytic reasoning, religion would continue to be vigorously pursued by most people. These grounds include the awareness that religion, whatever else it may be, purports to deal with man's felt helplessness and is a gratifying activity which, despite its demands, offers many promises and consolations. Though often insisting that abstinence be practiced under particular conditions, religion is not very strict in demanding radical renunciation of infantile wishes; on the contrary, it condones them rather quickly by symbolic satisfactions. For this reason, religion *per se* is not a sublimation but, rather, a problem-solving effort *sui generis*, although certain sublimations may be found in some gifted person's activities within the religious framework he espouses.

Religion is likely to be continued also on account of its pointed preoccupation with expunging or mitigating guilt feelings. Religion is psychologically speaking a kind of rescue operation in which people crying "Help!" find some palliative for their predicaments. In a word, religion is an immensely relevant, useful, powerful tool for ameliorating what man feels to be his lot in life. Apart from religion's astoundingly diverse traditions and institutional trappings, its rescue motif alone is enough to make it forever popular. But therein also lies its gravest danger: As we can see rather clearly today, being popular means being open to racketeering, profiteering, and fraudulence—all under a pious cloak. On account of these and other exploitations, religion not only has a seamy side but has such an extensive one that it needs to be pointed out again and again. "Thank God," we should say, "for the critics of religion."

The pitiful origins of religion in man's personal and collective histories of misery should not becloud the grandeur of themes and tasks to which the religious question might address itself. Since I am not impressed by personal salvation as a grand theme because of its almost inevitable contamination by self-aggrandizement, I [1971] suggested that the religious quest in the 1970s might concentrate on the reassessment of man's place in nature—that man be moved from his callous dominion over nature to a role of loving partnership with it. I advocated a concentration on realigning the relations between men and women. I urged an attitude of greater realism toward death and dying. I suggested that religion might seek to change the relations between clergy and laity and reassess the role of authority, power, obedience, and liberation in the light of Bonhoeffer's observation that the Gospel is an appeal to people to come of age and act accordingly. I find these themes grand precisely because they transcend the rather stereotyped polarizations between social action and evangelical piety, liberalism and conservatism, formalistic and charismatic penchants, quietism and activism. Indeed, they have the power to narrow the gap commonly assumed to exist between faith and reason.

Sacrifice of the Intellect

The phrase "faith and reason" leads me back to the question I raised about neurotic and healthy religion. Considering what I have said thus far, could we hold that neurotic beliefs characteristically separate and oppose faith and reason, leading to tenets and practices that demand the ultimate sacrifice of the intellect? Is *credo quia absurdum*, taken as a single proposition isolated from Tertullian's other writings, the acme of neurotic belief? I am inclined to answer "Yes" to these questions in light of the following observations. Numbers of people attest to a blind faith: formerly, blind faith in *incubi*, alchemy, or the messianic pretensions of a Sabbatai Zevi who, to save his life, had the gall to become a Muslim; currently, blind faith in such singularly undeserving persons as an obese adolescent from India and a right-wing agitator from South Korea, both of whom go blatantly to the pockets of their followers. Numbers of professing Christians see manifestations of the Holy Spirit in such unreasonable acts as babbling and having fits, as if the Third Person had no intelligence, no shrewdness, no reason. Others meditate on, of all things, nonsense syllables, plumbing their depths for revelations. Still others take single words, their translation from ancient languages fixed into the more recent archaisms of seventeenth century English, rather than sentences or paragraphs as carriers of scriptural truth. And I have recently seen a young man who in all seriousness professes that he himself is the Messiah whom the Almighty is bestowing upon the world; he takes the fact that the world is rejecting him as proof of his divine appointment.

Yes, the psychopathology of religion is most extensive and has many shadings. I intentionally have chosen examples that portray the range from corporate fantasies to private delusions, from a vague public numbing of judgment to an eagerness to be deceived, from the love of explosive abreaction that abolishes reason to a piously defended feigned dumbness that fears reason. Sacrifice of the intellect, demanded by a good many religious movements and blithely if not joyously made by a good many religious persons, is surely one of the ominous features of neurotic religion.

Wishful Compromises

Why should a great human asset, a glorious function of the human mind, a marvelous talent ever have to be curtailed, let alone sacrificed? The answer to this question lies not, I think, in pointing out the various alleged abuses of reasoning and intellect that have led to such deplorable phenomena as technocratic dominance, the backlash of insect control, the silliness of mass entertainment, and the current width of the generation gap. Reason itself can spot these hapless spin-offs from limited or shortsighted applications of the intellect and correct them. The answer must be sought elsewhere: namely, in the poor compromises some people make between their dearest, deepest, and earliest wishes and the fabric of reality. Some of these compromises, the neurotic ones, are mediated by an untutored fantasy and dominated by the pleasure principle. It is so easy to wish and to persist in wishing when the private fantasy stands always ready to provide a modicum of satisfaction, at least temporarily, in pleasurable daydreams. And it is so easy to bend the great myths of mankind to one's own pleasure purposes by selecting from them some thin fragments that have a good ring, screening out their more challenging or demanding parts which represent reality and require intellectual work. Favorite fantasies are: an ornately furnished heaven, a tranquil paradise, a disembodied soul, a god who combines the nicest features of father and mother and has none of their nastiness, an ethereal state of pleasurable sameness without change. These pacific libidinal fantasies are sometimes buttressed by spiteful and aggressive ones: apocalyptic visions of slaughtered enemies, of exploiters hurled into the pit, of the rich condemned to gnashing their teeth. The wishfulness of apocalyptic fantasizing and its flaunting of reason are brought out by comparing apocalyptic with eschatological thought or hope. Eschatology spurns unbridled fantasy—it soberly acknowledges the unknown and leaves its content unspecified, affirming solely that the future is in the divine hand and, therefore, to be trusted.

I hasten to add at this point, however, that fantasy as such should not be condemned as a neurotic function. To do so would be to write off the arts, literature, music, charm, religion, and probably much of science as well. A distinction must be drawn between what I called the "untutored" fantasy which, entirely under the sway of the pleasure principle, is autistic, private, unspeakable, and infantile, and what I shall call the creative fantasy which is stimulated by curiosity, spurred by aesthetic, moral, or numinous feelings, makes active use of human talents, and respects the nature of reality. Following a formulation by Winnicott,[5,6] we may say that man does not have to make a forced choice between the solipsism of individual, private hankerings and the publicness of a verifiable outer world; there is another option. Between the inner and the outer world man finds a third world, which Winnicott calls the transitional sphere, containing transitional objects—the world of symbols, of novel constructions that transcend both infantile fantasy and the entities of nature. It is the world of play, of the creative imagination in which feelings are not antagonistic to thinking, in which skills and talents are used to the utmost, and where pleasure is found without categorical abrogation of the reality principle.

Thought Control and Freedom

And so we will have to transpose our search for criteria of neurotic religion to a new plane. Inasmuch as the transitional sphere not only generates culture but is at the same time the arena in which cultural goods and traditions are transmitted by the old to the young, should we not expect to find much corporate make-believe and nonsense handed down and reinforced (although formally they can no longer be called autistic, they nevertheless reach back to autistic sources)? The answer is "Yes." Freud[7] addressed this point in "The Future of an Illusion." As many others before him had done, he exposed and assailed the imposition of and the readiness to accept religious doctrines. In his view, doctrinal religion is a form of thought control which capitalizes on the human penchant for accepting mellifluous or consoling promises to alleviate the distress of the helplessness he feels.

Freud's unmasking of the authoritarianism found in many religions should prompt us to ask whether the shedding of thought control, doctrinaire attitudes, and authoritarianism is a sign of health in religion. I, for one, tend to think so; but I would like to use Freud's critique differently by relating it to the transitional sphere. If an attitude of play is germane, nay essential, to the transitional sphere, the grim business of thought control and authoritarianism is *ipso facto* inimical to the viability of that sphere. Doctrinaire and authoritarian thought turns symbols into things, ideas into concrete entities, suggestions into decrees, leaving in the end nothing to the imagination—creating a closed system that holds people captive. In contrast, the transitional sphere, by its openness, liberates people from the fetters of autism and the strictures of reality.

At this point we should heed Fromm's[8] ominous message. Is the inability to tolerate freedom a neurotic trait? Fromm thinks so, noting that freedom comes at a price: It demands hard mental and moral work, it isolates the individual in moments of personal decision making, and it may alienate him from the masses. While freedom is pleasant, it is also taxing, if only because it demands vigilance toward the outer world and a good deal of self-knowledge. It requires renunciation of some impulses and the capacity to delay certain gratifications. And so freedom can be squandered away or sold for a mess of pottage. The biblical story of Esau's impulsivity and Jacob's deceit lucidly illustrates that pious blessings can be obtained by extortion if the victim is given a chance to gobble. The story conveys a low image of man—beset by lust and avarice, willing to degrade both himself and his brother—and prompts us to recognize the existence of religious shenanigans, perpetrated by both victors and victims, which frequently involve the surrender of personal freedom. I do not hesitate to suggest that reverence for and the fostering of personal freedom is a prime sign of healthy religion and to propose that religious neuroticism can be measured by the degree to which it holds people captive through some exploitative scheme or sadistic trick. Fromm sees neurosis as the misuse of freedom, which includes the impulsive act of surrendering what freedom one has.

Surrender of Agency

Retreat from freedom is not only played out on the stage of external relations but is often duplicated on the internal stage of the self, in which case it leads to hyperemotionalism. Accepting authoritarian impositions is frequently paired with succumbing to paroxysms of impulsive emotionality, variously rationalized as the "Spirit" or its bad counterpart, the "Devil." There is not much difference in psychological structure between feeling that "I've got the Spirit" and "the Devil made me do it"; in either case one surrenders the ego's controls and is temporarily swept away by a regression in which the self is no longer held accountable.

Lesser regressions may preserve some degree of accountability by making the self a slavishly obedient agent of the "Spirit," doing its work through compulsive rituals. I remember one day when I was the only customer in a bookstore. As I entered the store to browse, a shy, lethargic young man behind the counter promptly started to recite passages of biblical prophecy in a mechanical, affectless voice. Although my entrance had obviously elicited his recitation, he showed no concern for communication. I soon discovered that the store was stacked with pious tracts and third-rate books of folk religion that resembled the *Whole Earth Catalogue* in their nostalgia for the good old moral days; however, I remained longer than I ordinarily would have in order to watch and listen to the young man. In an experimental vein, I went out at one point and observed that he stopped his prattle. As I reentered a few moments later, he promptly resumed his mechanical, doomful prophesying, to cease only after I left for good. What struck me in this episode, besides the man's compulsivity, was the general atmosphere of literalism, traditionalism, and naive realism (in the sense of Piaget's observations on children's thought) that exuded from the works and the salesman on display; everything was tied to simple, indubitable canons that scorned both the intellect and freedom.

Renascence of Folk Religion

This passage on regression enables me to mention a feature of the contemporary religious scene that some people who are otherwise not stupid pursue with gusto. In an article entitled "The Lure of the Primitive," Woodcock[9] points out that among many intellectuals there is a wholesale fascination with primitive culture, precisely at a time when fairly accurate information about the miserable conditions of life in primitive cultures is available. In former days, some intellectuals sought to construct or reconstruct an image of primitive humanity by idealizing and romanticizing, e.g., Rousseau's fiction of the noble savage. Today's intellectuals seem to admire a primitivity that we know was harsh, bleak, and in many ways offensive to human dignity.

It seems to me that Woodcock's observation can be extended to a "lure of the primitive" in the religious ambitions of otherwise intelligent and educated people. Some of these persons are ready to swap the intricate organ for a simple guitar in worship services; they substitute simpleminded versions of half-understood Eastern religions for articulate formulations of Western theologies; they turn to platitudinous folkways and lore in disdain of spiritual giants such as Aquinas, Calvin, Luther, Spinoza, Kierkegaard, or Teilhard de Chardin. Within Judaism, Hassidic lore and the Cabala are plumbed for their presumed depths, and suspicious eyes are ready again to see the Golem wandering through dilapidated cities. In these cases, the intellect is not wholly sacrificed but, rather, is frittered away in an enthralled dabbling with archaisms that are of no consequence to the modern world. Moreover, fascination with the primitive is frequently enhanced by ethnic consciousness, in which case there is an additional risk of ethnocentric narrowness.

Coping with Stress

To understand better the dire needs and fears involved in neurotic behavior patterns, I suggest that we view human life as a ceaseless attempt to maintain a vital balance between forces that emanate from a person's inner and outer environment. Both these environments are in flux and of great complexity. To the ego we ascribe the role of an executive whose tasks are to be in touch with both worlds, to settle conflicts, and to maintain an organismic balance as well and as long as possible in the face of death, which always lurks around the corner. The ego must be attuned to libidinal and aggressive drives that well up from within; it must pay heed to the prescriptions and proscriptions sounded by the superego and ego ideal; it must engage us with other persons for satisfaction of longings; it must foster a sense of competence in the person as a whole; and it must tackle the demands and opportunities coming its way from the outer worlds of nature as well as culture. As executive of the organism, the ego must cope with all the stresses and strains inherent in life, and to do so it is equipped with a great variety of coping devices built into life and perfected or acquired by learning. Most of us are fairly well outfitted to deal with the average upsets produced by average life situations; after the constant, innumerable small and moderate imbalances, we are able to restore our dynamic equilibrium. But from time to time we meet with emergencies in which our habitual tools for coping are taxed. Such emergencies are experienced as stress, and the awareness of stress is distress—a most unpleasant feeling which requires mitigation if not abolition by emergency reactions.

Since psychological stress is hard to define objectively, despite its patently subjective actuality, let me focus on one factor found in all emergency reactions to stress. It has to do with the question: What makes stress so distressing? The answer is that stress, however provoked, invariably upsets the often tenuous control we have learned to wield over our own aggressive impulses. Awareness of stress is coupled with upwellings of anger; and this increment of anger, contaminated by other negative feelings, now threatening to be unleashed and directed at some object, presents us with an inner emergency situation requiring some drastic means for reestablishing our equilibrium. All psychopathology can be seen as emergency coping behavior where drastic tools are applied which entail risks, produce boomerang effects, and demand outlays of energy disproportionate to the slim satisfactions they procure. Worse, they put the person at greater risk of ultimate destruction for they weaken his capacity for staving off death. Even if intended and used as salvaging maneuvers, the emergency coping devices of psychopathology are to a greater or lesser extent only bungling efforts at self-defense and reequilibration.

Prevalent Forms of Religious Pathology

By and large, neurotic styles of coping manage to keep aggression covert. The increased aggressive energies that constitute the subjective stress, frequently merged with libidinal ones, are dealt with in one of four ways: (1) by dissociation and disavowal; (2) by displacement of the body; (3) by magic, ritual, and symbolism; or (4) by reinforcing an already established undesirable character trait.[10] Let me discuss how these neurotic ways of coping are manifest in and through certain religious beliefs and practices.

Dissociation and Disavowal

Dissociation and disavowal are no strangers to religious attitudes and practices. Not only are quite a few religious experiences attributed to transcendent origins and argued to come from beyond the self, but some may be *felt* as ego-alien, occurring without the person's agency or consent. They remain isolated episodes that cannot and should not be assimilated to the individual's consciousness. For instance, I know a person given to bouts of glossolalia who has not the slightest concern for finding out the significance of this experience to himself or for any role it may play in his life; all he knows is that "it happens" and that he has no power over it. It does not arouse his interest, and he is utterly blocked and becomes anxious when others raise questions about its meaning or implications. Since he acts as if it were of no concern to him, the episodes are clinically equal to a hysterical symptom.

Disavowal and denial are reflected in Pollyannaish attitudes of piety that entail blindness to evil and misery and that argue death away with a blasé optimism. These attitudes go beyond a suggestion to look at the bright side of things; they are so flat-footedly cheery that they fly in the face of reality. People who cope in this way tend to feel that God is always on their side; they simply cannot conceive it to be otherwise. Their aggression leaks through, besides hortatory preachiness, in their inability to have any empathy with those who feel in a quandary. To others they often exude a forced niceness, overwhelming them with seemingly friendly and godly words that blatantly bypass not only these other person's feelings but actual situations as well.

Denial is, of course, a favorite way of coping, as long as one can, with the unpleasant fact of death. Tinkering with the status of death, seeking to modify its impact on the individual or at least give it an acceptable meaning, is a salient feature of most religions. But abject denial of death by giving it no ontological status at all and refusing even to think of it amount to a significant truncation of reality and a refusal to face up to unpleasant feelings. Various heresies in Christology, particularly Docetism, can be seen as historical, corporate uses of denial regarding Christ's death; their continued popularity suggests a penchant for using this mechanism.

Also included in this first type of neurotic religiosity is the conspicuous use of counterphobic mechanisms in some cults. A prime example is snake handling. In counterphobia, the fearsome object or condition that one would naturally seek to avoid is forcefully approached as if it were strongly enticing. It is a way of dealing with fright by a piecemeal, controlled confrontation with it: Each time the snake does not bite, the person is somewhat reassured by perceiving that he is unharmed after all and therefore need not fear it as much as he did before. Instead of the fear abating, however, the urge to confront the fearsome situation persists, giving rise to ritualistic repetitions under a compulsive impetus. One can observe this compulsive counterphobic maneuver in the prayers of people who loudly testify to their sinfulness and profess that they deserve to be smitten by the Almighty, only to settle at the end on a soothing note: They have proven to themselves that their barking God does not bite!

Displacement to the Body

Some religious activities and beliefs involve the second type of neurotic mechanism, namely, displacing conflict laden urges onto the body. Outstanding examples are those who actively seek martyrdom and self-punishing asceticism. It is one thing to accept torture as it comes, for the sake of principle; it is another thing to seek martyrdom as an end in itself and trap oneself into it. Undemanded and self-imposed, such suffering bespeaks a wish for self-destruction either by masochistic urges or as a necessary atonement for some real or imagined wrongdoing which an implacable conscience demands. In the latter case it is more than likely that the implacable conscience also reflects belief in an implacable god whose major attribute is vengeance. A milder, doctrinally reinforced form of asceticism is the refusal of some believers to seek or accept help when they are suffering, e.g., using viable and easily available medical interventions for pain, symptom relief, or cure.

Displacement to the body takes a special form in religious doctrines which hold that bodily existence is of no account and therefore should not be fostered and in those which espouse that the body or parts of the body are manifestations of evil and thus should be whipped, maimed, starved, or otherwise extinguished. Such Manichaean attitudes are today often coupled with the self-administration of toxic substances which numb, excite, or grossly alter consciousness—not only at a price to the body but to the detriment of consciousness itself, which loses its power of discrimination by becoming habituated to excessive fantasy material. Ecstatic phenomena such as fits and convulsions also involve displacement to the body; the level of consciousness is lowered to a point where motor automatisms and reflex actions are allowed to take over. The paroxysmal nature of these religious acts shows them to be a rupture of ego control, temporary to be sure, but with drastic regression. Exactly as in hysterical attacks, when these ecstatic motor discharges are over, the person typically disclaims agency or responsibility for them.

I think that the appeal of such regressive states is in the several short-term benefits they render. Not only do they provide release from excessive, hard-to-manage tensions, but they are stylized to appear less as acts than as conditions in which one is overcome by some superior, divine power. These rationalizations provide an ideal stage for acting out, under a pious cloak and with God allegedly on one's side, those conflictual impulses in behavior that are not usually tolerated either by the person himself or by his audience. He can thus ventilate his anger and take revenge on hated persons, hated traditions, and hated religious institutions and precepts. He need not fear retaliation: With a "better than thou" smile, he can proclaim that he really takes religion more seriously than his hypocritical parents or teachers ever did.

Magic, Ritual, and Symbolism

Magic, ritual, and symbolism are the historical "stuff" of religion from which modern, developed religions have sought varying degrees of emancipation. Yet, despite refinements in ritual and symbolism and the abolition of the crassest forms of magic, these three retain a strong regressive pull even on modern minds. Witchcraft is thriving again; Satanism is practiced[11]; occultism is blooming; horoscopes are consulted; exorcism is advocated; and thousands of worthless pills and potions are sold to gullible people seeking to change their fate by swallowing some potent-looking substance. One theme underlying all these practices is that nature is full of diabolical forces which need to be detected, seized, and controlled—if need be through a partial identification with them, leading to a partial appropriation and reenactment of their power. To outsiders, at any rate, many religious practices appear to be patently in the service of controlling such agents of aggression.

Whenever a ritual connected with one of these practices becomes an end in itself and is performed repetitiously and compulsively, in fear that its imperfect enactment will bring disaster, it has deteriorated from a conventional ceremony into a symptom. To give a few examples: A ceremonial cleansing gesture is one thing; a handwashing compulsion that leaves the hands feeling sullied is a symptom. Instead of combating evil, the witch and the Satanist identify themselves with a personified form of it and partially enact its intrusive horror without offering the hope of redemption. To stake one's life on horoscopes and anxiously put one's daily activities under their control is to indulge in avoidance mechanisms. Pharmacists know that for pills to look potent they should be small, spherical, and highly buffed—like the popular image of a Gnostic microcosm. Such pills are ingested not only with exorbitant faith in their power but often ritualistically with a need for their perpetual readministration.

Just as compulsions do not really resolve anything but drive a person to exhaustion by depleting his energies, obsessional thinking is an unceasing preparatory activity that does not lead to a consummatory solution. Religious topics, particularly those related to sin and guilt feelings, are the choice fare of obsessions. Scrupulosity, acedia to the point of feeling guilty over one's lack of enthusiasm, hyperrepentance for minor errors, incessant acts of placation—they all occur in people with rather circumspect behavior and moral disposition. Their thinking labors under severe moral apprehensions with a forbidding tenor. But when it is remembered that the strength of a taboo is commensurate with the intensity of the desire it seeks to curb, religious obsessions also point to the person's hidden wish to engage in the forbidden thing. He is very likely, indeed, to satisfy his evil wish covertly in fantasy.

Reinforcing Undesirable Character Traits—Fraudulence in Religion

In today's culture, neurotic dysfunctions do not always appear as discrete symptoms forming the basis for a complaint. Increasingly, clinicians find them interwoven with character patterns, having become rather fixed traits of an individual's personality. Such traits can be understood as frozen emergency reactions—as ways of coping that have become habitual long beyond the time they were originally needed in an erstwhile stressful situation. Traits of this order are often ego-syntonic: The person has not only come to accept them as part of himself and thus does not complain about them, but he may prize them as necessary or desirable features. From a welter of recognizable types, let me select a neurotic trait germane to my topic, namely, one that seizes upon religious content and contaminates religion.

Given the enormous psychological power of religion over the minds of men and the mounting presence of religious exploitation in today's world, it should come as no surprise that I focus on fraudulence and dishonesty. One can observe at a glance that some contemporary founders of religious movements and sects and some so-called evangelists live in conspicuous material comfort from the donations they demand—if not extort—from their followers, who apparently allow themselves to be duped. A statement attributed to one such leader is: "I am a thinker, and I am your brain." Its brutality is clear enough, but what makes it stick? Why do people accept self-appointed, grandiose leaders of sects and settle for a total, uncritical obedience? Why do they accept, and perhaps even enjoy, being manipulated; or why do they fail to see the difference between suggestion, exhortation, persuasion, and manipulation?

I suggest that the fraudulence of leaders, in religion as elsewhere, is tied to the fraudulent dispositions in their followers. Deception is not only an act perpetrated by one person upon a victim; it is also an intrapsychic defense mechanism that some persons apply habitually to themselves. Cheating on himself can momentarily spare a person some pain or discomfort. As Ibsen and Adler knew, lives can be organized around lies, and the sudden exposure of such lies can precipitate the personality's collapse. Hitler was a past master in the art—applied to himself and others—of concocting a myth and parading it as reality, especially myths of threatening content which he personified as a tangible enemy who was about to sap the moral fiber or the vital juices from good Aryan blond beasts. The best lie is the accusatory lie that allows us to project our own nastiness onto others and that justifies aggressive, retaliatory action. And when fraudulence becomes habitual or addictive, it forces us to practice it compulsively—each and every occasion tempts us to use it, each little triumph or manipulative efficacy reinforcing the character trait. As in malingering a person feigns to suffer from disease, the fraudulent character feigns to be oppressed, discriminated against, persecuted, overlooked (e.g., Nixon's "silent middle Americans"), misunderstood, or exploited.

One indirect test of a religion's proclivity for fostering characterological deceptiveness lies in what the various sects and movements make of sex. Extremes are telling. Severe restrictions on sexual behavior and horrified rejection of homosexual penchants are found in movements beset by suspiciousness and hypervigilance. In fact, these movements often make homosexuals the scapegoats, targeting them as the infiltrating enemy. To hallow such fearful rejection, these sects take recourse to Deuteronomic law and make frequent allusions to the "unnatural" and "unmentionable" qualities of this enemy. The enemy must remain collective, a cliché, for fear that encounter with a concrete specimen might persuasively expose the basic lie. The other extreme lies in the extolling of polymorphous, uninhibited sexual activity—even hyperactivity—pursued with cultist enthusiasm. In this feast of fools, intimacy, privacy, and the value of personhood are denied by a deception which equates sensory touch with depth of feeling and spermatozoic industry with affection. Both extreme positions are built on lies about the value of sex, which is vested in the ego's ability to exercise both freedom and restraint and to differentiate personal encounters from mere contact with the masses.

I need to add a few words about attempts to control intense anger by sudden flights into religious ideation and by taking recourse to mysticism. Some time ago, on the fringes of a university, I was accosted by a man in his early twenties who tried to solicit me into some local Jesus movement. Feeling at first irritated by his intrusive manner, I was curious enough to listen to him. While talking profusely about love and peace, his body was taut, his eyes glowered, and his voice was punctured with rage. His responses to a few questions and remarks I put to him showed him to be religiously illiterate, unperceptive, and ill-informed. He provides a good example of someone who has taken a flight into religion, for he was, no doubt, frantically clinging onto some small group or controlling leader whose strictness, coupled with a soothing promise, reinforced his failing self-control by impersonating some early phase of the nascent superego.

I find pill-induced instant mystical states *ipso facto* more tainted by magical means and expectations than those resulting from a slow and effortful ascent by systematic focusing and ascetic preparation. A paper by Hartocollis[12] runs parallel with my own clinical encounters which indicate that, particularly in religiously naive persons, such instant mysticism is often sought in order to control dangerous excesses of a fierce, chronic aggression that has become a character trait. Through this type of mysticism, the individual attempts to come to terms with a hated object imago by inducing a temporary regression to a developmental level which preceded the object's distinctness as a discrete entity. By merging with the imago in a lapse to a less differentiated mode of thought, the imago is robbed of its threatening features; its aggression is fused with the anger of a more primitive self-vestige and then turned into a feeling of triumphant omnipotence which knows neither victors nor victims but only raw magical power—momentarily! The aftermath is, of course, a letdown necessitating further trials at mystical states or a continuous dissolution of the personality.

Criteria of Neurotic Religion

And so, having sought to illustrate and describe prevalent forms of neurotic religion, I return to the task of finding criteria for spotting unhealthy, sick, or dysfunctional religious penchants. Be aware that members of a culture do not have to create their religious ideation and practices *de novo* but, rather, find their minds shaped by the culture's driving trends as well as its more sporadic and far-out options. These cultural features derive some of their potency from the fact that persons at very early stages in their lives, in the so-called transitional sphere, practice all kinds of operations with transitional objects, notably symbols. Symbols are therefore charged with affect, often approached by childish modes of thought, and sometimes poorly differentiated from autistic fantasy on the one hand and testable reality on the other hand. Individuals in the process of growing up cannot take their culture for granted but must learn to discern viable from spurious symbols. To lack such discernment is itself a psychological deficit or dysfunction, albeit an exceedingly common one.

Dysfunctional religion at the corporate level is therefore matched by religious dysfunctioning at the personal level. My course in this paper has been to elucidate the former by the latter. The religious coping styles, mechanisms, and ideational content which I have described participate fully in the structure and function of clinical neuroses and can thus be judged by the same criteria. Neurotic coping devices are:

(a) costly to the individual for the energy depletion they cause;

(b) coarse, heavy-handed interventions beset with boomerang effects;

(c) incommensurate in their psychic cost with the slim satisfactions they preserve or procure;

(d) ill-adaptive in that they tinker with and distort both the demands and opportunities of reality, i.e., the natural and cultural environment;

(e) growth stunting in that they impose a sacrifice of capacities and talents;

(f) regressive, fixating the person to an archaic mode of thought, attitude, or action;

(g) poor and costly compromises that only disguise but do not effectively neutralize aggression;

(h) bungling cries for help or SOS signals sent by an individual in distress;

(i) disguised ways of getting back, in anger, at some persons or groups who are forced to bend to the individual's excessive demands, dependency, immaturity, lack of efficiency, or cantankerousness.

To these psychodynamic and psychoeconomic criteria I should add the captivity and enslavement that neurotic coping styles entail: They shrink personal freedom, reduce the vision of the world's richness, and curb human potentialities. They turn an open system into a closed one.

Outspoken as I am on sick religion, I cannot be sanguine about healthy religion—not only because health in any sense is more difficult to define than illness and because deviancy of any kind is more eye-catching than the norm, but because of the enormous latitude that religion gives, and has wanted to give throughout the ages, to human hankerings and ambitions. Religion has much to do with the dream, in its pedestrian as well as its sublime sense. Religion has also to do with the cosmos, with the nature and scope of reality, ranging from the seen to the unseen. Using Tillich's parlance, I would hold that the religious circle is, above all else, vast; in Otto's phrase it is the sphere of the *tremendum*. But if pressed to state one criterion of healthy religion I submit that it lies in the biblical declaration that "the truth shall make you free." This statement implies that healthy religion is a search demanding the greatest curiosity, the full use of all human functions, talents, and gifts, and the belief that the search, long and arduous as it may be, holds a promise. The striking thing about this promise is that its approximation can be registered subjectively, experientially, existentially—in whatever form the truth may be revealed. I regard an enlarged sense of freedom as a sign of psychological, moral, and spiritual health.

Notes

1. Presented in the Cole Lecture Series at Vanderbilt University's Divinity School, Nashville, Tennessee, on March 9, 1977.
2. The author was Henry March Pfeiffer Professor, The Menninger Foundation. Topeka, Kansas.
3. Freud, S. (1907) Obsessive Actions and Religious Practices. *Standard Edition 9*:117–127, 1959.
4. Pruyser, P. W.: A Psychological View of Religion in the 1970s. *Bull. Menninger Clin., 35*(2):77–97, 1971.
5. Winnicott, D. W.: Transitional Objects and Transitional Phenomena. In *Collected Papers: Through Paediatrics to Psycho-Analysis*, pp. 229–242. New York: Basic Books, 1958.
6. See also my use of Winnicott's ideas in *Between Belief and Unbelief* (Pruyser 1974).
7. Freud, S. (1927) The Future of an Illusion. *Standard Edition 21*:5–56, 1961.
8. Fromm, E. *Escape from Freedom*. New York: Farrar & Rinehart, 1941.
9. Woodcock, G. The Lure of the Primitive. *Am. Scholar 45*(3):387–402, 1976.
10. Menninger, K. A. et al.: *The Vital Balance: The Life Process in Mental Health and Illness*. New York: Viking Press, 1963.
11. Nunn, C. Z.: The Rising Credibility of the Devil in America. *Listening: Journal of Religion and Culture 9*(3):84–100, 1974.
12. Hartocollis, P. Aggression and Mysticism. *Contemp. Psychoanal., 12*(2):214–226, 1976.

4

Narcissism in Contemporary Religion

The myth of Narcissus is both vague and complex enough to allow various points of emphasis. In my apperception of the myth the following points stand out: Narcissus met his fate through an act of divine *punishment* for his cruelty in rebuking the amorous advances of a handicapped girl, Echo, who had lost the power of speech and was saddled with the symptom of echolalia. While the formal cause of his death was *being addicted to the adoration of his own image*, the efficient cause was exhaustion. Frazer[2] saw the origin of the Narcissus myth in a *taboo* prevalent in ancient India and Greece against looking at one's own reflection in water (sometimes extended to mirrors) and ingeniously linked this taboo to the primitive belief that the soul is a *shadow* or *reflection*. Therefore, the water spirits may take one's reflection away and render a person *soul-less*. In Frazer's line of thought, which I share, Narcissus is punished for his heartlessness by becoming soul-less, i.e., *dead* to humanity; he is turned into a flower.

Although I am not an advocate of soul-language, because of its proven whimsicalness in the history of religions, I do find Frazer's reconstruction of the origin of the Narcissus myth in a taboo worth pondering. We have learned from Freud[3] that behind every taboo lies a wish, and that the strength of a taboo is proportionate to the strength of the desire it seeks to curb. Therefore, the taboo suggests that man must have an ardent wish to behold his own image and

Reprinted with the permission of the *Journal of Pastoral Care*, 1978, *32*, pp. 219–231.

bestow adoration upon it—if need be, unto death! Not only is there a strong empirical case for the dynamic actuality of primary narcissism in everybody's life, but the pursuit of self-adoration, self-enhancement or self-absorption can be so relentless that one dies from sheer exhaustion. Excessive narcissism is also a psychiatric syndrome[4] or a dominant trait in certain character structures that comes to public notice and may demand social intervention. These considerations come from a treasure trove of observations and conjectures which the psychoanalytic movement, over the years, has been at pains to sort out under the rubrics of the psychodynamic and psycho-economic theories of love, object relations and energy flow. Since the word "narcissism" is a technical term deriving its meaning from these theories, I shall make an effort to use the term only in this technical sense, with appropriate qualifiers.

Narcissistic Motives in Historical Religiosity

Narcissism in contemporary society is a fashionable topic, but it is not often discussed in regard to religion. I shall pay close attention to the religious scene and shall do so from a distinct perspective, namely, psychoanalytic psychology of religion.[5] From this angle, the first question I wish to raise is: Are there any patently narcissistic motives or clearly narcissistic benefits in religious thoughts or actions perceptible at the level of the masses? This question goes beyond the contemporary scene to religion in general, across the ages. To make the question manageable I shall confine myself to the Western world and focus on what is called the Judeo-Christian tradition, which is large enough anyway.

Staying at the mass level, which is often at variance with the niveau on which responsible and articulate theological formulations are made, one can find in many religious believers a vast *preoccupation with the indestructibility of their souls or personalities.* Worded in different ways and often buttressed by vaguely understood shreds of philosophy or well-understood forms of Platonism, the religious scene teems with ad hoc beliefs which grant a person opportunity for tinkering with the eventual fact of his own demise, and for reassuring him of his perpetuity. Whatever one makes of such beliefs and their multiple variations, it is clear that they address the narcissistic issue par excellence, namely, the infantile intuition that one is the center of the universe.

Tinkering with the reality of death (i.e., one's own death) by softening its blow is indeed such an overwhelming preoccupation in religion that it is not surprising to find certain aspects of it articulated in specific themes. These themes have such theological labels as salvation, providence, election, and sin, with which I shall deal here, at the level of popular belief, as fantasy clusters or illusions.

One of these illusions centers on the word *salvation* or its cognates. Scores of people labor under the conviction that they must be saved—saved from something untoward or nasty, and saved unto something desirable. This grand theme, which runs through several of the world's major religions, is at times appropriated in blatantly narcissistic ways, namely when it takes the form of a proprietary concern over one's own soul to the utter neglect of redemption of communities, nations or mankind at large. The most florid expression of such a personal concern came to me some years ago when I heard a radio-evangelist preach on the text: "In my Father's house are many mansions." This preacher attacked the editors of a new Bible translation which had substituted the word "rooms" for "mansions," which he felt sold people short of the promises that God had made them. In a nutshell, since the King James version had promised him a mansion, he was not going to settle for just a room! He was holding his God to an alleged promise as if it were a business contract on which he was going to cash in.

Another fantasy theme dear to many believers is the notion of *providence* sentimentalized as an all-nurturing Father in heaven who cares for sparrows, has counted the hairs on one's head, and acts as a shield and buckler against one's enemies. These are all poetic phrases from the Psalms which need to be taken in context. But they can be pried loose from their contexts in the service of bolstering an image of the self as invulnerable under preferential divine protection and wallowing in narcissistic bliss. Some songwriters have presented such bliss as a leisurely walk with Jesus in a flowering garden: "He walks with me and He talks with me . . . "

From being saved or damned and from being nurtured to being left in one's own devices the mind can associate freely and with ease to the theme of *election*. A Jahweh chose his people, that is, a whole people, his Christianized counterpart can be imputed to choose individuals, with a discerning eye, of course. Without denying the desirability of being among God's elect, I note that some people behave prematurely as if they were given a guarantee for such exalted status—if only because they feel that they deserve it. The question of merit—much argued in theological history—can and has been phrased in simplistic contractual terms: If I maintain proper behavior my payoff is sure to come. Prayers can become negotiations, as the Romans recognized when formulating the principle of *do ut des*: I will give this, so that you, God, will give me that. Faced with reams of writings about the Puritans' alleged anxiety about election and its connection with the rise of capitalism, I cannot shed the impression that these staunch Calvinists behaved on the whole like a proud race, holding their heads high and acting like lords of the manor—despite occasional fits of depression.

In fact, we should also take a look at some religiously toned depressive states for clues about narcissistic motives. Some years ago I dealt with a middle-aged depressed patient who, upon admission to the hospital, shared with me his conviction that he was a *sinner*. He spelled out his sins for me as episodes of minor malfeasance in a job he had held several decades earlier; to my ears they had the makings of a screen-memory. After discharge to his home he was readmitted to the hospital some months later, this time more agitated and vastly preoccupied with anal themes. On this occasion he used stronger language by telling me that he was a *great* sinner who deserved to be punished; he was indeed already punishing himself lavishly by his depressive symptoms. Once more brought to his senses, he was again discharged, only to return after about half a year in still greater despair and with more profound regression now preoccupied with oral themes. When I saw him again he asserted, with an enigmatically blissful smile, that he was *The Greatest of all Sinners!* This time he was very difficult to manage for he had become grandiose enough to want to reorganize the whole hospital. In talking with him I ascertained his belief that he was beyond rescue; no love in the world could ever forgive him, who had now made an identification with the Devil, and no grace could ever have a hold over him. In holding himself thus refractory to any grace, he communicated the blatantly narcissistic view that he was the sole and ultimate judge of his own life and fate—no divine power could overrule his self-judgment. Cases like this alert us not only to the grandiose core in certain types of depression, but also illustrate the propensity for making mental associations between cosmic or religious ideas and the infantile core of the self.

Although the *mystical* literature shows a great variety of object-relations patterns, ranging from attempts to fuse with the divine object to lucid visions of the divine's otherness, there are mystical experiences in which the oceanic feeling and notions of grandiosity stand out. History has also shown quite a few self-styled Messiahs, saviors and prophets who had a gross disdain for their audiences and showed a vulgar self-inflation. And is there not a dangerous conceit in Angelus Silesius' assertion: "I know that without me God could not live one moment" (*Ich weiss dass ohne mich Gott nicht ein Nu kann leben*)?[6]

In view of such observations I find that Freud was not off the mark when he formulated what I call his "indulgence theory" of religion: religion, he held, is a unique form of coping with man's felt helplessness in life, which starts by partially giving in to his infantile longings—whatever it might add to this indulgence later. Instead of first demanding man's renunciation of infantile wishes, religion begins by granting them; too quickly and too lavishly in Freud's view.[7]

Though I do not aim at completeness in this sketch of narcissistic motives in religious experience, I should call attention to the fact that the history of religions provides a splendid example of what Freud[8] called the *narcissism of minor differences*. At group levels, the more people are like each other in outlook or conviction, the more they accentuate fine differences between themselves and their nearest semblances in an effort to appear special or unique. I find the endless thrust in religion toward sectarian movements and schisms unexplainable without due consideration of this motive. In addition, some thought should be given to narcissistic motives, again at group levels, that underlie mission work, particularly Christian mission work to peoples who stand themselves in highly developed religious traditions and articulate faiths.

Anti-narcissistic Motifs in Historical Religion

The second question I wish to address turns the tables on the first one: Despite the presence of narcissistic motives in religion, is it not true that the great religions abound with pointedly anti-narcissistic themes and programs? I have no hesitation whatsoever in answering this question affirmatively.

The anti-narcissistic motif in religion has been trenchantly expressed in recent years by the church historian Sydney Mead:

> . . . no man is God. This is what I understand to be the functional meaning of "God" in human experience. Whatever "God" may be—if indeed being is applicable to "God"—a concept of the infinite seems to me necessary if we are to state that all-important fact about man: that he is finite.[9]

In my words: the function of the infinite, of God, is not merely to be there, but to teach something, namely, that *man is not it*. The function of God is a pedagogical retort to the anthropological observation that man—if not curbed by a taboo—has an uncanny urge to play God, to assume that he is infinite and to act as if he were the center of the universe. If given a chance, he will lord it over his fellowman and all creation.

The anti-narcissistic motif of responsible religious thought is clear in the Hebrew myth of *the fall of man* in Paradise. Partaking of the forbidden tree will make man like God—this is the mythical language for the narcissistic longing in men's hearts. The tempter inveigles man to break the taboo, knowing that he speaks to man's deepest, aboriginal motive and therefore has a good chance to ensnare him. I detect in this scenario a deep conviction that man's fall is not to be seen as an accidental lapse from weakness, but as the outcome of arrogant striving. Man falls from strength, not weakness: he falls because he climbs! He wants to be God, over and over again in the mytho-history of the Jewish people recorded in the Old Testament. Or to put it in the modern theological phrase of Karl Barth: Man refuses to let God be God.

With this shrewd analysis of the human situation and powerful theological retort the Jewish Scripture opens. It defines the root of sin, the Ursin, as rebellious arrogance to assume omnipotence and omniscience, and it portrays man not as a weakling but a tower of strength, albeit a suspect strength.

If the concept of *original sin* is to mean anything, its dynamic import is to be found—in the Judeo-Christian tradition—in that basic genetic disposition which psychoanalysis conceives as primary narcissism,[10] a disposition that must be curbed. Hence, religion cannot remain an entertainable but inconsequential *Weltanschau-*

ung, but must become an ethic also. The aboriginal condition must be changed, by prescriptions and proscriptions, in the direction of more viable, productive and noble object relations than the narcissistic position poses. Man must be transformed from his collective and personal origins, voluntarily if possible, by taboos if necessary. The essential business of religion, which differentiates it from philosophy, is not understanding, but transformation.

Hence, the inevitableness of *concepts of sin*, in one form or another. More or less elaborated by various religions, and sometimes ridiculously particularized, lists of sins tend to attain a rank-order in which certain sins are considered cardinal, or seen as the ultimate cause of other sins. Old Testament major prophets spoke of sin as rebellion against God and his Law, the latter seen as an expression of God's affection for man. In this view, sin is rejection of divine affection, and is thus an aspect of the psychology of love and object relations. The Christian conviction is that sin is always committed against God and not just against other people. The Pauline emphasis is that sin is a power. The Reformation theologians saw sin as lack of faith, the failure to love and trust God. Together with Judaism and Christianity, Muslim doctrine singles out pride, in the sense of opposition to God, as the arch-villain. In these ideas lie clues that theologians in their grappling with the notion of sin have time and again hit upon love relations, being a disposition of the heart as well as an object choice, as the essential definers of sin or righteousness.

This emphasis on sin as incorrect object choice and lack of loyalty to something outside of and larger than the self has received much reinforcement from further ethical notions about selfishness, self-concern and self-preoccupation. Next to deity, the self attains a sharp focus in religion, mostly as something that has to be transformed from its natural state into a more dignified, more loving and ethical one. Typical religious words about the self as new Adam, transformed from the old Adam, are: selflessness, self-sacrifice, self-denial, self-examination, and self-surrender—all to be interpreted in the light of the ancient Hebrew epistemology which holds that knowledge of God and knowledge of self are reciprocal: no one can know himself without knowing God, and no one can know God without knowing himself. This epistemology makes allowance for the possibility of encountering "God" in other people, in the community or in the wonders of nature. Psychoanalysis finds little to criticize in these conceptions, except for the radicalization they tend to undergo in theological thought. For instance, it is a psychodynamic truism that loving engagements with external objects always provide narcissistic returns for the lover, even if unasked. The psychodynamic equation is that to love is to be lovable, and to be lovable is to be loved.

If the function of "God" is to tell people that they are not it, and that they have to get off their narcissistic hobbyhorse, it is not surprising that much theological thought has been given to the finer points of the love relationship between God and man. Moralists have accentuated the ethics of this relation: one should *merit* God's love, so that one's lovableness to God consists in one's moral meritoriousness. Others have accentuated the *spontaneity* in the love relation between God and man, apparently feeling that love and spontaneity have much to do with each other, as they tend to do in the human experience of falling in love. This emphasis is strong in doctrines of predestination, which may strike one as feats of theological tightrope-walking in an effort to preserve an aspect of spontaneity in the nature of God, in addition to his impeccable goodness and sense of justice. It seems to me that these otherwise quite tenuous theological constructs are attempts to say something about freedom and choice, perhaps the freedom-to-choose, that is experientially inherent in adult love relations at the genital level. There is no doubt in my mind that engagement with others in love relations sets a person subjectively free, i.e., increases his or her sense of freedom, however binding the relation will turn out to be through fidelity and loyalty. What, then, does one get freed from in such a love relation? Again, theological reflection will answer this question by noting that one gets liberated from self-preoccupation, selfishness, or excessive self-concern.

Much more could be said, of course, to highlight the anti-narcissistic concerns of theological thought, but this sketch will suffice. It is worth noting in addition, however, that even the narcissism of small differences manifest in sectarianism and schisms has found a counter-message in the ecumenical movement.

Narcissistic Trends in Modern Society

Sober observers of the contemporary scene, if they are old and wise enough to have a sense of history, cannot fail to register a sharply increased concern with the self and a claim to pleasures of and for the self during the late sixties and the decade of the seventies.[11] Note my cautious phrasing of this sentence: I start with drawing a line between people with and without a sense of history, for one of the most striking observations I have made as a teacher is that the successive cohorts of students to which I have been exposed during these years manifest an increasingly ahistorical or even antihistorical outlook on all things, including their professions. Historical reflections about their fields of study produce ennui, if not a belligerent disdain. To me, an old-timer with great interest in the historical unfolding of ideas in my basic sciences, and a clinician as well, these new student attitudes come through as cockiness, for they seem to convey two messages: "Don't bother me with the old rubbish, but get with it, tell me quickly what is alive now," and: "History begins with me and my world, the past is just a lot of nonsense."

I think we have here the beginnings of a rising cult of self-centeredness in which many young people assume that the world has been waiting for them, the past having been only a prologue to their birth. To the extent that they have access to higher education it is likely that they have been exposed to psychological literature, respectable or pop, that has told them a great deal about the desirability of self-actualization, self-enhancement, self-awareness, sensory self-stimulation, and taking pride in their bodies; they have been instructed to believe in the superiority of action to thought, and especially to cherish extemporaneous action and feelings of spontaneity. They have learned to equate tactile sensations with feelings. They consider themselves sexually liberated, and are anti-elitist mostly in the sense that they claim for themselves the prerogatives of former elites without wanting to limit these to a special coterie. They have gone through Daniel Bell's "revolution of rising entitlements,"[12] seeing no formal boundaries to sharing the good life, often defined in jarringly hedonistic terms. They are likely to have had some form of "therapy" in some kind of "workshop" or "seminar," on a self-referral basis, in which they were asked to "let themselves go," or to "get in touch with their feelings," perhaps amplified by baths, nudity, eccentric dress, ethnic diets, screaming, or orgiastic abreactions, especially those that can be recorded on video- or audio-tapes for rehash in another self-confrontation (sic) or for the pleasure of the empathic community. The taboo on looking intently at one's own image has been broken. While using the worst of psychiatric and psychoanalytic jargon, they reject "establishment psychiatry" and of course psychoanalysis, allegedly because of the latter's metapsychology, but more likely—I would think—on account of the hard (and for them tedious) work it demands.

If this picture seems somewhat overdrawn, I hope you have noticed the absence of the word "narcissistic" in my descriptions thus far. I grant that I bring to this picture the import of my clinical exposure to a rising tide of narcissistic syndromes and gross changes in the prevailing psychopathology during my years of practice. Though we are much in the dark about the exact relations between culture and personality, there is ample evidence that each cultural epoch produces a prevailing symptomatology in its disturbed members, in addition to the perennial psychic disorders of mankind. Clinicians have no doubt about the current increase in narcissistic disorders in young and middle-aged patients, nor are they surprised about this fact when they observe the culture in which they practice. I also grant that certain strokes in my sketch derive from acquaintance with professional colleagues who appear to have completely identified themselves with the patients they are called upon to serve: their "therapies" are meant to be as extemporaneous, sensual, spontaneous, hedonistic and orgiastic as their patients' behaviors, and are possibly also a form of acting-out. This sad observation in my own professional circles puts the clincher on my conviction that there is a strong covariance between culture, personality and psychopathology, on account of which the use of nosological terms in describing personality traits and cultural trends has its legitimacy.

Narcissistic Features in Current Religious Beliefs and Practices

In view of the ample experience which the great historical religions have had with self-serving attitudes, and these religions' vigilance against the narcissistic twisting of pious ideas, the current religious scene may be worrisome but is not really shocking. Quantitative changes in such a complex psychosocial dynamism as narcissism are hard to verify; one has to proceed with qualitative impressions which, if buttressed by parallel observations in other segments of life, may round off to a widely recognizable *Gestalt* or a culture-historical *Leitmotiv*. I myself find the current scene worrisome more for the blatancy of narcissistic strands in religious beliefs and practices than for their imputed novelty. At any rate, I will take a close look at the forms of narcissism manifest in contemporary religion.

Let me begin by noting the popularity of a certain type of mysticism which is not object-focused and does not require strenuous soul-searching, but consists of a kind of reverie induced by chemical alteration of the state of consciousness. I am speaking of *pill-induced, instant mysticism* without hard cognitive preparatory work, without examination of conscience, without theological background or supervision, and without clear pedagogical goal; the kind of mysticism that its practitioners find libidinally self-validating because it gives momentary pleasure in an otherwise empty or dull existence. One finds penchants toward this instant-mysticism in persons with chronic aggression to a hated introject which they cannot shake off; the mystical experience, as a temporary regression, is an attempt to merge with the image.[13] The introject's aggression and the person's anger fuse, and a moment of triumphant omnipotence is experienced; often to lead to a feeling of letdown afterwards which impels the person to seek repeats of such mystical states. The pattern may indeed become an addiction,[14] which in itself proves that the psychological problem remains unresolved. At any rate, what stands out in these states is the momentary narcissistic regression as well as the more permanent narcissistic nostalgia of the unhappy intervals.

Regressive phenomena always foster prominence of narcissistic motives. While the hapless mystic or pseudo-mystic seeks his regression privately, scores of others expose themselves to *collective disinhibitions* which entail the resurgence of narcissistic preoccupations. For instance, in *states of ecstasy* engendered by group action (sometimes mass action, as in evangelistic revival meetings) religion offers the possibility of diminishing an individual's sense of agency by regarding the person possessed by some indwelling spirit (whether divine or demonic), by demanding the sacrifice of the intellect, and by luring the person into primitivity[15] through exhorting him to "become like a child."[16] In some cases this exhortation speaks to the Oedipal child-in-the-person, i.e., the child with guilty and rebellious feelings who is to be led to confession and self-abasement as preconditions for forgiveness. As the hortatory slogan has it: "Repent, and you shall be forgiven!" But in other cases the lure of primitivization speaks to the pre-Oedipal child, whose concerns are with gaining acclaim and winning indulgence so as to enhance that cheery "Up with People" optimism which the pious literature often refers to as "abundant living" in the unruffled love of a heavenly father who gives himself unstintingly to his favorite child. To put this in the terms advanced in Rudolf Otto's *The Idea of the Holy*,[17] religious movements may find themselves stimulating bliss at the expense of awe—leaving no room for that profound dynamic ambiguity between awe and bliss which is essential to man's encounter with the Holy because the nature of the Holy is both grandeur and benevolence.

My impression of the so-called *charismatic movement* is that it cannot but attract both types, and possibly more of the latter than the former. It does so, moreover, by emphasizing a theological construct which refers to an intermediary entity between God and man so hard to define that it almost begs for human projections to give it experiential content. The charismatic movement centers its life and activity in The Spirit, surely one of the most elusive, difficult and strained religious notions which led to the most whimsical apperceptions already in the apostle Paul's time, so that a good deal of Paul's ministry was addressed to correcting its popular misinterpretations! I am not denigrating the idea of the Spirit—in fact I have a high enough opinion of it to have published a scholarly article on its symbolism a dozen years ago[18]—but I am pointing here to its inherent difficulty for rational understanding and therefore its vulnerability to subversion. It is so easy to project one's subjective feeling states and psychosomatic reactions onto the notion of the Spirit and then to excuse oneself from agency, accountability and responsibility by attributing one's feelings and doings to the indwelling of the divine. Subject and object can be so easily confused in Spirit-parlance that the danger of self-inflation is always present, especially in persons who drift into the charismatic movement without the screening which theological diagnosticians such as Jonathan Edwards or Soren Kierkegaard would require.[19]

And so we have to envisage the likelihood that some charismatics speak in tongues, jerk their limbs, writhe their bodies, break out in shouts, sing loudly to the Lord, and claim to receive the Spirit in notably pre-Oedipal ways, which may amount to an apotheosis of their selves. I think this danger is especially great in neo-charismatics who come from anti-Pentecostal traditions, because their search for an exciting and elevating religious experience has received much impetus from dullness and stultification they allege to have undergone in their former church-affiliations. They have something to contend, sometimes quite vehemently, and recourse to the Spirit permits acting-out their negativism under the safety of a pious cloak. With clinical discernment it is not difficult to see grandiosity in the cheer of some Spirit-filled people.

One may—and should—ask why it is that so many *"born again" believers* beat the drum so loudly about their alleged rebirths and are so prone to hard-pressure, intrusive salesmanship methods in proclaiming their faith to the world, or seek to make money of their experience by writing books about it. Does their lack of a sense of privacy and modesty toward self and others attest to a feeling of triumph they experience when putting over their ideal? Are their manners manipulative[20]—formerly symptomatic of a narcissistic character disturbance, but now zestfully engaged in under the claim of divine sanction? I think we must reckon with these possibilities, given the nature of man. How far can anyone identify himself with the divine intent anyway without becoming grandiose? Narcissistic characters are notorious for their promiscuity and shallowness in human relations, and their fantasies of omnipotence are reinforced every time they "do somebody in." Obviously, such people can feel "born again" without fundamental character change; only the auspices of their narcissistic motives have been enlarged and hallowed.

If anything characterizes the current religious scene for me, it is the naive indulgence with which large numbers of people accept the *obtrusive narcissism of self-styled leaders* of new movements who demand total, non-thinking subjection to their dictates and go without any scruples to the pocketbooks of their flock. Is this popular indulgence to the narcissism of others indeed as naive as it appears? I am afraid that it is based on identification with the admiration of the lordly, manipulative manners of these leaders and the public hedonism of their lifestyles. Manipulations, like other forms of fraudulence, is a two-way street: manipulators always find people who want to be manipulated because they have basically the same disposition for deceit. And if one wonders about the masochistic streak in those who allow themselves to be manipulated it is important to remember that a certain form of masochism, namely, ascetic pride, has very close ties with narcissism. Says Fenichel: "The analysis of ascetic pride regularly exhibits the idea of self-sacrifice for the purpose of regaining participation in omnipotence. . . . 'I sacrifice myself for the great cause, and thus the greatness of the cause falls on me.'"[21]

I mentioned earlier the ancient taboo on looking adoringly at one's own image. It is typical of narcissistic personalities that they are greatly concerned with the impressions they make on other people, not to invest their emotional energies in others and enjoy intimacy, but because they need others as reflecting surfaces that will mirror their self-love back to them. I am speaking of the so-called *reflective narcissism* that is familiar to preachers, teachers, actors and public speakers who are greatly dependent on the upturned, shining and smiling faces of their audience. Such dependency on admiration and flattery, mixed with a little awe, can be spotted in certain Jesus-freaks and in some Jews-for-Jesus who feel the compulsion to proclaim their new-fangled faith by rather intrusively accosting others in unlikely places and under untoward circumstances. It is one thing to find one's ears entertained by a Salvation Army band at a street corner; it is another thing to be nearly arrested by a self-styled, lonely proclaimer of Jesus-lore who proceeds to put one into the heathen role. Where does this *compulsion for proclamation* in that manner come from?

While it may come from a sense of obligation or loyalty to the divine object on whom one's faith centers, in which case it could have the same infectious or winning quality that we all experience on being exposed to a person who is in love, the people I am now describing appear to lack exactly such charm. Instead they come through as grim, overbearing and intrusive. They appear to labor under great tension and are hardly attuned to the psychological state of those they accost. Are they trying to reassure themselves that their faith is worthwhile by seeking affirmations from others? Do they seek proof of the correctness of their faith by testing out their magical power to win souls for it? Do they secretly triumph when rejections come their way because these prove to them that they themselves are indeed the Messiah or Jesus for which the world has been waiting? I recently saw a psychiatric patient who openly stated that the latter situation was true for him: claiming to be the Messiah, he used every critical question or rejection as proof of his divine appointment. And I have no difficulty finding cases, clinical and nonclinical, to exemplify the other psychodynamic possibilities I raised: I dare say that most experienced pastors are rather familiar with such cases. Reflective narcissism is a very common phenomenon in all walks of life, including religion, and it tends to beset precisely those religious activities generally described as "witnessing" and "testifying."

In casting our eyes on the current religious scene we should be arrested by the sudden popularity that the word *celebration* has gained. The religious world today seems full of joyful noises and happenings. Or should I say that it is full of strenuous talk about these desirable things and replete with strained efforts to produce them, often with rather hapless results? That a good deal of liturgical experimentation is taking place is beyond question: much of it in the direction of folk art and folk religion, some of it in the direction of high art and high religion, with a sizable group in the middle anxiously safeguarding its ailing liturgical traditions but hoping that these will come alive again with new enthusiasm. Theological scholars today write books about celebration, joy and feasts.

I see a wide gap, however, between *wishing* to celebrate and knowing *what* to celebrate; the cart seems to be put before the horse. A wish to celebrate may come from sheer boredom; it is a longing for affective experience per se, which may prompt one to going through celebratory motions so as to capture some emotion. It is like saying with a yawn, "Let's have a party!" without having an occasion, reason or disposition for one.

In boredom, as in sleep, libido is withdrawn from objects onto the self. Bored people will look for distractions but typically are refractory to them, because they are actually in a state of subjective excitement over a repressed wish which remains unfulfilled by the distraction at hand. The inhibited unconscious wish in boredom is usually aggressive: a lingering anger at others for not gaining their love or admiration and at oneself for not having found ways of getting one's libidinal dues. That is why narcissistic personalities who lack social savvy or find themselves without responsible friends tend to suffer from states of boredom. And being prone to action anyway, they will act out their conflicted feelings by engaging in promiscuous, superficial, shallow contacts that provide some temporary excitement.

I think we have here a paradigm for the haplessness of much

so-called celebratory activity in religion—the rituals and liturgies that are advocated, fought about, tried out, promiscuously tinkered with, syncretistically arranged, artfully managed, but generally fail to come off as hoped and thus lead to ever more fanciful experiments with expanded multi-media use, bigger balloons, larger banners, and more decibels. The paradigm of boredom and its frequency in narcissistic disorders points up the tragic weakness in contemporary religion namely, the insidious retrenchment in most churches and sets from action for social justice and from concern with corporate human woes. Evangelical concern with the individual and his soul is the watchword today, and in the light of our paradigm we can see the risk this program entails: It tends to condone, steady or augment the narcissistic penchants which are already so abundant in the culture at large.

I am sure that more features of the contemporary religious scene can and must be explored. But the scope of a paper is limited—and so is my angle of vision. But in view of the preceding paragraphs on boredom and its narcissistic components it will not come as a surprise when I reserve for a final line an age-old question that both Judaism and Christianity have struggled with since their inception: Is redemption an individual affair, meant for personal souls, or is its tenet the whole human community engaged in interpersonal love under God? I think this is the sixty-four-dollar question about narcissism versus object-love in religion.

Notes

1. Presented at the annual meeting of the American Association of Pastoral Counselors in Chicago on May 4, 1978. The paper was originally part of a symposium on Narcissism in Modern Society, held at the University of Michigan, Ann Arbor, on November 16–18, 1977.
2. Sir James Frazer, *Taboo and the Perils of Soul*. Ed. 3. (*The Golden Bough*, Vol. 3) (New York: Macmillan, 1951).
3. Sigmund Freud, *Totem and Taboo* (Standard Edition 13, 1913, 1–162).
4. H. J. S. Guntrip. *Personality Structure and Human Interaction; the Developing Synthesis of Psycho-dynamic Theory* (New York: International Universities Press, 1961). See also Otto Kernberg, *Borderline Conditions and Pathological Narcissism* (New York: Jason Aronson, 1975); and Heinz Kohut, *The Analysis of the Self: A Systematic Ap-*

proach to the Psychoanalytic Treatment of Narcissistic Personality Disorders (New York: International Universities Press, 1971).

5. P. W. Pruyser, "Sigmund Freud and His Legacy: Psychoanalytic Psychology of Religion," in *Beyond the Classics? Essays in the Scientific Study of Religion*, ed. by C. Y. Glock and P. E. Hammond (New York: Harper & Row, 1973), pp. 243–290; *Between Belief and Unbelief* (New York: Harper & Row, 1974).
6. Angelus Silesius, Selections from his poetry, by Willibald Koehler (Munich: Georg Mueller, 1929), p. 27.
7. P. W. Pruyser, "Sigmund Freud and His Legacy . . . " *op. cit.*
8. Sigmund Freud, *The Taboo of Virginity: Contributions to the Psychology of Love III* (Standard Edition 11, 1918/1917), pp. 191–208, see esp. p. 199.
9. S. E. Mead, "In Quest of America's Religion," *Christian Century*, 1970, 87, 752–756.
10. Sigmund Freud, *On Narcissism* (Standard Edition 14, 1914), pp. 69–102.
11. Christopher Lasch, "The Narcissist Society," *New York Review of Books*, 1976, 23, 5–13.
12. "Daniel Bell, *Coming of Post-Industrial Society: A Venture in Social Forecasting* (New York: Basic Books, 1973).
13. Peter Hartocollis, "Aggression and Mysticism," *Contemporary Psychoanalysis*, 1976, *12*, 214–226.
14. P. W. Pruyser, "The Seamy Side of Current Religious Beliefs," *Bulletin of the Menninger Clinic*, 1977, 41, (4), 329–348. [Reprinted as chapter 2, this volume.]
15. George Woodcock, "The Lure of the Primitive," *The American Scholar*, 1976, *45*, 387–402.
16. P. W. Pruyser, *Between Belief and Unbelief*, op. cit.
17. Rudolf Otto, *The Idea of the Holy*, tr. by J. W. Harvey (New York: Oxford University Press, 1928).
18. P. W. Pruyser, "Life and Death of a Symbol: A History of the Holy Ghost Concept and Its Emblems," *McCormick Quarterly Special Supplement on Myth and Modern Man*, 1965, *18*, 5–22.
19. P. W. Pruyser, *The Minister as Diagnostician* (Philadelphia: Westminister Press, 1976).
20. Ben Bursten, *The Manipulator: A Psychoanalytic View* (New Haven: Yale University Press, 1973).
21. Otto Fenichel, *The Psychoanalytic Theory of Neurosis* (New York: W. W. Norton, 1945), p. 364.

III

RELIGIOUS FUNCTION

5

Religion in the Psychiatric Hospital: A Reassessment

The years 1983-84 are anniversary dates for the Clinical Pastoral Education movement. In 1923 Anton Boisen started his studies of mental patients and of psychiatric theory at the Boston Psychopathic Hospital and in July 1924 went to Worcester (Mass.) State Hospital to pioneer a psychiatric hospital chaplaincy that quickly became also an organized training course for clergy interested in dealing with the mentally ill.[1] In the intervening sixty years of specialized mental hospital chaplaincy and Clinical Pastoral Education much has been done with and written about Anton Boisen's legacy.[2] It has gone through some significant transformations, and some aspects of Boisen's original agenda and work have even been forgotten.[3-5] To the best of my knowledge, very little attention has been given lately to the general premises for and the ways of dealing with religion in the mental hospital, and the anniversary of Boisen's enterprise is a good occasion for revisiting these topics.

Now that most mental hospitals have clinically trained chaplains, and now that most clinical work is being done by multidisciplinary teams that include chaplains, it is appropriate, and perhaps even urgent, to ask: Who does what in regard to the patients' religious needs, habits, ideas, feelings, practices, including their possible religious delusions, compulsions, or terrors? What can or should religious persons—or for that matter irreligious persons—count on when they become patients in a psychiatric hospital? How are tasks

Reprinted with the permission of the *Journal of Pastoral Care*, 1984, *38*, pp. 5-16.

and roles to be divided, if any, between the professional in religion and the professionals in such other disciplines as social work nursing, psychology, psychiatry and others which lay claim to standing in a physical-science or social-science tradition?

In an attempt to give contemporary answers to these questions I will successively pay attention to (1) the multidisciplinary mental health team and its workings; (2) historical patterns that have guided mental institutions' explicit or implicit contracts with religion; (3) defining the scope of chaplaincy; (4) the symbolic nature of religion; (5) the prevailing diagnostic neglect of religion and of the patient's personal agenda. The purpose of reviewing and defining these topics is to make some suggestions for a responsive and responsible flexibility on the part of all team members toward the patient's religious needs.

In setting myself to this task I will draw on my experience as an educator involved in training programs for virtually all mental health professions, as a clinician, as a student of the psychology of religion,[6,7] as an administrator, and as a friend of the Clinical Pastoral Education movement.[8]

The Multidisciplinary Mental Health Team

I do not see the human enterprises of science and religion as antagonistic to each other, but neither do I see them as fusable. Though both are symbol systems, science is science and religion is religion, and one should know what symbol system one uses for what purpose. I espouse a perspectival point of view in which each of the arts, sciences, religion, philosophy, professions, and disciplines adopts its own thought pattern and language game in order to make reality, and especially the human condition, a bit less chaotic and more understandable. The perspectival view holds that all disciplines and professions deal with reality, that each one is autonomous, and that each one creates its own data, leaning on a long history of efforts to make the universe understandable and hence meaningful. The perspectival viewpoint holds that nothing is anything in particular unless it is seen from a particular viewpoint, caught up in a special language game that names it, and becomes a function in some praxis.

As most readers will know from their own practical involvement, multidisciplinary operations have come to be adopted in mental hospitals and clinics. The major rationale for multidisciplinary teams is not just that two heads are better than one when one has to address the complexity of human misery, but that only an organized multiplicity of organized disciplines is fit to do justice to human suffering, which is always multifaceted. It is my conviction that all patients know deep down in their bones or bowels that their plight has more than one side, that it cannot be caught in one phrase, that it cannot be exhaustively labelled by a uniform system, and that each chosen approach to the alleviation of their plight can be complemented by another approach, and still another one after that, almost *ad infinitum*. For human suffering is mysterious and cannot be reduced to a single system of explanations. Sufferers need, and often speak, many different languages in dealing with their condition, just as they adopt many different behaviors in making their misery manifest.

But good multidisciplinary work is sometimes counteracted by managerial and administrative minds that see the so-called team in terms of an organization chart. I think that a well-working team is much closer to a living organism than to a bureaucratic system for the division of labor. A good team, just as an organism, is a self-regulating unit in which the effective leadership and integrative functions are disseminated throughout the whole. In fact, the effective team leadership is somewhat different in each clinical case. Each party to the team has a unique agenda that is nevertheless playing a role in also formulating a superordinate "agenda of agendas" of a holistic kind. And let us be frank about the crucial point that not a single one of the collaborating disciplines and professions has a corner on holistic thought or action—all team members have been trained to be specialists and to identify themselves with what they think a nurse, a psychiatrist, a social worker, an occupational therapist, a music therapist, a psychologist, or a chaplain should and can do, with loyalty to their own discipline. But they also proceed with fidelity to the team whose main task is to bring about transformations in the patients' presenting conditions, in the direction of betterment.

In a good team there is a dynamic balance between two options: the sharpening or the levelling of the differences between the disciplines represented. If too much sharpening occurs the team amounts to a Babel of tongues and the unity-in-diversity is lost sight of. If too much levelling occurs everyone thinks and acts in nearly the same way, which amounts to a costly reduplication of work, and fails to do justice to the patient's complexity. Moreover, levelling usually occurs in the direction of adopting the parlance and concepts of one discipline which for a complex set of good and bad reasons is considered to be culturally, if not politically, dominant.

Some Historical Patterns

Thus, to address now directly the topic of religion in the mental hospital, in an excessive sharpening situation religion would be left entirely and exclusively to the chaplain as the acknowledged and appointed expert in that perspective on humanity. The other team members would avoid making inquiries about religion and pointedly shun the making of religious suggestions. Conversely, in a situation of excessive levelling, everybody would adopt basically the same orientation and inquire about everything, oblivious of specialization and expertise. In such a levelling situation everybody could get busy with and about religion, whether to support it indiscriminately or to denigrate it as a fictional enterprise. In either case, the possible result is that the patient becomes flooded by suggestions that his or her religious ideas or the absence thereof are of the greatest diagnostic or therapeutic momentum. More likely, however, the patient may become bewildered by the diversity of religious voices addressing him or her, for most religiously attuned people are not uniform in their religious questions and suggested answers, except when they are doctrinaire.

Indeed, some church-sponsored hospitals have attempted to cut through the difficulties precisely by openly adopting a doctrinaire attitude: their staff members are asked to sign statements of religious belief and to bend their professional expertise by allowing it to be Christianized in some special denominational form, usually in a fundamentalistic or evangelical vein. Honest traffic with the vanguard in the professions' world of ideas is thereby curtailed, from sheer fear of getting enmeshed in ideological conflicts. For instance, from fear of underlying assumptions of psychodynamic principles or procedures of behavior modification a denominational hospital may restrict itself to seemingly "safe" and "unproblematic" somatic therapies—thereby selling the patient short of optimal treatment.

Along with this doctrinaire and highly ideological pattern, which in effect subordinates the sciences and humanities to religion, a hospital may restrict its services (actively or passively) to a clientele of the same religious constituency. Though this policy is difficult to enforce in the modern world and is economically not very feasible, it banks on the human propensity for like-seeking-like in personal troubles, in the belief that only like-minded, like-situated, and like-believing persons can be of true help to each other. I have seen much evidence of that propensity myself, and have learned something about its deeper motives: on the prospective patient's side it is in some cases dominated by the narcissistic theme that one is a very special person who warrants very special helpers; in other cases it is assumed that a like-believing helper will not raise probing questions about one's beliefs or practices. The result is that under the aegis of such a restrictive policy, whether demanded by the hospital staff or sought by the prospective patients, the superficial religious habits of patients may well be indulged, but the deeper needs for religious soul searching and conflict exploration are rarely addressed. And if they are, the staff's religious answers tend to be valued more highly than the patient's religious search.

An alternative pattern is the public psychiatric hospital. While not beholden to any religious group, public hospitals have nevertheless availed themselves of religious officers, perhaps in part because they cannot escape the public pressure of civil religiosity. Before the era ushered in by Boisen, hospitals were wont to lure ministers and priests, often only part-time, to hold religious services for the patients, to serve some public relations purposes, and to give the institution an aura of dignity commensurate with the civil belief of "a nation under God." Boisen changed all that by insisting on special clinical training for such dignitaries and by turning the chaplaincy into a functional direction and a specialized career choice.[9] The father of Clinical Pastoral Education had himself been a patient in several Massachusetts psychiatric hospitals and knew the score: he himself had suffered from religious delusions and saw a considerable amount of religious psychopathology around him. He did not care much about pastoral counseling, but felt that his trained chaplains should shoulder two major tasks: to make diagnostic investigations about the patients' religious histories, ideas, feelings and practices, and to make the patients' otherwise dull lives in the hospital stimulating and rewarding. Boisen believed that in many cases of severe mental derangement and in many profound religious crises a similar set of mental dynamisms is involved that can be addressed both psychiatrically and pastorally, and sometimes leads to a turning point.

Defining the Chaplaincy

And so we have had for some time a specialized professional ministry, that of the clinically trained chaplain who is an integral member of the psychiatric team, diagnostically and therapeutically. The chaplain's tasks are many: personal pastoral attention to the patient and the patient's relatives; liaison with the patient's local pastor or church, if any; making religious services available; doing pastoral counseling and engaging the patients in religious education or reeducation; serving individual staff members in their personal problems; shoring up the whole staff's morale, if needed; helping in the clarification of ethical and moral issues and consulting with staff members about their efforts to understand the patients' religion; and as a responsible professional giving training opportunities to other ministers who want to attain pastoral care and counseling skills in their parish ministry or who seek to embark on a chaplaincy career. Under all circumstances the chaplain's ministry must meet ecumenical standards in addition to professional and technical qualifications, on account of which the chaplain is responsible not only to the hospital but also to many outside parties: e.g. his or her church of ordination, a ministerial association, a council of churches, a professional society.

Unfortunately, the perception by others as well as the self-definition of the chaplaincy is often fuzzy. In mental hospitals from time to time the question is heard: What does the chaplain do that other team members do not or cannot do? Cannot the social worker deal with the relatives and the local pastor, cannot the psychologist spot religious ideation in the test protocols, cannot the psychiatrist take the patient's religious history and explore his present religious thoughts and acts, cannot the nurse quiet some religious furor and reinforce sound thoughts and habits? Liturgical church members and sacramentalists will of course single out worship and sacramental rites as the exclusive prerogative of ministers and priests and thereby vouchsafe the chaplain's place on the team, but such an exclusive and limited emphasis may only deal with the ritualistic side of the patient's religion, and fail to address the patient's cognitive questions and emotional longings. Moreover, for non-liturgical groups this answer simply does not hold and therefore the question still stands. For them, there is still an impasse, which not infrequently leads to the next question which many people feel is a better one: Does not the theological principle of the priesthood of all believers enlist all staff members, irrespective of profession, in serving the patient's religious needs or in helping the patient toward a viable religious perspective on his or her life; in other words, in doing some evangelizing?

I am not sure that I can give an unqualifiedly affirmative answer to this question. I myself am not an evangelizer, but those who are often give the impression of being overly verbal, rather zealous, somewhat meddlesome, and sometimes very unclear as to whom they are serving: themselves or others? For evangelizing is, alas, not infrequently done in the service of reinforcing one's own convictions and promoting the strength of one's ingroup. And its worst feature is its activism, nay, its hyper-activism; short shrift is made of listening to the other person and emphatically registering the nuances of the cognitive, emotional, moral, and relational facets of that person's belief system. Beliefs are very complex process entities that appear to lead a life of their own and are subject to ebbs and flows, regressions and progressions, fixations and developments.[10] And religious beliefs in particular are very vulnerable to two kinds of distortion: (1) autistic intrusions that are well documented by the content and form of clinical syndromes, and (2) displacements of their delicate content from the symbolic into the realistic sphere, by means of which the symbols are turned into mere emblems or shibboleths, as happens in certain forms of fundamentalism and literalism. Thus, undertaking a priesthood of believers is beset with problems.

The Three Worlds of Autism, Realism, and Symbolism

Religion is an illusionistic undertaking, as are the other great cultural worlds that humankind has shaped for giving meaning to its place in the cosmos: the arts, the sciences, and the humanities. All these great domains of culture partake of special cognitive and emotional processes that are grafted on the capacity for healthy and constructive playing and are therefore illusionistic. The illusionistic or symbolic world that is the home of these cultural engagements is different from the autistic subjective world of dreams and private fantasies that are doomed to be ineffable, on the one hand, and on the other hand from the realistic world of things, nature, food, concrete objects, and powers that is meant when we speak of ordinary reality contact and reality testing. All of us live in all three worlds: the autistic, the realistic, and the illusionistic spheres, and it takes perspicacity and skill to differentiate the special entities and processes germane to each. Art vanishes when it becomes too autistic or too concretistic; science becomes mere technology when its ideas are turned into gadgets; and religion loses its point when the autistic fantasies of a crazy leader stampede the faithful into mass suicide, or scripture is taken as a rule book or a compilation of facts about the origin of species.

The idea of the priesthood of believers then, should not be turned into a license for mental health professionals to dabble in religion in any way they want, and least of all taken as *carte blanche* to satisfy their own religious needs or fortify their own weakness of belief. The complexity and subtlety of religion and religious beliefs should not be obscured by anyone's myopic vision; they need to be addressed by expertise and empathic capacity. The phenomenology of religion is exceedingly rich in nuances, which are prohibited from coming into view by denominational hyperactivity. To put it bluntly, anyone bent on soul-winning should first pay minute attention to the soul he or she seeks to win by letting it express and manifest itself. But unfortunately, such desirable phenomenological sensitivity is rarely practiced, for a variety of reasons.

Diagnostic Neglect of Religion and of the Patient's Agenda

Thorough assessment of the patient's past and present religious beliefs and practices is a neglected part of diagnostic work. Apart from the ascertainment of some superficial indices (e.g. denominational affiliation, changes in affiliation, frequency of church attendance, strictness or lenience of upbringing, admiration or rejection of persons who transmitted beliefs) diagnostic explorations of the finer points of patients' religious beliefs have been hampered by a kind of taboo ("too personal" or "I want to keep this private") as well as a conscious fear or unconscious apprehension that the patient may turn the table on the questioner and ask about the investigator's religious orientation, which could raise countertransference problems.[11] And maybe many diagnosticians simply consider religion unimportant in the psychodynamics of living and therefore confine themselves to the exploration of object relations, superego motifs, or impulse control, as if religion played no role in those dynamisms. Or else some mental health workers simply do not know enough about religion to be comfortable with exploring that aspect of the patient's cognitive and emotional household.

Granted that for some people religion appears to be of no importance and throws no light on the misery that brought them into the hospital, and granted too that the scope of diagnostic work is limited by constraints of time and economics, one may miss important diagnostic clues by leaving the patient's religious ideas, values, and practices unexplored. And since all clinical work is in essence in the service of aiding the patient in undergoing some transformation, it is very important to know as much as one can about the patient's present situation as shaped by the past, with an eye on promoting a more wholesome future. But how can such desirable diagnostic knowledge be obtained, and who on the psychiatric team will do what to foster it?

Before this question can be answered we need to take a closer look at the patient's expectations when they enter the hospital and meet the various members of the psychiatric team. They soon discover from their successive exposures to the team members that each of the latter, despite overlapping topical interests and concerns, takes a somewhat different focus, uses a different technique, follows different leads, raises different questions, and may strike a different tone or parlance in coming to grips with their complaints. And the patients soon learn what interests each of the team members most; they bend their conversations to suit the individual staff member. For this to happen is a sign of some intact functioning; its absence is a sign of profound and widespread disturbance. But at heart, the patient's capacity to respond selectively is and should be a function of two realizations: the subjective, experienced multidimensionality of their problems when these have become big enough to warrant hospitalization, and the objective, organized multiplicity of perspectives on the problems stylized by the specialities represented on the team.

I infer from the patient's experienced multidimensionality as a problem-laden person that before *we* enter the picture the patient has already engaged in some kind of self-assessment and has come to realize that there are many aspects to his or her plight.[12] In other words, the patient comes to us after having made several kinds of self-diagnoses, albeit perhaps in a confused and bungling way, and now, upon entering the hospital, is given opportunity for refining and revising those self-diagnoses, by the use of various professional experts. No matter how dire the symptoms, and how costly his failings, the patient is still valiantly trying to rescue or shore up the battered self and prevent it from disintegrating. I mention these things to suggest that the crucial holistic efforts that are made in any clinical situation reside in and emerge from the patient, and that the staff must defer to those efforts that the patient is already making. The staff can sustain and foster those efforts, but it is not in a position to take over the patient's self-generated integrative effort or impose a model of alleged wholeness that rides slipshod over the patient's uniqueness.

What I am really trying to develop is a new clinical ethos in which the patient holds the center stage and in which we mental health professionals allow ourselves to function as counselors in selected perspectives to the patient. An old English title designates lawyers as "counselors at law." Could we see physicians similarly as "counselors at medicine," psychiatrists as "counselors at psychiatry," social workers as "counselors at social reality and institutions," psychologists as "counselors at mental processes," and chaplains as "counselors at religion?" If so, we can make our respective forms of expertise available to the patient as aides in the patient's ongoing self-explorations and as advisors in the patient's self-healing efforts. I remind us of the fact that the patients' rights movement and the current social criticism of the health professions necessitate a change in traditional authoritarian attitudes and a revision of our styles of functioning. But even apart from such recent external pressures I must confess that I have long felt uneasy about writing test reports about patients without ever verifying my reports with the patients' own self-assessments, and have lately begun to share my report drafts with the patients. I think that all our clinical work should appeal to the patients' demonstrable quest for self-knowledge and self-healing. It is the patient who sets the agenda for our work; we have no right to impose our agendas on the patient, and are anyway bound to fail if we try to do so.

Suggestions for Responsive Flexibility

If this ethos is taken seriously, it will allow us to find fresh answers to the question about religion in the mental hospital. The emphasis is then no longer on what staff members like to do, but on what patients would want us to do, and this requires a flexible approach. Some patients would want, in addition to other perspectives, to scrutinize themselves and their problems in the light of their faith or religious tradition. Some may want to place their problems exclusively in the light of their faith, but in that case a psychiatric hospital would not be their first choice. In either case, however, the helping perspective they seek is a pastoral one and the choice expert is obviously the chaplain. Other patients may simply seek in the hospital some opportunity for continuing their customary religious practices, devotions, confessions, readings, or even reveries—without conversations with the chaplain. In that case, a chapel, a visit to a local church, reading material, or just a quiet place in which to be by oneself may be made available. Since some patients are too shy to ask for anything, nurses are in a good position to orient them toward the available services, and a chaplain may take the initiative for visiting the patient. In fact, chaplains have some unique social prerogatives that they should exercise: the right of initiative and the right of access. No one else has such rights, which may be one more reason why some people consider religion a private affair that is not to be discussed with psychiatrists, social workers, the recreation therapist, or the greenhouse staff.

Other patients, especially those who have an aversion to ministers or church, may avoid the religious perspective entirely or demand for themselves a moratorium on religious thought, and such wishes may have to be granted. Still others put their trust in a particular member of the staff, irrespective of profession, and proceed to share all kinds of confidences with him or her, turning that person into a kind of omnibus helper. While this can be taxing for the staff member involved, the patient's indiscriminate sharing with one person can provide salient information for the team and lead to referrals for more organized discussions with specific team members. In fact, despite all their attention to professionalism, clinicians see daily that selective friendships develop between patients and staff members, which put some of the latter into a position of spontaneity that pushes against the limitations of strict role behavior. And I think that patients, like most others, tend to discuss religion with people they consider friends.

Let us not underestimate the leadership that patients assume in the diagnostic and therapeutic processes. They drop hints about what they want to discuss and with whom; they shop around among staff members for willing ears, and also avail themselves of other patients in whom they find a responsive chord for their troubles. It generally pays off to follow the patient's leads, that is, to be responsive to the patient's initiative. Therefore, if a patient opens up to the nurse about some religious theme in a visible attempt to ventilate some anguish or to gain some clarification, or for that matter as if begging to be contradicted, I see no reason for such an incipient conversation to be cut off, except when a grossly delusional paranoid idea is being phrased. It all depends on how comfortable the nurse feels with such conversations. Similarly, when in the course of psychotherapy with any qualified professional a patient mentions religious ideas or practices, the therapist is entitled to inquire or make conjectures about how these are linked with other ideas in the stream of thought or with the feelings prevailing at that moment. I also feel that confrontations are occasionally indicated; for instance, when a certain type of behavior or an intention is contrary to a patient's stated beliefs or values the therapist may well ask: "How would that fit with your belief?" or even "From what you said before I thought you were against doing anything like that!" In other words, when the patient does not compartmentalize religion but freely weaves it in with other expressed concerns or feelings in any professional contact, any team member can address it in the context of his or her professional expertise and personal comfort. Such occurrences do not bar, however, a concomitant referral to the chaplain when the issues are rather technical and require a stylized pastoral touch.

I hope it is becoming clear that in the perspectival model which I uphold there is no limit on the *topics* that any team member can address. *The professional expertise represented by the team members is perspectival, not topical.* Any perspective can potentially address anything, but does so in its own way, by the profession's special package of basic and applied sciences, skills, techniques, and language game. The perspectival view radically discards the older ontological and epistemological models that stage the disciplines as tightly bounded territories each representing a special kind of substance or neatly divide human nature into bodily, mental, and spiritual layers. Reality is far more fluid and holistic than these old models assume.[13]

Let me repeat something I stated earlier: in all strictness, in the perspectival view of reality nothing is anything in particular unless and until it gets recognized, captured, named, and operated upon by an organized discipline or profession. One can look at people chemically, mathematically, physiologically, psychologically, economically, theologically, ethically, neurologically, philosophically, linguistically, psychodynamically, behaviorally, etc. and each perspective makes sense. Moreover, each perspective creates its own data. Without perspectives there are no data but only confusion.

Hence, any discipline can deal with religion, as it can deal with art, morals, development, growing old, pleasure, suffering and a host of other relevant human themes, *but each discipline will do so in its own way*, in terms of its gradually evolved conceptual system, its basic premises, its aims, operational procedures, and its language habits. Though a psychologist may know quite a bit about theology, he or she is true to the trade when he or she looks at religion and patients psychologically. Though a psychiatrist may be a firm religious believer and an elder in the church, he or she should not address patients pastorally, but in the style and language of his or her chosen psychiatric orientation. Though a chaplain may be psychiatrically or medically well informed, he or she should address the patients pastorally and make use of theological knowledge. Though a social worker may also be a church school instructor, his or her patient contacts should be guided by knowledge of the social sciences and any discussions of religion should focus on the social processes that are fostered or thwarted by the patient's religious attitudes.

It is presumptuous to think that we mental health workers can integrate our patients or make them whole. Boisen knew better; his whole life and work demonstrate that the only one who can do the integrating is the patient himself or herself, albeit at times with a little help from the professionals. The rest should be left to the Almighty who is thought to be, after all, both more inventive and more holistic than any human being—and maybe not as religious as some of His creatures!

Notes

1. A. T. Boisen, *Out of the Depths* (New York, NY: Harper & Brothers, 1960).
2. E. E. Thornton, *Professional Education for Ministry: A History of Clinical Pastoral Education* (Nashville, TN: Abingdon Press, 1970).
3. A. T. Boisen, "The Present Status of William James' Psychology of Religion," *The Journal of Pastoral Care*, 1953, *7*, (3) pp. 155–158.
4. S. Hiltner, "The Debt of Clinical Pastoral Education to Anton T. Boisen," *The Journal of Pastoral Care*, 1966, *20*, (3) pp. 129–135.
5. P. W. Pruyser, "Anton T. Boisen and the Psychology of Religion," *The Journal of Pastoral Care*, 1967, *21*, (4) pp. 209–219.
6. P. W. Pruyser, *Between Belief and Unbelief* (New York, NY: Harper and Row, 1974).
7. P. W. Pruyser, *A Dynamic Psychology of Religion* (New York, NY: Harper and Row, 1968).
8. P. W. Pruyser, *The Minister as Diagnostician: Personal Problems in Pastoral Perspective* (Philadelphia, PA: Westminster Press, 1976).
9. A. T. Boisen, *The Exploration of the Inner World* (Chicago, IL: Willet, Clark and Co., 1936; New York, NY: Harper & Brothers, 1952).
10. P. W. Pruyser, "Psychological Roots and Branches of Belief," *Pastoral Psychology*, 1979, *28*, pp. 8–20.
11. P. W. Pruyser, "Assessment of the Patient's Religious Attitudes in the Psychiatric Case Study," *Bulletin of the Menninger Clinic*, 1971, *35*, pp. 272–291.
12. P. W. Pruyser, "The Diagnostic Process: Touchstone of Medicine's Values," in W. R. Rogers and D. Barnard (Eds.), *Nourishing the Humanistic in Medicine: Interactions with the Social Sciences* (Pittsburgh, PA: University of Pittsburgh Press, 1979), pp. 245–261.
13. P. W. Pruyser, *The Psychological Examination* (New York, NY: International Universities Press, 1979).

6

Anxiety, Guilt, and Shame in the Atonement

Nearly every comprehensive theological handbook makes it plain that speculations about the atonement have produced several alternative models or theories, each with its own intricate strengths and weaknesses, its own metaphors, analogies, historical accidents, and cultural images. They are roughly classifiable into three main groupings which have shown many permutations in the course of time: the Ransom theory, the Satisfaction theory, and the Moral Influence theory. This curious theological situation is not unlike the predicament of modern physics, in which two plausible theories of light, the particle theory and the wave theory, vie for supremacy but are forced to live in a kind of peaceful coexistence and are used alternatively, depending on one's purposes, opportunities, and perhaps even one's moods.

To the psychologist of religion, these three main theories of atonement constitute three types of thematic material, three thought structures of men pondering the divine intentions towards mankind, three fragments of religious ideation, three symbol systems. About these, he can ask what he asks about any psychological datum: what is its structure, function, and purpose? How is it motivated? What economic role does it play in the psychic household? What conflicts or problems does it solve, if any? How did the theme or the symbol originate? What are its vicissitudes during the life of the individual or of the religious system? Can one consistently abide by one of the three theories, models, symbols, or themes only, while rejecting the alternatives?

Reprinted with the permission of *Theology Today*, 1964, *21*, pp. 15–33.

While I am far from being prepared to answer each of these questions exhaustively, I do believe that the questions themselves are valid and that some preliminary knowledge can be gained by comparing the three major theories of atonement and placing them in a clinical-psychological context. Let me begin by trying to describe concisely each major theme.

I

In the thinking of the Greek fathers the image of the "powers of darkness" plays a large role. Whether personified into Satan, Devil, or Adversary, or described as Death, Realm of Darkness, or the idea of mortality, one main trend in Greek-Christian thought is a duality between powers, one of which is thought of as genuine and true being, while the other is not. Man is alienated from the true ground of being, and has fallen into the captivity of a faked owner who has power over him. He is in bondage to a foreign master from whom he cannot liberate himself. In this cosmic setting, the atonement became dramatized as a set of power transactions between the righteous and the unrighteous owner of men in which Christ, with varying emphases on his birth, life, suffering, and death but with equal emphasis on the dual nature of his God-manhood, was seen as a ransom. In the works of Origen, to whom we owe a succinct description of this cosmic power struggle, the death of Christ is the ransom price which God pays to Satan in order to reclaim his creature estranged from him by original sin. Man's bondage to the foreign potentate is now abolished; his alienation from God gives way to re-alignment with the ground of being. But the power of darkness was fooled in the barter, since Christ, the perfect God-man, triumphed over Satan's temptations during his life as well as in his resurrection and thus abolished in principle the ultimacy of death.

While much of this imagery recalls the deals which buyers engaged in on the slave market, the elaborations introduced by the Cappadocian fathers, especially Gregory of Nyssa, added an element of clever deceit on the part of God. Since God did not want to use force in reclaiming his rightful ownership over captivated man, he used, as it were, the lure of a more perfect, more desirable, more tempting possession in barter, and Satan fell for it without foreseeing what he was in for. Indeed, Gregory the Great freely used the image of the fishhook in order to describe Christ's dual nature: Satan, lured by the bait of his humanity, sank his teeth in the hook of his divinity and found it too much to swallow.

The point I want to make is that this group of theories of atonement assumes a dualism and for this reason runs counter to the dominant monotheistic position. It is also frankly demonological, assuming as it does the existence of a powerful, pseudo-divine adversary in heaven, on earth, or in man himself whose essential goal is destruction, i.e., death. But perhaps most noteworthy of all is the image of God in this context: he is seen as creator and rightful owner of man, who pities his creature's predicament of alienation, estrangement, slavery to a foreign master, captivity, or bondage. His love for man outweighs his anger over their corruption. He works for their delivery by identifying himself with their plight through his divine son who became man. His work of deliverance starts at the incarnation and ends in the resurrection with promise of the *parousia*, at which time man will be completely renewed by a final recreation. In this scheme, the major points of emphasis on incarnation and resurrection of the God-man parallel the two choice points by which man discovers his own contingency: birth and death. In Heidegger's ontology, man's *Geworfenheit* whereby he feels thrown into existence and out of it without any power of decision of his own, is experienced as anxiety. In Tillich's terms, anxiety is the awareness of our alienation from the ground of being.

The ransom theory seems to address itself to the anxiety aroused when man feels himself in the dominion of foreign powers, which eventually produce death. These powers can be seen as cosmic, in the form of Satan and the tortures which he inflicts, or as the internal powers of all that is ego-alien in man, especially his unconscious anti-social instinctual impulses which are bent on destruction. In either case, the emphasis on the demonic nature of these powers is to be seen in the context of ancient cosmological myths which hold that the powers of darkness are real since they derive from the misappropriated power of God.

II

But human relations are not confined to the slave market, and human experiences are not confined to anxiety. Another choice of metaphor in describing the mystery of redemption and the need for deliverance from evil is possible. From a cultural point of view it is small wonder that the Latin church fathers began to take hold of another image of great antiquity, derived on the one hand from the institution of sacrifice elaborated in the Old Testament, on the other hand from the Roman institution of the judicial process. These two trends are merged into the one idea of satisfaction. They derive from the image of God as just and holy, sovereign ruler, supreme judge and lawgiver, whose domain in priestly terms is the altar of sacrifice and in civil terms the law court. While the theme of satisfaction is as old as Christianity and can be found, together with the ransom idea, in the Pauline epistles, its clearest and most elaborate form was reached much later in the work of Anselm, whose *Cur Deus Homo* I will take as paradigmatic.

The satisfaction theory portrays, in essence, a God who is both just and forgiving, angry and merciful, offended and long-suffering, whose wrath demands reparation, satisfaction, penalty, or repentance from offenders and transgressors of his holiness and his law. It portrays man as an offender of law, blasphemer of the holy, rebel against sovereign, disobedient and obstreperous child, violator of rules who stands in need of punishment and correction. Sin, according to this theme, is basically transgression of rules and boundaries, with a great deal of rebellious arrogance. In a Barthian phrase, it is refusal to let God be God, i.e., sovereign being. The result of original sin, thus interpreted, is life under the curse of work and pain, and death as inescapable punishment.

Crucial to Anselm's reasoning are his adhortations to his interlocutor: "You have not yet considered what a heavy weight sin is," and his emphasis on the centrality of willing both for the sinning of man and the saving done by the God-man. With hairsplitting logic the necessity for the death of Christ is proven and yet it is said that he died freely, of his own will, in order to render for man the sacrifice exacted by an offended God. But most important to the satisfaction theory is the idea of punishment and penalty: sinning is likened to thievery, and merely to give back to God what was stolen from him may provide restoration but not satisfaction. Since God's dignity and honor are at stake, more than restitution must occur. His justice is necessary and his mercy optional.[1]

Subsequent variations on the satisfaction theme have placed greater emphasis on the penal element and upon the Son as the propitiatory victim, whereas in other versions the ancient theme of sacrifice was re-enlivened. Both had the effect of keeping the satisfaction theory associated with blood and suffering. This elicited an understandable reaction in thinkers like Socinus who found the tension between God's mercy and justice in these portrayals so intolerable that he denied the possibility of their combination.

Throughout the satisfaction and penal theories the model for sin is disobedience, arrogant rebellion, transgression, and violation of God's laws, with a parallel emphasis on Christ as a model of obedience who renders himself a sacrifice, fine, penalty, Paschal lamb, or vicarious criminal for man, depending upon the particular version. Through this process of atonement God's honor is restored and death is abolished because the punitive reason for man's perdition has been taken away by the divine pardon. Man is now justified and a life of rectitude is made possible in principle.

What is the experiential matrix, the basic feeling tone out of which this theme might have emerged? There can hardly be any doubt that guilt feelings were preponderant, with a sense of transgression and disobedience as the essence of human misery. Whereas the ransom theory is based on anxiety over the uncanny phenomenon of death, the satisfaction theory is based on guilt feelings over incorrect conduct. The redemptive side of the ransom theory turns anxiety into joy over adoption and deliverance; in the satisfaction theory it relieves guilt feelings through justification and expiation. To the extent that man's own felt intrapsychic contents have served as a model for these themes, the ransom theory is a typical expression of conflict between the Ego and the Id, whereas the satisfaction theories are typically modelled after conflicts between the Ego and the Super-ego.

III

There is a third group of atonement doctrines, essentially as old as the others and also to be found embryonically in the Pauline writings, but which took a longer time to become clearly formulated. Its central theme is taken from another sacrosanct social institution: government with public justice and positive law, projected onto God who is now seen as governor and guardian of the social order. With antecedents in another Cappadocian father, Gregory of Nazianzus, and in scholasticism through Abelard, it found a competent systematizer in Grotius who was also the founder of international law. It has also one root in Athanasius' conviction that the consequence, if not the purpose, of the atonement was to restore the defaced *imago dei* in man so that moral and social betterment might ensue. Two notions are crucial to the theory: it ranks God's goodness as his highest attribute, making his mercy necessary and his justice optional (the opposite is true of the satisfaction theories). God punishes not out of wrath but for the common good, for except from this end, said Grotius, punishment has not the character of being desirable. In the second place, it sets up Christ as an example to be followed rather than as an expiatory sacrifice, though elements of the latter are not missing.

The influence of the governmental theory extended even to such a staunch Calvinist and penalist as Jonathan Edwards who let God be a ruler who maintains order and decorum in his kingdom and Christ a benevolent mediator who seeks man's welfare by offering to pay his penalty for him. Christ identifies with man out of sympathy and mercy, whatever his function toward God might be, and this has the moral effect of making man desire to identify with Christ, his life, his teachings, and his perfection. In these and other versions of the moral influence and governmental theories rings the echo of Augustine's compassionate idea: "Christ did so much for us—what can we do for him?"

Most of the governmental and moral influence doctrines maintain in some way the major tenets of the satisfaction theories, but they add something essentially new; namely that among God's attributes mercy and goodness prevail and although he also is just, he is not absolutely tied to his own laws since the wise governor dispenses justice with the common good in mind. It avoids the classical pitfall of *summum ius summa iniuria*, whether or not it betrays a Socinian streak.

Although these theories involve an element of fear of punishment for sin and an awareness of guilt feelings (to the extent that they are intermixed with satisfaction theories of one sort or another), the new stratum of human experience they tap is selective identification with Christ as a model to be followed, the desire of belonging to him and the new life, and feelings of shame. In psychological terms, the underlying conflict situation is one between the Ego and the Ego-ideal with shame as the essential affect.[2]

IV

To the student of personality who adopts a psychoanalytic frame of reference, the major structural divisions within the personality are conceptualized according to frequently observed clinical conflict situations. For psychoanalytic theory is a conflict theory which starts from the premise that personality is more like a house divided against itself than a homogeneous substance of one sort or another. It capitalizes in its concepts on the paradoxical nature of man. One of the major congenital givens of the personality is the Id referring to the instinctual drives of love and hate, libido and aggression, strivings for union and urges toward destruction. These tend to follow their own course, driving more or less blindly toward discharge of their tensions, were it not for the controls imposed upon them by the environment, the reality of other persons, and an internal psychic constellation of control, regulation, and integration called the Ego. The task of the Ego is to regulate the internal forces of the Id in line with material and social reality, to make incessant bargains, as it were, between inside and outside demands and thus guaranteeing the most favorable form of adaptation.

Cutting across this division is the qualitative distinction between conscious and unconscious mental processes which runs throughout mental life. But the Id and its strivings, in their raw form, are unconscious and therefore usually outside the Ego's awareness. Their power is great, and feared by the Ego. In the relations between Ego and Id the affective experience of anxiety plays an important role, since the quality as well as the intensity of the original instinctual promptings is often felt by the Ego as dangerous. Through various so-called defense mechanisms, especially repression, the Ego may be able to keep these impulses at a distance from itself and find various innocuous opportunities for their modified discharge. Under the impact of various forms and intensities of anxiety, the Ego can overshoot its mark, as it were, and repress all too vigorously, with the result that the Id and its tendencies become almost completely alienated from the rest of the personality and produce a painful symbolic expression in mental symptoms, such as slips of the tongue, mistakes, hysterical paralysis, or in dreams, by which the Ego feels partially victimized.

In the course of personality development, the Ego is aided in its task of control by a new internal psychic structure, the Super-Ego. This is the product of largely unconscious and pre-verbal identifications, starting very early in life, with the do's and don'ts of significant adults which control the person at first from the outside, until by learning and habit formation the rudiments of conscience are established as a new structure within the personality. While this greatly simplifies control and gives the Ego aid in its judgments, the Super-Ego usually attains a certain degree of independence and can even become so dominant that new lines of conflict are engendered between Ego and Super-Ego. This is especially the case when moral demands have been put before the developing child in great strictness, with forceful punishment or threat of punishment upon transgression of the original proscriptions. Such conflicts engender a particular affect, namely, guilt feelings which are painfully felt by the Ego.

For the elimination of such painful feelings of guilt the Ego uses the time-honored devices of self-punishment or the seeking of external punishment, expiation, retribution, either literally or symbolically, until a balanced relation between Super-Ego and Ego has been restored. Crucial to this type of conflict situation is the realization, entirely within the personality, that some boundary has been trespassed, that some transgression in deed, word, or thought has occurred, and that punishment is in order, painful as it may be. The sting of this particular form of anxiety (i.e., guilt feelings), is the threat of bodily harm or mutilation. The situation of the self in this type of conflict has been described as "I am no good—I will be harmed!"

But as development goes on, the examples of others who are important to us make a further impact, in the course of which we come to identify selectively and often consciously with special traits and characteristics of those whom we admire and whose behavior and values we want to make our own. The ideal standards for thought and conduct which we thus acquire and thereafter follow almost routinely, constitute another psychic structure, the Ego-Ideal. This too aids the ego in its adaptive function and makes the task of acculturation easier and richer. One knows better what to aim for in life after having admired something in one's heroes and loved ones.

But the Ego-Ideal too can occasionally lead to conflict situations, for instance when a person fails to live up to his standards and ideals. This too produces a special kind of anxiety, namely a feeling of shame. In that situation, one feels that one's goal has not been reached, one senses failure, and has the feeling that one does not belong any more to the cherished company of one's erstwhile models. Behind shame lies the fear of contempt and exposure, with the ultimate threat of abandonment. A sense of one's own inadequacy prevails, until one has a chance to prove once more that success in one's ideal strivings is possible. I have suggested in a previous article[3] that at some deep level the theme of death and dying is inherent in shame.

This sketchy exposition of basic theory must suffice to undergird my thesis that each of the three described groups of theories of atonement is a parallel to each of the major types of intra-psychic conflict situations characteristic of human life. It seems to me that the ransom theories of atonement are germane to the psychological situation of anxiety produced by Ego-Id conflicts, in which the Ego feels in captivity by strange symptoms and has lost access to the motivating grounds of personality. The healing of such a conflict situation and the reduction of this anxiety proceed in principle by the therapeutic demonstration that the feared impulses are not really as dangerous as they seemed, and that greater awareness of them rather than shutting them out of awareness is a better mode of control over them. Instead of bondage to autonomous impulses there is now mastery over them, with much greater all around satisfaction. On this basis, new love relations become possible with more lasting gratifications which in turn mitigate fears, both realistic and irrational ones. Significantly, the ransom theories portray the old life as estrangement, and the new life in terms of *deliverance* and *adoption*, by a God whose attitude toward men is one of *pity, compassion*, and *concerned sympathy*.

The satisfaction and penal theories show a definite parallel with the conflicts engendered by a strict and forbidding Super-Ego. Their major emphasis is on guilt feelings and the horror of transgressions, whether in thought, word, or deed. The Ego feels haunted by the internal task master, is forced to damn itself and to live in a world of doom, and is preoccupied with real or imagined corruption, violation of rules or orders, transgression of laws and other heinous crimes or vices. To the relentless demands of the Super-Ego, sacrifices must be made, purifications tried, fines and penalties paid, in the hope that these will serve to alleviate the nagging guilt feelings. Some suffering must be shouldered to effect a tolerable correctness of the person.

The healing of this type of conflict usually proceeds by bringing Ego and Super-Ego closer together, which in principle can be done by clarifying, softening, or refining the demands of the one as well as by heightening the capacities, effectiveness, and versatility of the other. The *differentiation of justice from love* is an important therapeutic goal in this situation, and the *reality of forgiveness* must be learned to counteract the perpetual fear of punishment. Sometimes these goals are not reached and all that can be done therapeutically is to offer possibilities for innocuous symbolic atonement for persistent guilt feelings.

The clinician who knows the symptoms and mechanisms of depression and compulsivity is in an entirely familiar sphere of thought when he reads the classical satisfaction and penal theories of atonement. They portray a God of wrath, whose love is deeply hidden behind insistence on his sovereignty, honor, holiness, and outraged sense of justice; who insists on sacrifice and penalty and to whom blood must be shed in order to restore acceptable relations. Typically the goal of salvation in this framework is stated as *justification* and were it not for his vicarious self-sacrifice, the love of this God could not easily be seen behind his face of wrath.

And what about feelings of shame? I think they play a large part in the moral influence and governmental theories in which the emphasis is on the sanctification of behavior. God, having the common good in mind and acting as a benevolent governor, exacts satisfaction from one who is to serve as a model and example for the many. He makes the perhaps all too optimistic assumption that people are educable. Whereas the satisfaction theories seem to assume that man is trainable through fear, the moral influence theories stipulate in addition (or instead) that man can be led positively to a sanctified life by being given the opportunity *to identify with an enlightening example* to whose circle they are moved to belong out of love.

To fall short of one's ideal and to let the example down henceforth produce shame, an unearthing experience indeed if one recalls how close to total abandonment one can feel in that predicament. But shame has the seeds of betterment in it and it may spur one on to love the example all the more and demonstrate one's intentions in changed behavior. It is future-directed and lives from hope.

It will by now have become obvious, however, that my categorizations of conflict are somewhat artificial and academic. One may object that intra-psychic conflict is rarely confined to discord between just two internal psychic structures. More often it is the whole personality which is in discord with itself, with an involvement of all its structures in a complex set of interactions. The point is granted and is precisely the one I wanted to make. Typology cannot be pushed too far, or we end up with static entities which have nothing to do with life. But while it is true that most psychic conflict is complex, it is also a clinical fact that in each case some lines of conflict are more focal or conspicuous than others.

Thus far I have pointed out a close parallelism between three typical intra-psychic conflict situations and three typical formulations of the atonement mystery. It is chiefly one of symbol structure, prevailing metaphor, predominant affect, and role behavior. As a psychologist I do not thereby take the position of those who assume an *anologia entis* between the structure of man, the nature of God, and the person of Christ. But I wish to remind the reader that in some philosophical contexts, such as extreme personalism, scholasticism, and some forms of gnosticism which stress structural identities between microcosm and macrocosm, the *analogia entis* idea can be applied in order to make assertions about God's nature in terms of man's self experience. One example of its use by a psychologist is Jung's speculation about God gradually resolving his own intra-psychic conflicts by an increasing awareness of some of his unconscious strivings.[4]

The parallelism which I found, so tritely obvious after it has been pointed out, poses many problems of evaluation and interpretation to the psychologist of religion. It also raises some pedagogical questions, especially to the religious educator who wants to know what difference it makes, if any, to stress one atonement theory over another in the appropriation of faith. While I am not prepared to give definite answers to such vast and complex problems, I will venture a few conjectures, which will probably be more revealing of my own bias than be directly useful in giving guidance to the perplexed.

In the first place, the observation of so close a parallelism between experienced human motives and the supposed motives, feelings, and aims of the divine could be used to confirm Freud's suspicion that much religious thought and imagery is a projection of man's own inner experience onto some external object, real or imagined. Especially since all three atonement models arose during the long era of frankly supernaturalistic thinking in Christianity (shared alike by "popular religion" and theologians) which reinforced the "old man in the sky" notion of God,[5] the projection hypothesis is a potent explanation of how the idea of God arises in the first place, and then becomes doctrinally articulated in modes of theological thought which retain a mythological, if not autistic, premise. The other side of this hypothesis is that all such thoughts are illusory in the special technical sense which Freud gave this word in *The Future of an Illusion*, namely "fulfillments of the oldest, strongest and most insistent wishes of mankind; the secret of their strength is the strength of these wishes."[6]

Assuming that some sort of supernaturalism continues to permeate the thought of many ordinary believers and that Freud's psychological interpretation of it is at least in part valid,[7] one is tempted to ask about the relevance of the dissemination of certain atonement doctrines for mental health. At first sight it would seem appropriate to say that since each atonement symbol represents only one aspect of experience, instruction might aim at appropriate richness by fairly representing all three models and their possible combinations. Favoring one while rejecting the others might not only lead to truncated religious development and closed system thinking, but also to over-stimulation of certain affects, eventually leading to preoccupations and perhaps even obsessions with at worst quite morbid consequences. For instance, one can think of irresolvable guilt feelings leading to flagellation, self-castration, and suicide or martyrdom; one can find in some persons or groups chronic feelings of shame and insufficiency; or paranoid delusions of evil invasions, persecutions, or demon possession leading to the mass madness of witch hunting or the cruelties of the Inquisition. Indeed, anyone who is informed about historical psychopathology[8] and the peculiar geographical and cultural distributions of contemporary religious psychopathology[9] knows that this is exactly what has happened, at least occasionally.

But what is perhaps more important than the teaching of atonement theories as such is to recognize the impact of each symbol system, even when not verbally taught, on related religious doctrines, practices, and experiences which the faithful learn, as it were, by osmosis. For along with each special view of the atonement goes practical selective emphasis on some special aspect of the life of Christ such as his birth, teachings, miracles, sayings, suffering, death, resurrection, ascension, or *parousia*. In the wake of this there is a further selective stress on certain fragments of the liturgical year, and even a special interpretation of the sacraments, especially the communion elements. Which of all these should a particular believer be most identified with? Should he rejoice at Christmas, or rather on Easter? Can he rejoice at all on Good Friday? Indeed, is there any ground for joy at all? Can he afford to neglect Pentecost or can he allow himself to over-emphasize it? Is there any special feeling to be emphasized about Advent? What do or should the communion elements mean to the contemporary believer? Is the wine a symbol of spilt blood, messy suffering, brutal aggression, or of new life, gentle nurturance, and rich vitality, or is it perhaps the seal of a promising new pact or covenant? The various doctrinal answers to such questions correlate far less with one's logical acumen or grasp of truth than with the whole cluster of interacting psychological, sociological, economic, theological, denominational, and ideological factors which determine one's concrete religious identity. The power of this correlation resides in the fact that each believer is immersed, as it were, in a vast symbol system around a given atonement motif.

VI

If mental health is a Christian value and mental hygiene one practical concern of the church (as many churchmen now hold), Christian education in the churches must be enlightened, among other things, by the data of religious psychopathology and the psychology of religion. If man's redemption is to be proclaimed, it is important that not only the positive symbol values, but also the limitations and even the dangers of each of the atonement theories be made clear. Since my own preference, in the last analysis, is for richness rather than precision of thought with a good deal of tolerance for paradoxes and open systems, I would be inclined to advocate a broad representation of all the atonement models with their associated religious symbol systems, with a frank discussion of the pros and cons of each, their psychological implications, their dangers, beauty, and limitations. I have found that such a process of teaching and learning which articulates the psychological substrate of the atonement theories, is in itself a valuable stepping stone toward the acquisition of a new, contemporary, and more creative mode of symbol thinking. It may not only help revitalize many now antiquated and quaint, but in principle crucial Christian propositions, but also aid people in overcoming the crude, unnecessarily primitive and un-biblical supernaturalisms which abound in yesterday's and today's Christianity.

Another warning is to be issued. If God is active love, as the fourth Gospel has it, and if loving and working are the essential ingredients of mental health, as Freud once said, it is pedagogically most important that God's image as well as man's behavior be continually purged of the traces of hostility, cruelty, pride, insolence, truculence, suspicion, and vengeance which tend to accrue. The words and ideas used in teaching must be commensurate with their object. Thus they must be chosen so as to set forth the enduring qualities of mercy, benevolence, charity, hopefulness, and cheerfulness for which Christianity stands according to its leading spokesmen. This does not imply taking the problem of evil lightly, or to play havoc with the question of authority and power, but it does mean that adequate symbols must be created which stress grace in graceful ways, mercy in compassionate terms, bliss in joyous metaphors.

Although it is rarely put this way, at the risk of being misinterpreted, I daresay that the idea of God must be therapeutic and that the imagery and language in which he is to be pondered, worshipped, and proclaimed must be a therapeutic imagery and language. It seems to me that several of the traditional theories of the atonement, for all their partial relevance, are also at variance with this goal and will remain so for most believers, until by some fortuitous route they may have reached the level of freely playing with each as an interesting but, in its one-sidedness, quite fallacious metaphor. Clinicians know that for some people it takes the toll of hospitalization or a course of psychotherapy (which need not have an explicitly religious focus at all) to become sufficiently detached from outworn and cumbersome symbol systems, in order to be free and creative enough for a more venturesome and wholesale appropriation of faith.

VII

There is an alternative type of approach to the psychological problems posed by our interesting parallelism. This is the phenomenological approach, which suspends explanation and proceeds toward a clearer understanding of the religious experience via a precise and detailed description. In this approach the first question is not who or what God is, what he does, or what might have motivated him to act as he presumably did, etc., but in what way does man consciously experience himself, his fellowmen, or his God when he thinks, feels, prays, worships, meditates, etc., on such themes as sin, redemption, atonement, grace, divine love, power, or justice. Following Otto[10] such experiences can be described at first in specific sets of parallel terms, one describing qualities, acts, and attributes of God, the other describing the correlative "moments" of human experience. In Otto's own work God is described in such terms as *Mysterium tremendum et fascinans*, the Majestic, the August, the Energetic, the Wholly Other, etc., corresponding to which there are descriptions of the human experience of awe, attraction, repulsion, terror, dependency, creatureliness, smallness, weakness, etc. In my general exposition of the three atonement theories I have tried to use the "typical" words and phrases, which allow one to penetrate into the atmosphere, imagery, and feeling tone of each symbol system in its own right. But these pictures could be deepened, and the language further refined in order to enhance a rich understanding of their many levels of meaning, in the hope of catching their essence.

Here phenomenology can go two ways. It can study the atonement portrayals painstakingly in great openness to the particular mood, sentiment, images, relations, themes, and dramatic unfolding of each symbol system. It can sink itself, as it were, into the content of what it studies, absorbing its language and imagery, with an almost reverential attitude to what it finds. In so doing it will appreciate the various atonement constructions as drama and as mythology, as world design, and as system of meanings. But since phenomenology itself is an attempt at refinedly naive "seeing" or "viewing," its esthetic tendency often ends up in freezing or fixing the things it studies as monuments of human experience, without concern for critical judgment to promote change, improvement, or correction. I am afraid that in this way a phenomenology of atonement symbols may deepen one's grasp and appreciation of the many meanings of each model, without ever noting their errors, limitations, and failures, and without helping anyone to correct their dated imagery and poetic nonsensicalness.

The second way of phenomenology (since it is a study of consciousness) is to note the form, style, and depth dimensions of perceptions, feelings, acts, and relations as experienced. This had led to the conviction that certain deep feelings, some penetrating thoughts, some lucid states of awareness, and some strata of valued knowledge or profound concern are inherently numinous, even when they contain no explicit or verbal references to "God," deity, "old man in the sky," etc. Linked with existentialism, as this kind of phenomenology often is, it points to a stratum of experience which because of its depth, existential relevance, ultimacy, or value is taken to be "religious" or numinously charged with mythology, poetry, and mood as its proper mode of experience and expression. In this perspective, anxiety, guilt feelings, and shame have their special numinous qualities and give rise to mythological forms of thought and action. I think this too has its dangers. While I am far from decrying mythology, I think that mythology and religion, despite their similarities, should not be equated. Nor should deep feelings and stunning insights be confused with the *numen*. It is not enough to show a symbol parallelism between intrapsychic conflicts and atonement theories, and to acknowledge that the private language and imagery of anxiety, guilt feelings, and shame partake in the corporate language and imagery of certain time-worn theological symbol systems. For this will keep us in the mythological circle and may even lead to perpetuating and condoning the various inadequacies of these symbols.

VIII

In addition to the grasping of essences some rational critique is necessary. I feel that sooner or later one must bring the clinical-psychological category of reality testing to bear upon religious thinking. How adequate and accurate is reality testing in those who abide by the three traditional atonement models? What adaptation value does it have to the exigencies of life in the work-aday world? Again, I am unprepared to answer these questions adequately, since the problems are complex. It is obvious that the term "reality" has a plurality of meanings and definitions, and that many people have already accommodated themselves to a completely compartmentalized view of many unintegrated realities or reality fragments. Nevertheless I suggest that reality testing cannot be very adequate and comprehensive if one takes at face value the apparent monstrosities of atonement symbols and the dated metaphors which permit God and Devil the trickeries of barter in the slave market, of fishes snapping for bait on the fish hook of a double-natured person, of heavenly law courts in which fines are leveled by a proud and demanding judge who ends up paying them out of his own pocket, of lordly castigations in which one is punished as an example for many. If these images are taken seriously as descriptions of reality events, much intellectual trapeze-work is needed to give them a place in the fabric of our daily reality assessments; if they are taken wittily or humorously, they have obviously no more than propaedeutic value, as something to be overcome and replaced by a better symbolism.

This raises a new question which to the best of my knowledge has not received much attention in the debate over demythologizing. This is the question of psychic development and age-specificity. Let me give it the following form: although anxiety, guilt feelings, and shame can occur with great intensity any time in life, and can be chronic, it is nevertheless true that there are certain developmental stages and crises in which there is a special proneness and vulnerability to any one of these affects. The course of personality growth is determined by the ways one learns to cope with these disturbing affects, by the successes and failures in dealing with them, by fixations to unresolved conflict situations. May this not imply that there is an appropriate and fitting *ad hoc* symbol system of the atonement for each age level, stage of development, or personality type (to the extent that the latter is co-determined by developmental factors)? Or to put it very crudely: Should the atonement narratives be offered to young children, "primitives," and the emotionally disturbed since they are "only mythologies" anyway, and should one aim at a careful matching of each theory with the anxious, guilt-ridden, or ashamed person, as a pedagogical or therapeutic "best fit"?

If one finds these questions ridiculous, as in a way they are, chances are that one's rationalism is getting the better of him and that he finds little room for the mythologies which apparently have been meaningful to millions of people in previous generations. If one finds the questions pertinent, as in a way they also are, one is likely to be tolerant of primitivism and may have given up hopes of reaching a unified view of reality. A third response to these questions might be to acknowledge the proper domain of myth, to acknowledge the relevance of the traditional atonement symbols, and yet to insist that they be more mature and contemporary, as rich and adequate as possible; that their message stand out clearly so that it will be heard, and that they be relevant to man's total existential situation. I think this demands, among other things, a new and creative theologizing about the atonement which is enriched by psychological insights, so that it can speak to the young and the old, the simple and the sophisticated, the well and the sick, the sure ones and the perplexed.

Notes

1. Mozley, J. K., *The Doctrine of the Atonement*. London, Gerald Duckworth & Co., 1915.
2. Considerable re-interpretation of the older thematic material has engaged the attention of theologians in recent years, as for example: Leivestad, R., *Christ the Conqueror*, London, SPCK, 1964; Aulén, G., *Christus Victor*. London: Macmillan, 1931; Whale, J. S., *Victor and Victim*. Cambridge, University Press, 1960; Pelikan, J., *The Shape of Death*. Nashville: Abingdon Press, 1961; Murray, H. A., "The Personality and Career of Satan." *Journal of Social Issues, 18*, 36–46, 1962.
3. Pruyser, P. W., "Nathan and David: A Psychological Footnote." *Pastoral Psychology, 13*, 14–18, February 1962.
4. Jung, C. G., *Answer to Job*. Transl. R. F. C. Hull. London: Routledge & Kegan Paul, 1954.
5. Robinson, J. A. T., *Honest to God*. Philadelphia: Westminster Press, 1963.
6. Freud, S., *The Future of an Illusion*. Transl. W. D. Robson-Scott, Garden City, New York: Doubleday & Company, 1927.
7. Some writers have also found this critique theologically liberating, e.g., Hiltner, S., "Freud, Psychoanalysis and Religion." *Pastoral Psychology, 7*, 9–21, November 1956; Tillich, P., "Psychoanalysis, Existentialism, and Theology." *Pastoral Psychology, 9*, 9–17, October 1958.
8. Huxley, A., *The Devils of Loudun*. New York, Harper & Bros., 1952.
9. E.g., Cannon, W., Voodoo Death. *Psychosomatic Medicine, 19*, 182–190, 1957; LaBarre, W., *They Shall Take Up Serpents*. Minneapolis: University of Minnesota Press, 1962.
10. Otto, R., *The Idea of the Holy*. Trans. J. W. Harvey. London, Oxford University Press, 1923.

IV

METHODS FOR STUDYING RELIGION

7

Assessment of the Patient's Religious Attitudes in the Psychiatric Case Study

It is often said in informal psychiatric shoptalk that there is a conspiracy of silence on two important facets of life in diagnostic interviewing and psychotherapy. They are not sex and body functions, which one could expect to remain veiled by a sense of privacy or modesty, but religion and money. The prevailing taboo on discussing religion and money is undoubtedly a cultural inhibition which has deep and ramified roots. But to assume, as we are prone to do, that it is the patient who hides these topics by a self-imposed taboo represents less than half the truth; for this fails to admit the likelihood that the interviewer labors under the same taboo, perhaps more stringently, as well as the possibility that he reinforces this taboo by special iatrogenic resistance.

We all know that religion and money are symbols of authority and power; that they are grounds of meaning, nuclei of values, sources of satisfaction, and frequently points of intrapsychic or interpersonal conflict. And yet, despite the important role which most of us are willing to attribute to religion and money in life, despite the demographic compulsion that forces us to check "religiously" whether our patient is "Protestant, Catholic, Jew, Other or None," and despite our interest in setting the right fees for our psychiatric services, we find time and again that our psychiatric case studies are devoid of articulate references to religion and money in the lives of our patients. To the best of my knowledge,

Reprinted with the permission of the *Bulletin of the Menninger Clinic*, 1971, *35*(4), pp. 272–291.

that startling lacuna in the case study was first reported in written form by Woollcott,[2] who also demonstrated that persistent interviewing about religion can yield interesting psychiatric data. Woollcott made these observations, moreover, in a clinical setting in which the guidelines of Menninger's *Manual for Psychiatric Case Study*[3,4] are mandatory; these guidelines contain suggestions for ascertaining the patient's religious concepts. But there is little evidence, ten years later, that these suggestions are heeded. Most psychiatric case studies are still as empty as ever in regard to the role of religion in the patients' lives, and attitudes toward money are rarely recorded, even if they are assessed. This curious paradox needs to be analyzed, but since the magnitude and ramifications of problems buried in that paradox are little less than overwhelming, I will confine myself now to a few sober, preliminary, if need be, obvious remarks, for the obvious always tends to be overlooked. I will do so in the hope of correcting our typical psychiatric attitudes just enough to enable us to get started on collecting some much needed psychiatric data. And after noting James Knight's book *For the Love of Money*,[5] which provides the diagnostician with important leads to ascertaining the role of money in the patients' lives, I will focus on religion, well recognizing that religion and money are closely interwoven ever since the invention of tithing. Indeed, words like stewardship, charity, sacrifice, giving and receiving, to name but a few, have both a religious and a fiscal meaning. I will present my thoughts under a few simple and practical headings.

Religious Attitudes Toward Mental Health, Illness, and Psychiatry

There was a time when psychiatrists, in attempting to understand religious factors in the attitudes of people toward health and illness, could follow a few rules of thumb or clichés which had some practical value. Puritanism was assumed to exist among mainline American Protestants, whose forcefully repressive superegos forbade some kinds of sexual expression, prescribed ambitiousness and exhorted youth to live life as a divinely imposed task. According to another cliché, Roman Catholics had an easier time of it, for they could occasionally unburden their consciences of the crusts of sin in the confessional, which was sometimes construed to mean that they could get by with periodic moral looseness without having to pay a serious psychic price. White fundamentalist and Pentecostal groups, usually of lower socioeconomic status, were not often private patients, both for financial reasons and because of their value system which gave the concepts of sin and forgiveness a heavier weight than the concepts of mental illness and psychiatric help. The so-called free Protestant Churches, including Mennonite and other small Anabaptist groups, tended to live in close if not closed communities which had little use for psychiatry. Of the Hutterites, it was even believed that they had an astoundingly low incidence of mental illness, until the study by Eaton and Weil[6] dispelled that myth. That study indicated that the Hutterites had a rather effective volunteer service among themselves in dealing with the depressions or *Anfechtungen* in their ranks.

Beyond these clichés, which were not worthless though somewhat trite, more sophisticated psychiatric personnel could take recourse to the *Handbook of Denominations*[7] in order to find concise statements about the creeds, belief systems, habits and organizational structures of religious groups to which their patients belonged. These beliefs included for some groups very special attitudes of distrust toward or wholesale rejection of medicine and psychiatry, or a metaphysically buttressed denial of illness and other evils. That approach still has some usefulness, provided one realizes that the *Handbook* shows only group data and modal patterns to which the individual may or may not subscribe, or with which he lives in conflict despite his affiliation.

The crux of this approach, or any variant of it, is that the interviewer uses a simple classification which helps him to be alert to certain expectations about presumed religious beliefs and entanglements in the patient he is dealing with. Noteworthy among these are the patient's expected attitudes toward psychiatry and mental illness, the possibilities of denial of illness, of poor motivation for treatment, of ostracism by the patient's religious group, or of a potential for zealous attitudes.

Typological Aspects of Religious Affiliation and Religious Experience

Beyond the very preliminary sorting process just described, more sophistication can be had by taking recourse to a few basic data from the sociology and psychology of religion. For instance, there is the vast body of studies showing that in pluralistic America religious beliefs and affiliation patterns are heavily codetermined by ethnic, racial and cultural factors.[8-16] The Scotch-Dutch Presbyterian and Reformed traditions are historically linked with an assertive mercantilism and an entrepreneurial attitude, with Church polities representing a republican form of government and an articulate theology that can be seen as a system of checks and balances. Mennonites, Brethren and other free Church groups tend to be agrarian in origin and outlook, gregarious in attitude, sober in habits, somewhat resistive to cultural assimilation, and prone to extol the extended family pattern under paternal dominance. Methodist and Baptist groups have a long history of emphasis on good works, missionary activity, personal warmth and dedication, and prize the experience of personal conversion as a test of sincerity. Negro religion and the religion of many white sectarians of low socioeconomic status tend to be more effusive, emotive and at times explosive than the religion of members of the white middle-class.[17,18] The latter, and their upper-class brethren, tend to emphasize decorum, orderliness, properness and tempered rationality.

From another branch of sociology we should heed the historical studies by Max Weber and others.[14-16] These studies describe the dynamic movements of sect development, with their cycle of left-wing, poor, oppressed and antirational beginnings, through a slow ascendancy process to social acceptance, gaining of status, gaining of wealth and the eventual reacceptance of middle-class values to the ultimate establishment of the bourgeois mainline Church with orderly liturgies, conservative attitudes and prestige status. This theory implies that every sect and church has to be evaluated in terms of its particular phase in its own historical cycle, with recognition of tension between the generations of its members. This sociological aspect of the psychodynamic tensions between parents and children should not be overlooked in psychiatric work.

From the domain of the psychology of religion[19-25] I will select only a few practical items of immediate psychiatric relevance. First the distinction which William James[21] elaborated between *once-born* and *twice-born* people. The once-born man accepts life pretty well as it is, with some optimism and often with a conviction of its basic goodness; the twice-born man finds temperamentally that there is something deeply wrong in his life and life in general, which necessitates him to seek a forceful realignment and a reevaluation of values. This observation does not only account for the hankering after or occurrence of conversions,[26] but may also throw some light on the dynamics of those who seek psychotherapeutic help and anticipate or experience it as a "second birth." There is also James' description of the "divided self" which attributes central importance to the dynamics of the will and marshals religious ideas and practices in order to straighten the will's determination or augment its power.

Recourse may also be had to the simple, but very useful typology of Goodenough,[20] which describes certain value options and clarifies certain themes in the superego and ego-ideal. *Legalists'* emphasize rules, taboos, folkways, or anything else that assists a person to do the "right thing." Legalistic codes are guides for conduct as well as defenses against the experience of terror. *Supralegalists* are also interested in right conduct but dig deeper for ultimate or ideal codes, well aware that these are often in opposition to the established rules of order. *Orthodoxy* puts a premium on truth as correct knowledge; having the right beliefs not only aids the person to staying in line with the proper authorities but makes him participate in their power. *Supraorthodoxy* digs deeper beneath popular truth for a truth that transcends what everybody thinks and that has been discovered in a highly personal or existential way, with strong conviction of its ultimacy. In the *aesthetic* type, the value of beauty is of the highest order, and emphasis is placed on perfect form and formal practices with craftsman-like perfection. Finally, the *symbolists* or *sacramentalists* prize the sacred rites which link the person with the divine power or guarantee his personal salvation, often to the neglect of social action and responsible involvement in the problem-laden facets of life.

In the many psychoanalytic writings about religion, the emphasis has been more on the phenomena of religion at large than on individual differences in religious experience. Nevertheless, the centrality of the projection and displacement mechanisms which psychoanalysis finds in religion alerts the clinician to the possibility of parallels between the God-image and father-image held by any patient; to the selective predominance of ego, superego, or ego-ideal factors in the religious ideation of any person; to the search for mystical union with the divine, or to ambivalences toward divine figures or ecclesiastical authorities which may mirror ambivalences in ordinary object relations.

Some of my own work in the psychology of religion[24] has dealt with the nature of religious thought and language as exemplars of thought organization and thought pathology. Since religion is not spared by thought disorder or affective disturbances, the religious topics, phrases, rituals or acts in which our patients engage can give clinical clues for personality diagnosis.

Religious Acts and Ideas as Coping Devices

Subscribing as I do to a dynamic-economic view of mental illness,[4] which portrays life as a continuous process of seeking a dynamic equilibrium in a biosocial field of forces and an existential matrix of meanings, I am prone to look at all acts, ideas, and attitudes in life as ways of coping with stress, or as attempts to redress a real or threatened imbalance. In this theoretical framework, a distinction can be made between many such diverse acts as eating, drinking, sleeping, walking, talking, gesticulating, thinking, forgetting, laughing, or crying which are normative at their time and place for almost everybody (though each of them may serve a defensive function as well), and the more exceptional and taxing acts that are commonly regarded as symptoms of mental disturbance. Though this distinction is patent in some regards (social, legal, etc.), it is only a fluid distinction from the psychodynamic and psycho-economic points of view. Indeed, coping devices in everyday life and emergency reactions to acute, strong, or prolonged stress can be placed on a continuum that spans from health to illness and from life to death. On this continuum one can map out certain way stations of coping devices, coping strategies, and coping costs which could replace the traditional classification systems of psychiatry.

At any rate, if personal or corporate acts of men are systematically regarded as coping devices, one is alerted to the possibility that engaging in any religious act and ritual can serve an equilibrating, homeostatic or defensive function. Whatever the theological or sacramental justification of the confession may be, it has clearly a functional psychological meaning as well. The same holds for praying, worshipping, communion celebrations, foot-washing rituals, the laying on of hands, baptisms, and purification rites. Simply going to Church or Temple once a week, whatever one does there, may be a tension-relieving coping device. Religious ideation and fantasy formation are not necessarily free exercises in logic or metaphysical speculation—they can be in the direct service of personal problem solving, with a poor outcome as Freud demonstrated in his comments on the Schreber case, or with a creative outcome as Erikson demonstrated in the theology of Luther.[27]

Since many religious acts are corporate acts, an individual often finds himself both supported and confronted by his religious group in regard to the practices he takes recourse to.[28] It is one thing to be praised for one's regularity in going to confession; it is another thing to be confronted by one's priest about a certain spuriousness in the sins confessed, as is bound to happen to the person suffering from scrupulosity. It is one thing to pray, but quite another thing to be noted for a compulsion to pray excessively, anxiously, or laboriously. It is one thing to feel low and less than saintly, but quite another thing to feel that one has committed the unpardonable sin.

Other classical coping devices, ordinarily not stylized by religion into a rite or practice, may assume religious connotations or sanctions. An example is the mechanism of denial, which may be reinforced by Christian Science readings or rationalized by its particular metaphysic. Withdrawal may take the form of mystical musings or a penchant toward the monastic life. Phobic reactions may accrue the content of a morbid fear of blaspheming, or panic at exposure to allegedly sinful circles in which card-playing, drinking, or dancing occur. Identification with the aggressor may take the form of a zealous and intrusive missionary activity in the name of a vengeful God, with the preaching of coming world disaster. Depression may assume the form of acedia (or accidia), a spiritual dryness and lassitude in which one feels estranged from his customary religious activities. Austerity may become asceticism or mortification to expunge a felt sinfulness. Any autism or thought disorder may assume religious content, as is abundantly evident in the psychoses.

The point that needs to be remembered when one speaks of religious acts as coping devices is the distinction between normal and symptomatic forms of coping. The normal acts are reality oriented, socially approved, not costly in terms of their psychic price, integrative and healthy; the symptomatic acts entail poor reality testing, social disapproval, a costly investment of energy, regression or a variety of boomerang effects which further endanger the person's success at equilibration.

Syndromes of Religious Psychopathology

The term religious psychopathology does not imply that cult or creed are the leading causes of the pathology shown, not that all religious ideas and practices found in these syndromes are forms of "sick religion," although these are possibilities in the individual case. I use the term to indicate that religious themes, ideas, acts or patterns of affiliation are manifest aspects of the presenting symptomatology or play a psychodynamic role in the production of illness.[23-29] The clearest example of what I have in mind is the syndrome of demoniac possession. This is only possible if one's belief system includes the existence of demons who, with force and impersonation, are held capable of taking hold of an individual and locating themselves within him as a foreign body, or of coexisting within him as a dual personality. The current rarity of this syndrome in our culture and the fact that it is not so rare in African cultures whose members are still close to animistic beliefs show how much it is dependent on specific forms and content of the religious imagination.

Much has been written about scrupulosity, an obsessional state in which one is beset by thoughts of one's own unworthiness in the light of divine commands. It is sometimes linked with compulsive acts of penance or with urges to confess. In the latter form, it is particularly reported by priests who observe in the Roman Catholic sacramental confession that certain penitents repeatedly confess sins which seem to have no basis in fact and which are in contrast to the person's circumspect behavior and thus sound strikingly irrational to the trained ear of an experienced father-confessor. This syndrome clearly evolves from certain interpretations (or misinterpretations) of the religious concepts of sin and forgiveness, and the patient considers himself refractory to grace. Scrupulosity can also lead to withdrawal from participation in other sacramental acts of one's faith, e.g. refusal to share the elements of a communion service, not out of rational enlightenment, but from a deep sense of unworthiness. For clinicians who know the dynamics of depression it will be no surprise to discover that beneath the expressed unworthiness (e.g., "I am a great sinner") may lie a hard core of narcissism (e.g., "I am the greatest of all sinners") through which the person in his pride does not deign to stoop down to sharing the communal activities or symbols.

That states of ecstasy and frenzy often have religious content is not only documented by the history of tumultuous outbreaks among religious sects, but it follows logically and with plausibility from the regression to the oceanic feeling, the expulsion of the superego and the reinstitution of the oral pleasure ego known from the dynamics of mania. The thrust of so much religious education is to convince a person that he is not God, much as secular training for maturity is in the direction of convincing him that he is not the center of the universe. If either of these lessons is undone by a profoundly regressive maneuver, the likelihood of attributing divine powers and splendor to the self is very great, quite apart from one's customary degree of piety.

More specifically religious, both in the sense of private piety and in terms of affiliation with public religious institutions, is the syndrome of moving from one denominational affiliation to another, sometimes in a whole series, with or without special conversions or mystical experiences.[24a] Particularly when the move is downward in the socioeconomic scale of stratified church life, chances are that the person moves on the basis of his needs one or more steps from a decorous to an enthusiastic group, from a rational to an irrational faith, from an intellectual to an emotional test of faith, from a delicately held faith-doubt dialectic to a more childish affirmation of simple faith propositions held beyond any doubt. Such moves, by individual choice which goes against family tradition, from mainline to sectarian churches are usually instigated by a frantic search for support when a person feels that his customary coping devices give out and his integration threatens to be dissolved. In an effort to bolster his failing defenses he seeks to lean on the strength of hortatory preachers who clearly distinguish right from wrong, who can describe sins in concrete details, whose flocks tend to have a repressive life style but are also very supportive of each other, and whose strictness is matched by a great deal of personal interest in any "lost sinner." Together with the greater motoricity and impulsivity displayed in the celebrations of many holiness sects, one can thus find in these new affiliations at once a greater tolerance of one's peculiar weaknesses and much external support to ego and superego functions, albeit at the price of a regression which is socially inconspicuous, if not actually hallowed by the new group into which one has entered.

The old syndrome of acedia, which Chaucer mentioned in his *Canterbury Tales*, is now a rarity, though it can still be found among people with a religious vocation. In acedia, fervently devout people with established religious habits would be overcome by spiritual torpor, with revulsion of their customary practices. Since this happened particularly to people whose religiosity was foremost a matter of feeling, the lassitude of acedia was felt as quite an ordeal. The modern diagnosis of this condition is likely to be depression. It seems to me, however, that a contemporary form of it can be found in a type of alienation, possibly associated with drug abuse. Certain people, once capable of deeply religious feelings, may find themselves increasingly ill at ease with the traditionalism or stuffiness of their religious group and drop out from their affiliation, not without guilt feelings and sometimes with a deep longing for the old effervescence. Meanwhile, alienated from their tradition, and possibly depressed, they may try to recapture some depth of feeling through flirtations with Eastern religions, through mystical states, or by seeking to alter their state of consciousness through drugs.

I would count as religious psychopathology the sudden occurrence of glossolalia in people whose religious tradition, personal upbringing and theology do not prize it or are averse to it.[24b] In such cases, the psychodynamic factors producing this regressive speech act are different from those in which it is a hallowed tradition and learned from childhood on, by parental example, as in Pentecostal groups.[30] The same warning must be sounded about sudden conversions in people whose religious traditions do not demand them. If one includes visions, which in some religious cultures are far more acceptable than in others, all such sudden transformations or rebirth experiences must be carefully evaluated in the context of the religiocultural background of the person. But in all cases, the final psychiatric judgment will have to be based on the outcome: i.e. whether the experience proves to be progressive and integrative or whether its result is regressive, autistic, or disintegrative in some other way.

With these observations we have come close to a syndrome which need not have religious content or meaning but often has, which is severely disturbing and disabling while it lasts, and which has the earmarks of a crisis: the catatonic crisis or catatonic schizophrenic reaction. Sullivan emphasized the crisis character of this syndrome so much that he considered it a turning point in the course of an illness: one either settles into a more profound or prolonged regressed state, or one emerges from it with a good prognosis for a fairly high level of reintegration. Experienced variously as panic, dark night of the soul, death and rebirth, or cataclysm, this state naturally invites cosmic associations and whatever religious meanings the person will bring to it through his history. A celebrated case of this kind is that of Anton Boisen, founder of the Clinical Pastoral Education movement, who advanced in his *The Exploration of the Inner World*[18] the viewpoint that the catatonic process and the religious conversion share a level of depth and a sincerity of existential meaning unequalled in other disorders and rare in normal life. His own disordered thoughts and actions during several catatonic episodes were full of religious themes, not so much because but in spite of his recent seminary training conducted in the liberal Protestant spirit of the second and third decades of our century.

As soon as the large cosmic schemes of good and evil, God and devil, male and female, life and death, etc. beset the stream of thought of a patient, religious ideas, words, images, and acts are bound to enter the picture of the illness. The counterpart of poor reality testing is often the flight of the imagination, and the imagination of most people tends to be structured somewhat by theological or metaphysical speculations. A good deal of logical thinking and a shrewd use of erudition can be applied to a few odd assumptions, so that an intellectual edifice is being built with a seemingly respectable use of religious and philosophical propositions. The paranoid conditions illustrate this very well, and these patients' thoughts and words tend to be replete with religious ideas. I remember a patient whose word salad involved the triplication of the first syllable of important words: she spoke of the hospital's canteen as the "ro-ro-rotunda." All this remained unintelligible to others for years until further interviewing and expert listening revealed that she thought herself married to the Pope, and that her mind thus dwelled on Rome ("ro-") much of the time. Her triplication of syllables was based on a trinitarian calculus, and her choice of the word "rotunda" involved a reference to her pyknic body type as well as the recognition that the hospital's social center was the canteen located in a Quonset hut with rounded ceiling meriting a dignified Latin or Italian name.

There is no point in trying to draw up a complete list of these syndromes of religious psychopathology. The older psychiatric nomenclatures contained such items as religious mania, religious melancholia, religious monomania, and religious delusions; the hysterical and obsessional states were often noted for their religious content, and it was long felt that in epileptics religiosity tended to be an outstanding trait. My purpose in describing these outstanding syndromes of religious psychopathology is to convince practicing clinicians that they should be familiar with them in order to arrive at adequate diagnostic formulations, whether or not they themselves have any interest in religion.

Transference Factors in the Diagnostic Process

In view of the basic science data and the clinical facts described in the previous sections, we must now ask again why diagnostic case studies tend to be so devoid of religious data and references in a culture many of whose members are so avowedly religious, and in whose institutions religion is so patently visible. What are some of the factors producing the conspiracy of silence about religion between patient and doctor in diagnostic work?

To start with the patient's contribution to this state of affairs, one can recognize both negative and positive transference reactions. If there is a cultural taboo on discussing religion, as I think there is, one of its implications is that it will affect the help-seeking behavior of persons who are aware of having problems. In the first place, like seeks like in time of trouble, which may account in part for the fact that a very large percentage of people in quandaries first seek the help of their clergymen and thus bypass psychiatric resources. Secondly, like seeking like in time of trouble may determine the flow of troubled religious people in the direction of denominational clinics and hospitals, or private practitioners known to have a religious affiliation matching that of the patient. Thirdly, the role divisions in society and in psychiatric institutions may foster selective behaviors in the patient such that he will be prone to discuss many things with psychiatric personnel but reserve mentioning religious troubles for pastors or hospital chaplains. When this occurs, completion of the case study depends in part on an actively sought collaboration between the psychiatrist and the clergyman, who will have to pool their data.

Beyond these possibilities there is likelihood that the patient, like everybody else, is a victim of clichés and stereotypes of psychiatric personnel by means of which he may assume that any psychiatric interviewer is not interested in religion, not knowledgeable about it, averse to it, or even scornful of it. By the same token, the patient may have stereotyped any pastor or chaplain as being interested solely in religion, to the exclusion of everything else. In some religious patients this selectivity may be reinforced by a conscious or unconscious fear that any clinical probing of the religious dimension in his life would lead to the undermining of a cherished belief system or expose and eventually curtail his religious practices. Such patients may deliberately remain silent about religion, vis-à-vis all secular clinical personnel.

One of the worst features of stereotypes is that they tend to be reinforced by their own recipients, by a process that has been described as the self-fulfilling prophecy. Apart from specific countertransference attitudes of psychiatric personnel, which I will describe later, any psychiatrist who surmises the patient's negative transference to him regarding religion and takes it for granted without attempts at correction, reinforces the stereotype and thus becomes living proof to the patient that psychiatrists are indeed not interested in the religious vicissitudes of their patients.

Special mention should be made of the selectivity in help-seeking behavior whereby a patient, even before positive transference processes can get started, seeks a psychiatrist of the same religious affiliation. He may do so in the hope that his problems may be more easily understood, that his religious beliefs and practices will be left unexamined, out of an assumed reverence, or even that they be reinforced by a healer who is also a believer. He may expect that his words and metaphors and associations will be quickly grasped by a co-believer, or that such an examiner may know from his own participation what specific stresses may be experienced from the belief systems and customs of the denomination, sect or religious community. If these things are assumed, it is likely that in the evolving positive transference reaction further assumptions arise about the therapeutic roles that the examiner will eventually play. For instance, such a patient may maneuver the therapist into the role of religious instructor, impose quasi-pastoral roles on him, or demand that he act as a moralist, consoler, inspirer or soul-winner according to the religious principle of the priesthood of all believers. All such expectations or transference moves are attempts to exploit an allegedly shared value system.

The diagnostician should be aware of the psychological traps in such budding positive transference patterns. An obvious trap is that the patient who insists on being seen only by an examiner of like religious persuasion and makes altogether too much use of religious phrases and metaphors may not really wish psychological help but seeks religious solace or advice. In other words, he asks in effect for pastoral counseling under false pretenses and under the wrong auspices. A less obvious but more dangerous trap is the patient's assertion, "Only *you* can help me," which always sounds flattering because of the naive trust it bestows upon the helper. But such denominational or sectarian emphasis on the helper's uniqueness and goodness of fit may mean that the patient feels particularly *safe* with him, that he expects some kind of magical intervention, some special divine presence, and above all that the helper will leave the patient's religion alone. These expectations suggest that the patient is not very well motivated for the hard work involved in getting psychological help and promoting psychological change.

A third trap in hyperselectivity (or choosiness) of religious patients regarding their prospective psychiatric helpers is grandiosity. To be choosy is to assume quite a bit about one's self-worth, one's uniqueness, one's rights and station in life. The patient who says "Only *you* can help me" because of a psychiatrist's known religious identity wants in effect special consideration and special treatment of a kind that lifts him several notches above his fellowmen.

It should be clear from this analysis of early transference manifestations that, when a patient insists on being matched by a fellow-religionist for psychiatric diagnosis and treatment, his finicky particularism can itself be seen as a symptom of his disturbance, *the* presenting symptom for the time being. How one might respond to such a tranference pattern will be discussed in the next section.

Countertransference Factors in the Diagnostic Process

When we now ask again why diagnostic case studies tend to be so inarticulate about the role of religion in a patient's life and illness, the other half of the answer must be sought in the psychiatrist himself and his clinical colleagues. What prevents so many clinical interviewers from coming to grips with religion as it affects the weal and woe of their patients?

Despite prevalent clichés, I do not think that the answer is to be sought in any alleged atheism of (some) psychiatrists. As Freud's case studies prove, an examiner's atheism can go hand-in-hand with his keen interest in the phenomenology and dynamics of a patient's religion. A clinician's own disinterest in sports does not typically prevent him from inquiring about his patient's recreational life and physical exercises, nor would a psychiatrist who is a conscientious objector fail to inquire about the military experiences of a patient who has been a soldier. If any, an explicitly atheistic interviewer who may privately judge all religion to be primitive and atavistic, would rather be inclined to carefully take note of his patient's religious ideas and activities as symptoms of neurotic conflict or personality disorganization.[31]

I think that the problem goes deeper and has many facets. In the first place, clinical interviewers may share in the cultural taboo on discussing religion simply as citizens, without giving it any thought, and without seeing the absence of religious data in their case studies as a clinical omission. My only critical comment on this automatism is that clinicians must be trained to recognize all taboos so that they can judiciously rise above them in the pursuit of their tasks.

In the second place, the fear of sounding moralistic is implanted early in psychiatric training, and for good clinical reasons. But like all fears, it has a habit of spreading beyond its proper focus. While religion and morality have close links, they are not identical, and, even if they were, inquiring about them is not practicing religion or morality. When these clear distinctions are allowed to be blurred and thus prevent adequate clinical inquiry, there must be a special countertransference problem. One of its origins may be the interviewer's own undigested experience in which religion and the do's and don'ts of early moral training are still childishly confused. Another cause may lie in an examiner's own God-image, which may be a compound of forbiddingness, strictness and authoritarianism. More subtly, an interviewer may recognize his own religious ideas as immature and his own morality as inarticulate, and in full awareness of his own confusion decide to skirt the issues rather than expose his ignorance, nobly rationalized by the feeling that he has at least not committed the professional "sin' of being moralistic.

Thirdly, countertransference reactions to religion may be based on the fear that questions about the patient's religion may be countered by the patient questioning the interviewer's religion. Such a simple (but not advisable) question as "Do you believe in God?" may indeed be countered by the patient turning the tables on the doctor. This could be an embarrassing confrontation and to avoid it out of fear is not unrealistic. Some patients *are* zealous. But some interviewers are too anxious on this point and may blissfully forget, while successfully avoiding questions about religion, that the patients are constantly testing them out anyway on all aspects of thought, values and behavior which they consider important.

A fourth countertransference reaction prohibiting inquiry about religion may stem from simple ineptness in raising cogent questions, finding proper words, or knowing enough about religion to have adequate images of and associations to the leads proffered by the patient. Clinicians usually develop the art of small talk so as to find easy points of entry into the world of their patients, but they must also be intellectually alert and become knowledgeable about the prevailing interests of a great variety of patients. Since religion is so prevalent and multiform, failure to be informed about religion, if it is a selective failure, is more likely due to blocking than to lack of opportunity and for this reason it merits to be categorized as a countertransference problem.

I noted earlier that patients may respond to the division of labor in clinics and hospitals by dividing their topics of conversation according to the roles they attribute to the various professionals. Similarly, the hospital staff may apportion the diagnostic interviews among the various specialists, leaving certain types of inquiry to psychiatrists and delegating religious inquiry to the chaplains. This runs not only the risk of territorial thinking, but tends to reinforce all the countertransference problems thus far described for it offers the rationalization that "someone else," the chaplain, obtains the "religious data" through a very neat arrangement. In practice, however, those "religious data" obtained by the specialist rarely find their way into the psychiatric case study so that the allegedly holistic assessment fails to be realized.

The instances thus far described are negative countertransference reactions, all to the effect that religious phenomena and dynamics are eliminated from the case study. There are also positive countertransference reactions among clinicians, with the opposite effect of giving undue or inappropriate weight to religious factors in the life of the patient. I dwelt in the previous section on certain religious patients, often sectarian, whose denominational particularism demands that they be matched with a like-believing psychiatrist. I mentioned that such particularism can be seen as the presenting symptom, which requires a judicious response from the interviewer. Two contrasting responses are possible to such a situation.

The first response, most often found in psychiatric workers who are themselves sectarian or keenly denominational, consists of fully accepting the patient's particularistic demands, and considering it an opportunity. The psychiatrist who knows that he is considered by the prospective patient as "one of us," or "safe," can reason that he must respond positively to such a matching arrangement, for otherwise the patient would not seek any psychiatric help at all. Indeed, he would consider it part of his Hippocratic obligation to allow himself to be thus sought out. But due to the patient's sectarian role perceptions projected on him, he may quickly find himself drawn into the roles of taskmaster, teacher, advisor, guide, scripture reader, or benevolent dispenser of blessings. When he assumes these roles unawares, his countertransference problem is one of role diffusion; when he pursues these roles consciously because of his religious convictions, his countertransference pattern entails the risk of role confusion.

An alternative response to the situation in which a patient claims the right to be matched by a like-minded helper is to regard this claim as the presenting symptom, and to accept the patient only provisionally for what one could call a short-term crisis intervention. The crisis consists of the patient's religious particularism which prevents him from using flexibly all the psychiatric facilities available in his community. The interviewer can deal (often very successfully in only one interview) with the reasons and the self-imposed limitations of the patient's particularism, trying to free him from this handicap first so that he will be set free for tackling his other, more serious symptoms in the most promising way through the available resources. One can discuss in the first interview the patient's magical expectations, the possible grandiosity behind his request, the dangerous restrictions which he imposes by his desire to match with one of his own ilk, and the likelihood that he is still setting up barriers against the diagnostic work-up and the eventual treatment recommendations. In other words, the diagnostician can choose in such a case to give first aid only, and then refer the patient to the best possible psychiatric resource that is available but which the patient may thus far have ignored.

It is plausible that the first choice tends to be made by psychiatric workers who enjoy a general practice role, who themselves have strong denominational or sectarian loyalties, and whose therapeutic techniques do not focus on transference phenomena and their analysis. The second choice is likely to be made by workers who may or may not be religious but who are aware of the dangers of role diffusion and confusion, who may have a keen intellectual curiosity in religious phenomena, and whose clinical techniques tend to take transference phenomena as a therapeutic focus.

Finally, it should be said that in all countertransference reactions to the topic of religion there can be a selective inclination to assess mostly the pathological features of religion to the neglect of its conflict-free, imaginative and creative uses, or to assume too glibly its positive features to the neglect of its pathological and destructive possibilities.

The Challenge of New Religious Persuasions

There is one more reason for the dearth of religious data in typical psychiatric case studies. It is capsuled in the word "irrelevance." The pronouncement of irrelevance may have several meanings. Clinicians could argue that, with the exception of the specific syndromes of religious psychopathology described earlier, there is no evidence that religion plays an active or important role in the life styles or problems of the majority of their patients. They could go a step further and say that their experience with patients confirms the observations of sociologists,[10,32] culture analysts, and theologians[33] who find secularization rampant in our society. In a more sophisticated vein, they could add that religious language today does not refer any more to circumscribed religious ideas or specific religious practices and therefore it is very difficult to know how religious factors in the life of a patient can be recognized as such. One could take a further step and fathom the possibility that genuinely religious convictions are expressed in secular decisions and social acts which occur outside the physical boundaries of churches and the assemblies of congregations.[34]

The judgment about the irrelevance of religion to psychiatric assessment can also be based on the recognition that much religiosity is an innocuous and inconsequential pastime, confined to an hour's worship attendance per week, while the rest of the week is filled with work and sleep, love and hate, earning and spending money, etc., all based on wishes and moral curbs and social regulations which seem to have little connection with that one religious hour! This observation is prone to be made, and stated loudly, by theologians; and it can be buttressed by psychiatric observations.

But while the irrelevance of religion is a serious consideration in explaining the dearth of religious data in psychiatric case studies, there is also much evidence that religion is cropping up in strange places (as in San Francisco's Haight-Asbury district), in strange forms ("Let Jesus be your next trip"), and at unusual times (in the third decade of life). While traditional and established religion may have become irrelevant to many people, there is also much experimentation with religion outside the establishment.[35] Some, particularly young adults, are flirting heavily with Eastern religions; others seek mystical experiences, Eastern or Western, with or without drugs; still others are engaging in meditation and other disciplined mental or physical exercises in order to achieve some personal renewal. To middle-aged people of today, these religious experimentations seem strange or new; but one needs only a little historical sense to realize that the French proverb *Plus ça change plus c'est la même chose* pertains exquisitely to religion. All these seemingly new things are very old. The attractions of sensitivity training, feel-ins, be-ins, and kneel-ins may stem from the same matrix of feelings and wishes that produced the revivalists' tents a hundred years ago.

In other words, on the basis of these observations, one can turn full swing against the argument of religion's irrelevance. To be sure, the new movements generally do not engage in the typical God-talk and the typical habits of the religious mainliners (although there are some notable fundamentalist conventions in the street societies which belie this). But psychiatrists must be professionally alert to new forms of expression, new symbols and new behavior patterns while spotting beneath the changing phenotypes the stable genotype of man's deepest wishes. That attitude will improve any psychiatric case study.

Notes

1. Dr. Pruyser, vice-president of the Society for the Scientific Study of Religion, was director of the Department of Education, The Menninger Foundation. He taught the case study course in the Menninger School of Psychiatry for over ten years, and this article reflects his concern with case study. Dr. Pruyser was the author of numerous articles and was co-author with Karl Menninger and Martin Mayman of the books *The Vital Balance* (Viking Press, 1963) and *A Manual for Psychiatric Case Study*, Second Edition (Grune & Stratton, 1962). His book, *A Dynamic Psychology of Religion*, was published in 1968 by Harper & Row.

2. Woollcott, P.: The Psychiatric Patient's Religion. *J. Relig. Health, 1*(4), 337–49, 1962.
3. Menninger, K., Mayman, M., and Pruyser, P. W.: *A Manual for Psychiatric Case Study*, Ed. 2. New York: Grune & Stratton, 1962.
4. ______: *The Vital Balance*. New York: Viking, 1963.
5. Knight, J. A.: *For the Love of Money*. Philadelphia: Lippincott, 1968.
6. Eaton, J. W. and Weil, R. J.: *Culture and Mental Disorders: A Comparative Study of the Hutterites and Other Populations*. Glencoe, Ill.: Free Press, 1955.
7. Mead, F. S.: *Handbook of Denominations in the United States*, Ed. 4. New York: Abingdon, 1965.
8. Birnbaum, N. and Lenzer, G.: *Sociology and Religion: A Book of Readings*. Englewood Cliffs, N.J.: Prentice-Hall, 1969.
9. Demerath, N. J., III: *Social Class in American Protestantism*. Chicago: Rand McNally, 1965.

10. Glock, C. Y. and Stark, R. *Religion and Society in Tension*. Chicago: Rand McNally, 1965.
11. Niebuhr, H. R.: *The Social Sources of Denominationalism*. New York: Holt, 1929.
12. Parsons, T.: *Structure and Process in Modern Societies*. Glencoe, Ill.: Free Press, 1959.
13. Troeltsch, E.: *The Social Teaching of the Christian Churches*. New York: Macmillan, 1956.
14. Weber, M.: *The Protestant Ethic and the Spirit of Capitalism*, Talcott Parsons, tr. London: George Allen & Unwin, 1930.
15. ______: The Social Psychology of the World Religions. In *From Max Weber: Essays in Sociology*, H. H. Gerth and C. W. Milles, eds. New York: Oxford University Press, 1946.
16. ______: *The Sociology of Religion*, Ephraim Fischoff, tr. Boston: Beacon Press, 1964.
17. Boisen, A. T.: *Religion in Crisis and Custom: A Sociological and Psychological Study*. New York: Harper, 1955.
18. ______: *The Exploration of the Inner World*. New York: Harper, 1952.
19. Allport, G.: *The Individual and His Religion*. New York: Macmillan, 1950.
20. Goodenough, E. R.: *The Psychology of Religious Experiences*. New York: Basic Books, 1965.
21. James, William: *The Varieties of Religious Experience*. New York: Longmans, Green & Co., 1902.
22. Johnson, P. W.: *Psychology of Religion*. New York: Abingdon, 1959.
23. Pattison, E. M., ed.: *Clinical Psychiatry and Religion*. International Psychiatric Clinics, Vol. 5, No. 4. Boston: Little, Brown, 1969.
24. Pruyser, Paul W.: *A Dynamic Psychology of Religion*. New York: Harper & Row, 1968. (a) p. 222, (b) pp. 137–38.
25. Strunk, O., Jr. ed.: *Readings in the Psychology of Religion*. New York: Abingdon, 1959.
26. Elkind, D. and Elkind, S.: Varieties of Religious Experience in Young Adolescents. *J. Sci. Stud. Religion, 2*(1), 102–12, 1962.
27. Erikson, E. H.: *Young Man Luther*. New York: Norton, 1958.
28. Lindenthal, J. J., et al.: Mental Status and Religious Behavior. *J. Sci. Stud. Religion, 9*(2), 143–49, 1970.
29. Group for the Advancement of Psychiatry: *The Psychic Function of Religion in Mental Illness and Health* (GAP Report #67). New York: Author, 1968.
30. Hine, V.: Pentecostal Glossolalia: Toward a Functional Interpretation. *J. Sci. Stud. Religion, 8*(2), 211–26, 1969.
31. In fact, it is interesting to note that quite a few psychiatrists hold

memberships in denominational professional organizations by means of which their own religious affiliation becomes a matter of public record. If psychiatrists as a group are held to be rationalistic or disinterested in religion, what shall we say of psychologists who go through the scientifically more rigorous Ph.D. mill and have hardly any denominational professional organizations?

32. Shiner, L. The Concept of Secularization in Empirical Research. *J. Sci. Stud. Religion, 6*(2), 207–20, 1967.
33. Cox, H.: *The Secular City*. New York: Macmillan, 1966.
34. Vernon, G. M.: The Religious "Nones": A Neglected Category. *J. Sci. Stud. Religion, 7*(2), 210–29, 1968.
35. Cavell, M.: Visions of a New Religion. *Sat. Rev., 53*, 12–14, 43–44, Dec. 19, 1970.

8

Psychoanalytic Method in the Study of Religious Meanings

In corporate symbol systems, meanings are anchored in bonds that a community recognizes to exist between a *sign* and a *signified*. The word "flag" is a linguistic sign for the thing that waves in the wind; a particular flag is in turn a sign for the country so signified. Rational systems of thought cannot do without such communally fixed bonds between sign and signified, for conceptualization and formulation depend on them.

Inasmuch as psychoanalysis is a rational system of thought, the meanings of its concepts, models and words presuppose such bonds. But the psychoanalytic meanings that are ascertained from an individual analysand by the method of free association are of an altogether different order. Clinical psychoanalytic semiology pertaining to the person on the couch rests on a unique system of connections between one idea, thought or image and another (in fact, dozens of others), produced by that individual, and yielding a pattern within which certain forms and frequencies of traffic obtain. What psychoanalysis produces in clinical practice is a lattice structure of ideas whose inner connections are idiosyncratic and do not necessarily match the objective convolutions and articulations of outer reality.

If such networks of ideas could be graphically portrayed, their rendition would come close to a map, showing highways and by-

Reprinted with the permission of *Psychohistory Review*, 1978, *6*(4), 45–50.

ways, connecting cities and towns with each other by a myriad of lines. Some connections are close, others distant; some are direct, others circuitous; some are like densely travelled freeways, others are more like tollways demanding a price, or veritable obstacle courses through flood areas and rockslides. A topographical map would add ascents and descents, and a host of landmarks over and beyond the length, width and shape of roads.

The essential point in free association[1] is that no single idea has a single meaning; that no single idea stands for anything in particular which is its sole referent. What free association yields is a conglomerate of linkages that stands somewhere between the extreme concretism of a particular this-ness and the other extreme of syncretism, spanning the vaguest all-ness. Meanings thus obtained are patterns of relevancies and irrelevancies relating to a particular self. To illustrate this point, while yet foregoing exposure of confidential clinical case material, allow me to proceed autobiographically. I shall try to free associate to the limited extent this is possible behind a typewriter, to a patently religious idea: Saint Francis. To begin with, that choice is not random, for a small statue of the man, which I bought years ago in Assisi, stands on my desk.

> It stands on my desk for many reasons: I know of no more beautiful city on earth than Assisi. I am inspired by the Umbrian landscape with its mysterious light and shadows. The Basilica with its many levels and inner spaces resembles my own psychic stratification. A saint who preached to birds, and loved sister moon, while defying the aristocratic clique of his father, charms some of my own penchants. I think of Francis's closeness to nature. His vow of poverty I could never accept, though I admire him for sticking to it. His haunting, worn-out face that Cimabue painted and his monk's robe and hood lead me to the remembrance of a childhood panic in which a Saint Nicholas's mask with attached beard (Dutch version) came tumbling down from a top shelf when I opened an old closet (why did I want to open useless closets?) in the attic of our home in Amsterdam, setting me running for life and inducing fear of dark stairways for some years to come. Fifty years later I dreamt that episode all over again, but then with the added revelation that Saint Nicholas's mask was the face of my father who had died a year before that childhood panic, on Christmas day. I think of tenderness, meekness, and nonviolence in the revolution that Francis brought about, which stand in contrast to my own choleric impulses. The stones of Assisi's houses

> are warm-pink, reflecting light—it is a feminine city with narrow, winding streets, but interspersed by candle-shaped cypresses and bell towers which attest to a streak of masculinity also. Francis and Clara—two saints, perhaps engaged in a love affair.

Most of these are conscious thoughts; some emerge in slight reverie from the pre-conscious. The discovery in my dream was a sudden apposition of two thoughts: one an available reminiscence, the other a repressed memory. The combination was a spontaneous product of the unconscious coming out of hiding after fifty years.

Enough to indicate that no single idea stands apart in this stream of thought. Everything is connected; everything contextually amplifies and modifies everything else. Yet there are themes which, like highways of significance, articulate my map of meanings. For instance: was my father's sudden disappearance through death an echo of young Francis's forswearing the world to becoming a monk, and becoming a saint? Had my father not been treated like a saint in the family during the years of my upbringing? Was my mother in widowhood a Santa Clara, platonically attached to a soul or ghost? To arrive at such themes, and to analyze their detailed meanings (i.e., their outline in the network of connections) psychoanalytic theory adds some systematic considerations derived from articulate viewpoints. But before stating these I must add a weighty caveat, namely that the method of free association and the angles from which its raw material is to be apprized are designed to elucidate only clinical, individual patterns of meaning, which allow some grasp of personal ideation and conduct. Their applicability to groups, masses, societies, cultures and historical movements or epochs is, for the time being, better kept an open question.

At any rate, the raw material of free association is scrutinized in specific vantage points having a conceptual structure of their own. For instance, in the so-called *topographic* and *structural* points of view, certain operations are performed on the material, in the form of special questions. What part of the material, verbalized by the ego, is felt or presented as impulse, urge, action tendency, or affect? What part bespeaks an ideal, an ought, or must from ethical precepts; What part or aspect alludes to identifications, what part to object love or object hate? What feature arouses hesitancy of verbalization, blocking, dawdling? What is laden with guilt feelings or bespeaks prohibitions and sanctions; what seems to act as a goad toward freedom of action and spur to spontaneity? What is presented to the functioning ego as freely available and consciously produced; what seems to come as a slight surprise, from pre-conscious strata; and what comes only as a hint, disguised, round-about, or vague, with an aura of strangeness that bespeaks unconscious origins? By systematically reviewing the topographical concepts of conscious, pre-conscious and unconscious, as well as the structural ones of Id, super-ego, ego-ideal and reality in their relation to the productive ego, the psychoanalyst attains, with the patient's help, a functional appreciation of the web of over-determined meanings with which he is presented.

For instance, in my association fragment, the mask is not merely disguise; it is an emblem of Saint Nick, a simile for the harried face of Saint Francis; and a symbol of my dead father whose "face" (portrait) hung in the house—each "sign" having a different status, different availability, and different significance.

The *holistic* viewpoint, concerned with relations between parts and whole, elicits questions of cohesiveness and integration. Are the body postures and acts of the free-associating person commensurate with the thoughts verbalized? Is affect harmonious with the pleasure or pain of the reminiscences? Does the person believe that his thoughts are coherent at bottom, even though they seem scattered and loose on the surface? Are some thought clusters tightly walled off from others, or do they malignantly invade the rest of psychic life from time to time?

The *dynamic* point of view produces questions about tension, force and counterforce, resistance and defense. If "wish" is the ideational form of the intentionality of drives, what happens between wish and wish-fulfillment or wish-frustration? What wishes are thwarted, deflected, censored, repressed or modified—and by what modifying forces? Coupled with the topographical viewpoint, what is the fate of a wish (or the outcome of a drive or urge) in the systems of the unconscious, pre-conscious and conscious? E. G. the wish for my father to be alive may have prompted my curiosity about closets; the ambivalent wish to see a departed one made the mask scary; the wish to see him dead created an affect (panic) but, for years, no conscious idea. How are the meanings inherent in a wish stratified by these three systems, and how does this stratification affect any wish's expression between the extremes of rawest immediacy and subtlest sublimation?

These considerations are prone to elicit the next systematic viewpoint, which is the *economic*. All psychic (maybe we should say organismic) activities are a form of work, and inasmuch as work requires energy, the outcome of battles between force and counterforce impinging on any idea is determined by the amounts of energy (and their mode of expenditure) present on either side. In other words, how strong is each of the various forces toward drive discharge (primary process), toward drive constraint and regulation (secondary process), toward defense, toward object cathexis, etc., and what room is there for sublimation or neutralization? Altered in a more holistic direction, these questions become: At what cost (in vital energy) does the person obtain the satisfaction he seeks? What energy price-tag is attached to his particular defense system or coping devices? How much does he gain in narcissistic input or return from the energy investments he makes in various objects, considering that one of these objects, the narcissistic self, is a kind of dead account accruing no interest? How well, how long and at what cost in wear and tear can he ward off the ultimate destructiveness of death, which from birth on always lurks around the corner?

The *adaptive* point of view adds to all these questions an important contextual frame: the presence of (external) reality. Reality extends both to the physical universe and the world of culture, each of which are particularized in any person's given environment. Adaptation to reality proceeds from birth on and the very process of it makes for the acquisition of psychic structures and the perfection of functions designed to enhance adaptational skill commensurate with age, toward ever greater complexity. Adaptation is a twofold process involving accommodation as well as assimilation, the latter designated by psychoanalysis as internalization. It follows that, depending on selectivity and modes of internalization, the adaptational skills are fostered or thwarted—each for a particular environment!

Pertinent questions evolve from this viewpoint: How adequate is one's reality testing in general, or for any given environment? How potent is the reality principle vis-à-vis the pleasure principle in this person's life? How adaptive in the short or long run are the person's ways of coping with reality? What reality pictures and concepts are attained? How well are reality and fantasy distinguished? How does one influence the other, e.g. toward broadening or deepening the grasp of each? What are the specific reality pressures in the person's life situation? Are some empirical realities for him different from an "average expectable environment?"

It seems to me that this angle of vision is critically pertinent to the psychoanalytic study of religion. It asks the psychoanalytic researcher to be fully aware of *the patent presence of religious precepts*, models, institutions, persons, teachings, pressures, etc., and their historical permutations, in the subject's personal orbit. Religion is, among many other things, something to which one is asked to adapt oneself in one form or another. Its presence and its pressures must be taken into account. I say this with some conviction because even in many clinical studies a genre of psychoanalytic thinking prevails which construes an individual's religious ideas and practices as personal inventions, e.g. by projections unique to that person, whereas they could very well be only a selection from extant cultural notions. In fact, some seemingly idiosyncratic or odd religious ideas may prove to be quite adaptive if one would know the details of the subculture in which they prevail, and within which they have been transmitted. Moreover, though the historical origins of many sects and faithgroups are replete with "crazy" features, subsequent reality testing and adaptation by generations of the group tend to modify, rationalize or even disown them.

In this concise presentation, the *developmental* point of view demands special and lengthier consideration. In the history of psychoanalytic theory building as well as in clinical practice, the developmental viewpoint has proven to be dominant over other perspectives, and its preferred position has sometimes led to over-extension and interpretative wildness. Not only must ontogenesis and phylogenesis be kept apart, but distinctions must be made between the concrete development of a particular analysand and the theoretical schemata of ontogenesis derived from compilations of individual cases. In clinical cases, interpretation of meanings under the aspects of fixation, regression, repetition compulsion, transference, etc. is done within the framework of one, specific, personal life that had its unique progression of vicissitudes. Generally, one will find cohesiveness of themes and meanings, which is an effect of "overdetermination." For instance, in my association fragment there is a theme of "spiritual marriage." The person's experiences and acts round off to a plot which unfolds in the stretch from his past to his present.

The developmental point of view insists that full articulation of meanings is possible only from *knowing how something has evolved*; that is, by tracing its odyssey within a particular psyche. Both the analyst and the analysand want to know the saga of an idea, theme, habit, symptom, etc., not to savor its epic qualities, but, so to speak, to empower the captain for better mastery at the helm. Bit by bit, the person comes to tell his own story, while the analyst seeks to make conceptual distinctions. What was the history of a drive, drive-derivative or wish as these presented themselves to consciousness? How was their urgency felt, with what affect? What external stimuli precipitated any particular urge? What unseen inner forces were brought to bear upon the wish? Was there automatic exclusion from consciousness, as in repression (e.g., active in excluding any thought of my father from my childhood panic)? Is there evidence of scrutiny by conscience leading to the counter affects of guilt feelings or shame? Was signal anxiety produced, demanding defense mechanisms, and if so, which (e.g. in my case, phobic binding to dark stairways)? What were the social consequences of wish fulfillment, and how were these faced? What of all this became automatized in habits or symptoms? Did some habits, originating in conflict, later shed their conflictual features to become autonomous acts, useful in other ways, (e.g., counterphobic development of my original phobia, leading eventually to something approaching courage in facing dangers)? What external conditions or inner preoccupations, including messages from the body, tend to elicit regressive reactions? What fixation points predominate in the person's course through developmental stages? What inventory of unsolved business can be made and how does its bulk or weight thwart the person in coming to grips with current demands for adaptation and further growth?

But *the developmental point of view is inherently a comparative method*, whose use hinges on the availability of norms. Ontogenetic norms are to be based on current or recent cohorts of individuals. Ideally, if these norms are to serve as checkpoints against which specific features of an individual's development can be assessed, they should be derived from raw data of identical or comparable order, obtained under the same procedures and circumstances. Unfortunately, we have very few normative data on the ontogenetic development of religious ideas and practices and hardly any that have evolved from free associations studied psychoanalytically in sizeable samples. This lack of solid comparative data presents a methodological impasse for psychoanalytic studies of religion. Compensation for this lack has been sought in three alternative comparisons, each having different virtues and vices.

The first maneuver is to accept the fact that the few ontogenetic norms which exist stem mostly from questionnaires, interviews or test scores. Admittedly, these tap a different order of experience than free association does, and are formulated with much greater definiteness than obtains for clinical psychoanalytic data, which tend to preserve ambiguities and ambivalences. Faulty as comparing these two unequal rubrics may be, one may give it a try. If, say, some Idea of God scale shows that 13-year olds tend to think of God as love and all-powerful, while 10-year olds think more often of God in terms of fear and as something impersonal, then our analysand, who is phobic of old, dark churches and hears God's threatening voice in thunder claps, is closer to the 10-year olds than the 13-year olds in that aspect of his religious ideation. And so forth. The price one pays for these hapless comparisons is forgetting that the process of free associating (which was the origin of our formulation of the analysand's idea of God) is itself a very special, slightly regressive mode of thinking that capitalizes on memories and holds the rules of reasoning at bay. All results of free association are ipso facto more primitive than answers to questionnaires and responses to interviews. They are given in a special state of consciousness, close to reverie, with defenses lowered, and with the observing part of the ego taking a theater-goer's interest in watching the happenings on one's own inner stage.

A second maneuver is to stay within the realm of psychoanalytic data and use whatever developmental norms have accrued from psychoanalytic investigations, acknowledging their unique, incomparable quality. This boils down to using the various epigenetic charts, the descriptions of libidinal stages, the sequence of age-specific defense mechanisms, the stages of evolving object relations, the age-determined progression of psycho-social tasks, or the diverse fixation points and regression levels of psychiatric syndromes, and bringing these to bear upon the prevailing religious ideation or practices of a given person. This can be done, even when none of these informal scales makes explicit reference to religious experience; Erikson's *Young Man Luther* is an excellent illustration of the use of this method.

The price one pays is that such studies do not contribute to the compilation of norms of religious development per se, for they are essentially biographical and remain true to the psychoanalytic precepts precisely by not separating out religious from other kinds of ideation or practices. I think the latter is a gain that more than compensates for the price one pays. For psychoanalysis, in its theories as well as in its clinical methods, assumes a priori the pervasive continuity of all experiences and tries to do maximal justice to it by its modes of interpretation. *Young Man Luther*'s importance lies exactly in showing the continuities between ideas of God and images of the father, between theologies of grace and a mother's singing, between satanic evil and bowel movements. And in my own fragment, saintliness has far more to do with openness to nature's play of light and shadow, and the oneness of all beings, than with having a sterling moral character.

This method also preserves the epic character of meaning, for it does not bifurcate meanings into private and public, fixed and fleeting, right or wrong, normal or deviant, but accentuates their unfolding. The emphasis is on growth or stagnation, progression or regression, i.e., on the *developmental* qualities of the meaning of any idea or practice. I find this quite an existential gain also, for the personalistic question is not: How far am I ahead of, or behind my fellowmen? but, How well do I live up to my own entelechy?

Moreover, it is well to remember that the ontogenetic stage descriptions of psychoanalysis, even if laid out on an age-scale, are closer to the ideal-types of *Verstehende* psychology than to the single-attribute rubrics that populate the scales of quantitative developmental psychology. They are essentially word-pictures of complex meaning clusters or symbol systems, which are only loosely age-specific, for much of each picture's particularity is also derived from its selective prominence in adult psychiatric syndromes. The usefulness of ideal types lies in matching a specimen with a type, for heuristic purposes, to sharpen diagnostic acumen. The latter is to note differences (poor fit) also, so as to better grasp the uniqueness of the individual studied. We always return from our comparative detours to an essentially biographical approach if we want to know the meanings of a person's religious ideas or acts.

A third method uses phylogenetic data to elucidate ontogenesis.

One thing we know from the start: phylogenetic data are not obtained by the method of free association conducted within a transference relationship. In addition, we are less sure today than Freud and his generation of anthropologists and sociologists of religion were in assuming that the primary process must have predominated in primitive man, and that symbolic thought is in all respects inferior to (modern) rationality. And our faith in Haeckel's law (ontogenesis repeats phylogenesis) has considerably dimmed since the days of the early psychoanalytic explorers. Nevertheless, what we know about archaic religious ideation and practices strongly suggests that archaic man's religion was greatly influenced by the phenomena of nature; that it apprehended the sacred in spatiotemporal terms; that it hardly differentiated between the offices of priest, healer and ruler; that it depended more on objects and pictographic representations than on verbal formulations of religious truth or divine beings—to name but a few defining features. Historical knowledge of art forms and texts of later, literate, societies confirms these reconstructions. E.G., in my fragment, architecture and iconic imagery play a large role in giving meaning to fear, panic, peacefulness and exaltation, in ways no words can capture.

It is thus quite telling when a contemporary person, living in a very different ambiance of meaning formulas, rejects them in favor of archaic representations and acts. This happens in severe psychopathology, and it happens symbolically in the occasional dreams of healthy people. However we imagine its workings, the unconscious of contemporary individuals seems capable of (re)producing material that has a striking resemblance to patterns of meaning and figurative representations that prevailed in earlier stages of human civilization. Note the ease with which the basilica became a symbol of my own psychic organization, in my association fragment.

Here is where history of religion, archeology, anthropology, art history and the study of myth can come to our aid, in providing long-range antecedents to contemporary experiences and formulations of meaning. The material provided by these disciplines tends to reflect collective rather than personal aspects of religious experience; the ascertained meanings will be corporate, public and eminently communicable through special media such as art, drama, liturgy, dance, architecture and, in later stages, written documents and oral traditions of myth and folklore. The outstanding feature of these materials, especially of myths, is their narrative character, which captures meanings by taking hold of their unfolding, and in this respect they are closer than anything else to the clinical method of psychoanalysis. And on finer scrutiny we may find that thought processes close to free association have gone into the making of just those monuments of human experience of meaning which the disciplines I mentioned use as evidence.

Moreover, religion itself is saturated with the narrative mode of presentation. Without stories no religion! Theological reflection is, among other things, a rationalization of stories and of the unfolding quality of religious meaning.

We find, then, that the developmental point of view as a comparative method in psychoanalysis may yield its best results for the study of religious experience and meaning when it insists on free association as the ultimate source of data, no matter how remote in time the terms of any comparison may be. The parties to be compared may indeed be very distant, but that is no handicap in the study of meanings. It seems to me that this insight, only recently gained, lies at the heart of the current interest in psychohistory also, and if its methodology may as yet seem somewhat muddled, that is a small price to pay for the promises it holds. Maybe the earlier sections of this paper will have clarified to members of the historical disciplines how psychoanalysis proceeds to operate on the rather unique data that come its way.

Returning now to the opening part of this paper we can formalize our findings by saying that eventually, in the successful psychoanalytic process, the initial free associations slowly begin to round off to a cohesive story. What appears first to the analysand as well as the analyst as "random connections" with a plethora of bits of ad hoc meanings, shape up into a cluster of meanings, in which purposive threads become visible. The fragments become a plot, a narrative, a history. At first, the story is full of lacunae and in that sense conceal and reveal—in the form of gaps—many things that are not told because these cannot (yet) be told by the would-be narrator. Meanings thus seem to have their being on a continuum between *told* and *not-told*, between *speakable* and *unspeakable* bits of knowledge. I would hold that, for this reason, the so-called ultimate meaning of any experience or event does not lie exclusively in the traumata or anguishes of the past, but also in the attempted reconstructions of the past which go on in the present, and in today's and tomorrow's appropriations of the remote and recent pasts. The ultimacy of meanings is thus not localizable in one particular time dimension, but must be approached by that radical existentialism of St. Augustine which caused him to coalesce all time-dimensions into one process-view: "a time present of things past, a time present of things present, and a time present of things future."

Notes

1. The term "free association" in psychoanalysis stands for saying anything that comes to mind, without customary inhibitions, in a transference relationship to the analyst. The term is somewhat of a misnomer, for a totally "free" process of associating would amount to speaking gibberish. What happens on the couch is better described as "associating" in the sense of letting ideas and images combine spontaneously in the stream of consciousness. In my own example, I let my mind wander; nevertheless, an awareness of purpose and some cognizance of the paper's prospective readers remained which gave my association fragment more coherence than would have been present in a purely clinical psychoanalytic situation.

V

RELIGIOUS DYNAMICS

9

Psychological Roots and Branches of Belief

Although the word *believing*, according to the dictionary, is an intransitive verb, meaning that the verb's action does not pass over to an object, a moment's thoughts helps us see that this verb does require an indirect object ushered in by a preposition or a conjunction: "I believe in . . . " or "I believe that . . . " I mention this grammatical requirement in order to clear away a pious abuse that features the noun *belief* and the verb *believing* and their derivatives as self-sufficient words suggesting a self-evident power, action or state of mind. A prime example of this usage is the Biblical passage describing the event of a father bringing his son "having a dumb spirit" to the disciples of Jesus, to be healed. When the disciples fail to heal the boy, Jesus comes forward and tests the father's conviction, saying to him "All things are possible to him who believes." Upon which the father says: "I believe; help my unbelief." (RSV, Mk. 9: 23–24) These are elliptical phrases, which omit mentioning the object for brevity's sake, but tacitly imply a reference to an object, e.g., "All things are possible to him who believes . . . in the power of God to heal" and "I believe . . . that you can heal" or "help my unbelief . . . in you."

Yet, a further thought presses for a hearing. Must belief and believing always have an object reference? Is it not at times appropriate to speak of belief and believing as a state of mind or a disposition of the heart independent of a specific tenet or object, as was perhaps intended in the quoted Biblical phrases? We can speak adjectivally of a "believing soul," both appreciatively in the

Reprinted with the permission of *Pastoral Psychology*, 1979, *28*, pp. 8–20.

sense of a person who has trust and confidence, and derogatorily when we mean a gullible character prone to falling prey to anyone's lures. This parlance is not foreign to clinicians, who can be heard speaking of a person "who has trust," or "who has faith"—without further specification, as if to imply that the trusting or believing disposition counts more highly than its particular subject matter. If one takes to this usage, however, I feel obliged to warn for the intellectual disaster that is likely to follow in its wake, illustrated by the inane messages on taxicabs telling us to "go to church" with the implied assertion that any church will do, or the flatfootedness of former President Eisenhower who exhorted everybody to be religious no matter how.

So, on further consideration, I stand on the platform of specificity of belief, both in principle and for empirical reasons. Any belief is ultimately a "belief in . . . " or a "believing that . . . " and the subject matters of belief and believing are of cardinal importance. I would not hesitate to say that credal subject matters are facts of life in the sense that any person growing up in almost any modern culture is, from birth on, bombarded not only by specific sets of beliefs, but also by specific sets of disbeliefs which he has to sort out. For every acquired loyalty to some idea or tenet there is an acquired aversion to another idea or tenet, imposed by those regions of the culture we call home, family, school, church, government, police, laws, etc. When we grow up with coins saying "In God We Trust" it takes almost an act of God himself to open our minds to our freedom to drop that phrase if we want to. When prayers in the public school have become a social habit or psychological automatism we can hardly imagine a virtuous ground for changing such a habit.

To formalize these considerations I propose that we take the bold step of thinking about beliefs, disbeliefs, and unbelief with their inevitable specificity of content as quasi-entities: as objects of love and objects of hate in their own right on which we bestow affection and aggression.[2] Beliefs and their counterparts are "hot subjects" eliciting strong feelings and demanding fierce loyalties or opposition. I find phenomenological support for this view of beliefs and disbeliefs as love or hate objects in phraseology which tells us that beliefs are at times highly eroticized. One *embraces* a faith and *cherishes* a belief; one holds his beliefs *dear*. One is *true* and *loyal* to his beliefs. One tries to *woo* others to his beliefs and hails converts as persons who are joining a new *family* of faith. One *pledges* to be faithful to a belief system much as one pledges to be faithful to one's spouse. Indeed, one speaks of being *wedded* to a belief. One can even eroticize the symbols and tokens of any belief: loving holy books, crosses, vestments, temples, statuary, or stained glass windows.

All of these erotic investments tend to have their aggressive counterparts in the despising of beliefs held by others, outside one's own orbit of faith. During the crusades, Christians called Muslims *infidels* and during the colonizing era European missionaries spoke blithely of *pagans* and *heathen* when they met religious persons of different persuasion. We also tend to hate the tokens or symbols of the beliefs we do not share: Protestants despise statuary and certain types of crosses, and at one time were moved to ventilate their hatred by massive iconoclasms in Catholic churches. Even today an Episcopalian may refer to Baptists with a denigrating or sarcastic chuckle and a Presbyterian may speak of Mormons patronizingly or with a wry smile. In our society hardly any child grows up without being told in myriad ways that *he* goes to worship on Sunday mornings and not on Friday nights or Saturday mornings as certain other people do; that the Virgin Mary is to be adored and not to be overlooked as others are wont to do; that praying is a significant act and not hogwash as some people say; that *his* parents and family are something distinctly nameable such as Protestant, Buddhist, Jewish, Greek Orthodox; something barely nameable such as "nothing," or only negatively nameable such as "atheist." Selectivity is the keyword, especially in a pluralistic society in which all kinds of beliefs and disbeliefs contend and ask for a hearing. One's beliefs are a determinant of one's identity, and every positive identity is matched by a negative identity: if one is A, one is not B or C, etc.

To put this in a different way: We acquire our beliefs and disbeliefs by a learning process. Our parents and teachers transmit beliefs and disbeliefs to us, in direct or indirect ways. Some aspect of belief are distinctly verbalized, by denominational labels, catechetical phrases or doctrinal formulations; other aspects are taught in non-verbal ways, by example, action and even facially through frowns or smiles in response to any belief proposition we ourselves venture to make.

But if it is true that beliefs are taught, it is also true that the educational process may succeed or fail in making the teachings stick. For a seed to sprout the soil must be fertile and of the right chemistry. What soil makes the seed of any belief sprout? What makes a transmitted belief plausible, if not heartily welcome, to the person who is to receive it? To answer this question, the psychoanalytic theory which I espouse would emphasize, as mentioned, that *beliefs function as love and hate objects*. But psychoanalysis would add to this observation the justifying reason, which is that the power of beliefs to function this way is psychodynamically continuous with the power that inheres in one's earliest emotional relations with other persons. Within our love or hate for any belief lies a trace of love or hate for the persons who had the greatest impact on our lives, especially during our first formative years. Beliefs are derived love and hate objects, behind which stand real human love and hate objects of flesh and blood. William James hinted at this dynamism when he said that often "Our faith is faith in someone else's faith," especially in "the greatest matters."[3] Erik Erikson implies the same motif in his emphasis on the critical importance of "basic trust",[4] acquired in infancy, for healthy development, and in his recognition that in the good relation between mother and infant the first inklings of numinosity, i.e., the sacred, are experienced.

Another formulation of the derivative status of beliefs proceeds from the basic psychodynamic thesis that the unconscious is prone to making equations which consciousness would not tolerate. As dreams and hallucinations indicate, in the unconscious a thing or animal may stand for a person, and even an abstract idea may be transposed to animated interaction between living entities. By condensation, displacement and symbolization various entities are amalgamated in the unconscious. The bearing of this peculiarity of unconscious processes on beliefs is that the latter, despite their abstractness, function as objects of satisfaction to the person holding them, much as his dearest longings are typically satisfied through engagements with other people. Taken in the technical psychoanalytic sense, an object is a satisfier, and thus, *a belief is a satisfier*. Various classes of satisfiers can be recognized, such as other persons subdivided into those of the same and of the opposite sex; oneself and one's body; things, ideas, and symbols. These classes have permeable boundaries allowing their content to overlap with each other in terms of their emotional significance to the subject, or if one wants, in terms of their subjective meanings. And if one asks what satisfactions these satisfiers typically offer, the answer is: A stratified range including the person's drives, his acquired needs and wishes, the demands of his conscience and value system, the requirements of his ego for a sense of competence and identity, his capacity to form ideals and his concerns about his fellow men—all modulated to form a workable compromise between diverse intrapsychic parties. There is no cheap hedonism in this notion of satisfaction.

So, especially in weighty matters by which one's life is to be organized and governed, such as beliefs and values, it always behooves us to ask what multiple satisfactions a person is seeking to obtain or maintain by holding certain beliefs. This search has, however, a counterpart. For beliefs can also have a *defensive function* as a means to avoid pain, or as ways to ward off any threat to currently customary satisfactions. For instance, it is telling how many beliefs, throughout human history and worldwide, center on the painful prospect of death, seeking to mitigate its horror. Many beliefs also center on the unpleasant facts of life such as illness, pain, war, natural disaster, oppression or anything else experienced as evil, purporting to aid people in coping with these nasty experiences and softening their blows. And it is extremely interesting to note how frequently any beliefs partake of descriptive or explanatory imagery in which persons, or person-like entities, are conjured up to convey their existential significance or cosmic meanings. The human mind becomes automatically mythopoetic when it has to contend with threatened or actual attack upon a person's organismic integrity. If we call this kind of thinking archaic we should not be fooled by notions of cultural progress into assuming that archaic thought is confined to man-at-the-dawn-of-civilization. Archaic thinking is as alive today as it was yesterday, for each one of us bears in his psychic makeup traces of mankind's long heritage as well as retains in his adulthood traces of his own infancy. If anything proves this psychodynamic continuity, beliefs do!

William James called attention to another function of beliefs, expressed in his phrase that beliefs "make easy and felicitous what in any case is necessary."[5] This statement gives beliefs the role of *adjuncts in adaptation* and reality testing. Certain things in life are inevitable and therefore must be tackled: man's contingency, the power of nature, the helplessness of infants, the task of growing up, the certainty of eventual death, the shifts of fate, the fragilities of our bodies, the cruelty of economic and political systems. No one can escape their impact for long. These things have to be met as they come and for James the all-important thing was to meet them with zest and courage, in a good mood. James felt that religious beliefs in particular enable a person to meet these reality situations with a modicum of liveliness in an active coping process, which he preferred to passive succumbing in lethargy. It is a nice point, true to life.

But it is also a dangerous point, if coupled with the defensive encrustations that many beliefs carry, or if tilted in one direction only. For one can overplay the "easy and felicitous" in James' sentence to the detriment of his note on "what is necessary." Reality testing may go by the board and the beliefs may deteriorate into pleasing fantasies which not only mitigate, but deny or falsify reality. For instance, Christian Science cedes no ontological status to death in its metaphysical world view; to adherents of this faith evil, death, illness, etc., simply do not exist but are only illusory fancies. I think this position amounts to a truncation of reality, based on the denial mechanisms. In other beliefs, falsifications are present in many versions of life after death which portray the hereafter as an ethereal Holiday Inn with wall-to-wall carpeted motel rooms for every registered guest meeting the admission test. Some religious bodies have their historical origin in a hoax. A plethora of beliefs of this order have titillated the pleasure-seeking minds of millions of people in all ages and they will doubtless continue to be entertained. In each one, the infantile-archaic motif is that the person demands to be indulged, blithely insisting on preferential treatment or slyly manipulating his deity into granting him some favor by showing up with a report card of significant merit.

Somewhat more complicated, but by no means rare, are beliefs that proceed from the opposite mood structure, in which malevolent forces have come to stifle the beckoning voices of benevolence. For some people, experience has been so bleak from the very beginning and throughout life that a pall of depression lies over their person. Going by their basic mood, they feel already half-dead or that they should be dead, or feel they ought to be smitten on account of something unnameably wrong with them. They may long to be reborn, to start all over again with a clean slate. I am sketching a basic feeling-tone about life that is apparently widespread and has affected beliefs—religious or otherwise—in which evil, death, suffering, and innumerable sins hold prominence. Such beliefs center not on bliss, but on the demonic in man, nature, society, and the cosmos and on the awe which the demonic inspires by its persistence and omnipresence. Some of the grim beliefs emerging from bleak moods and unfortunate life experiences are tainted by imagery of forbidding or vengeful gods, of the coming end of the world, or hell-on-earth populated by devils, incubi or witches, all of which have to be constantly placated. Or else, these experiences tilt refined and complex theologies into a simplistic direction, as has happened with certain Puritan excesses of Calvinism which distorted the mystery of divine election into the flat-footed belief in the damnation of infants. Currently, the Church of Satan is a demonstration of such gruesome onesideness.

From these sketchy portrayals of certain beliefs it is apparent that *beliefs are embedded in and responses to moods and the basic feeling tones we attach to our "Sitz im Leben."* Whether they are adaptive or defensive, corporate or idiosyncratic, realistic or fantastic, *beliefs are coping devices* enabling a person to make sense of his existence, improve his lot, endure his fate, obtain an identity, and procure a modicum of happiness for himself. This does not mean that all beliefs are ultimately selfish; on the contrary, many beliefs contain noble wishes for the betterment of mankind at large. Indeed, the question focally addressed by many faith groups is whether salvation—if that is the major tenet of one's beliefs—is meant to be for the individual, for his community, or for mankind, and there has always been much contending about the right proportion in which these entities are to be saved. Outside the pale of religion, philosophical or ethical beliefs can address the parallel issue of whether it is the individual or the society that merits primary concern. A striking note in Stoic philosophy is the willingness of the individual to subdue his self-interest by granting priority to corporate or cosmic order, and thus to be resigned to his personal fate.

In the course of my work I have become increasingly fascinated by the question *how beliefs are instilled and incorporated*, particularly those cardinal beliefs that represent core convictions throughout one's life. These beliefs need not coincide with one's allegiance to voluntary associations such as churches, sects, ethical groups or philosophical schools. In fact, marked changes in such allegiances may occur during one's lifetime, sometimes with startling turnarounds and the public forswearance of former positions. My concern is with the deeper, characterological attitudes and tenors that run as a golden thread through the diverse beliefs one entertains during the various phases of life. To illustrate: although Kierkegaard is noted for the sharp distinctions between the aesthetic, ethical and religious orientations which he described in *Stages on Life's Way*, giving the impression that one grows or should move sequentially from one to the next, it is also apparent that Kierkegaard's distinctions are dialectical ones which explicate by a kind of optical enlargement various facets of his one even more basic conviction that one must have the courage to choose, with risk. Similarly, can one not perceive in the successive works of Spinoza, Whitehead, Tillich, Barth, Freud, Marx, James and other productive thinkers certain invariant, perhaps temperamental, beliefs that earmark their whole oeuvre? Even Darwin, who is known to have gone through a radical change from pristine Bible belief to outspoken disbelief in the Genesis story, had some deeper belief-constant working in him, namely to regard with abiding wonder and wide-open eyes, with enormous curiosity, the goings-on about him in nature, reading the book of Nature as if it were his bible, invested with ultimate authority.

I shall try to answer my question about the instilling and incorporating of cardinal beliefs by taking recourse to some homely observations anyone can make about early childhood, but which needed the acumen of the pediatrician-psychoanalyst Winnicott to record and formalize them.[6] Winnicott's observation is that infants use parts of their own body to stimulate and satisfy another part; they use fingers and fist to rub against the lips or to stick into their mouths. After a few months, they tend to become strongly attached to a piece of blanket, a soft toy, a rag doll, or some other special object which they keep close to their bodies, often their mouths. Sometimes they suck a finger while the rest of that hand holds the special object. Such action often occurs before the child falls asleep or when he is overtly frustrated, fidgety, anxious, or depressed. It took a Winnicott to emphasize the corollary of this plainly observable situation: that the mother and the rest of the family appear to realize instinctively that the baby's special object stands in a very precious, intimate, and intense relation to him that has (in my words, not Winnicott's) an almost sacred connotation.

That odd piece of blanket or that much-fingered rag doll is to be kept near the baby as his possession. It should not be laundered as often as his clothes and bed covers, for it is unlike all the other objects in the baby's world: It is his talisman, his cherished symbol. Perhaps it combines many fragmentary elements of the total mothering situation and elements of his nascent selfhood, but for the child it is not an internal object in the sense of a mental image nor an external object at par with all other things in the world. The mother does not argue whether her infant has a right to that special object, or whether it is internal or external to him, and the whole family takes a ritualistic attitude toward it without questioning right of possession or propriety of choice.

Winnicott infers that the transitional objects and all the goings on around it (which he calls the transitional sphere) are the origin and first practice of illusion. In my words, *the transitional object is the transcendent*; it is beyond the ordinary division we make between the mental image produced by the mind itself and the objective perceptual image produced by the real world impinging upon the sensory system. Illusion is neither hallucination or delusion, nor is it straightforward sense perception. Illusion also includes mystery: since it is beyond the merely subjective and the merely objective, it has a special object relationship endowed with many surplus values about whose legitimacy one does not bicker. Its validation lies in the encounter with the special object itself. And illusion also includes the holy: the special object is held as something sacred and so regarded by third parties also. It may become a fetish. It is held reverentially. One's dealings with it may become rituals. In the transitional sphere a language emerges which takes certain attitudes for granted as expression of a unique verity, which cannot be reduced to mere "subjective nonsense" or "cold, hard facts of perception."

The transcendent, mystery, and the sacred are not equivalent to the so-called security blanket of the infant merely because they have primitive origins. The security blanket is only the beginning of an infinite playful relation between mind and world, and the first illusion focusing on the first possession will typically disappear in a few years. Some of the infant's early illusions will lead to disillusionment, but in the meantime a sphere and a manner of relation have been created in which things are not merely what they are perceptually, and not simply flimsy imaginings either. Winnicott himself sees in the transitional sphere and the transitional objects the beginnings of human play, and the origins of religion and art, but to the best of my knowledge he has never articulated their contact with religion as I have.[7] His statements on this point have remained programmatic.

Movement from the pleasure principle to the reality principle is a lifelong endeavor. Relating inner world and outer world to each other produces some strain. Winnicott has pointed out that relief from this strain comes from an intermediate area of experience whose inner or outer reality is not challenged. This intermediate area, and the actions engendered within it, are *sui generis*. Nevertheless, as Winnicott has also suggested, only a fine, thin line divides the illusory intermediate reality of religion and art and the hallucinatory projections and delusional ideas which indicate madness. Adequate reality testing is needed to keep the transitional sphere properly bounded, and its content and language consensually validated.

As Winnicott has described the special characteristics of transitional objects, the infant assumes rights over the object, with the agreement of his parents. Yet there is some abrogation of primitive infantile omnipotence. The object is cuddled and excitedly loved, or mutilated. It may not be changed, except by the infant himself. It must survive instinctual loving and hating. It must seem to give warmth, to move or do something to show it has vitality and a reality of its own. In addition, the infant's playful dealings with the transitional object find some clues in the mother's attitude: she also initiates play and deals with certain objects in a special way. She too adopts a language, a ritual,and a mood of playing in which she elaborates the transitional sphere. In other words, the style and content of the transitional sphere are not entirely the child's own creation *de novo*. There is external reinforcement and outside encouragement or initiative. As Erikson has said, all ceremonies begin with the greeting rituals which mothers spontaneously adopt upon revisiting their infants after a short separation.[8]

I think that Winnicott's notions of transitional objects and the transitional sphere provide us with a promising vantage point on the early instilling and incorporating of beliefs. The transitional sphere provides the first practising ground for beliefs in which, on the one hand parents transmit and enact their beliefs, while on the other hand the child furtively entertains and enacts some beliefs of his own. Both processes interact with each other, in a setting of a serious playfulness where some verbalized intellectual content, but, more importantly, mood and disposition, tone of voice, facial expression and other non-verbal means of communication add up to significant patterns of positive and negative reinforcement that channel the nascent beliefs while enhancing the child's capacity for dealing with symbols.

The child obtains training in illusionistic thinking and imagining and attains a sense of the values inherent in beliefs. But he also develops a sense for the un-values attached to the alternative beliefs which his parents reject or ridicule; he acquires some set of disbeliefs. His as well as his parents' beliefs and disbeliefs are building blocks of his growing sense of identity. And both the beliefs and the disbeliefs are experientially embedded in all the verbal and non-verbal suggestions that come his way: the frowns and smiles, the suppressions and encouragements, the blockings and outpourings, the blames and the praises, the no's and yesses and the do's and don'ts with which his own ideas meet. In a word, definite links are formed between the content or tenet of any belief or disbelief and the emotional tones inherent in his object relations, i.e., the feeling tones attached to his parents and to his own nascent self. His wishes and ideals become canalized to follow a certain direction and to assume a certain form which will subsequently influence many of his later ventures into belief and disbelief systems.

I regard the illusionistic sphere as a kind of "third world" that lies between and above two other worlds with which human beings have to contend. These other worlds are, of course, the *external* one of nature, things, and sense data in the broadest sense, and the *internal* one of the mind engaged in personal wishes, fantasies, longings and primitive thoughts, too private to expose and too ineffable to be communicated in ordinary language.[9]

Psychological theories of belief, and most belief systems as well, have tended to proceed from the givenness of these two worlds only, often assuming in addition some basic incommensurability between these two. Hence, the words *fantasy, illusion, wishful thinking, day-dreaming*, and *idealization* have mostly been handled as if they were functions of the private mind only. Similarly, such words as *reality, rationality, logic, common sense, perception*, and *actual entity* have referred almost exclusively to the external world of nature and things. The individual mind has been portrayed as chaotic and impulsive, if not utterly whimsical if left to its own devices, and thus in need of curbing and structuring by the patent realities of the outer world. The private mind is held to be solipsistic and autistic, and the outer world is the ultimate reference for everything that is common and communal.

The thrust of my essay is to help us overcome this stark duality in favor of seeing an intriguing multiplicity. We do live in a world of symbols too,[10] and symbols are neither autistic fantasies nor external things. Symbols are very special entities that transcend both the autistic mind and the realistic world of sensory data, though they may bear traces of human longings as well as phenomena of nature. The third world I am trying to define is the world of culture, i.e., the psychic and social "space" reigned by ideas that man lives by in his search for meanings. To set this world off from the other two, it can be described as the *illusionistic world*, for the symbolic entities germane to this world are properly definable as illusions. I repeat: Illusion is neither hallucination or delusion (both of which are spawned by the autistic mind), nor is it straightforward sense perception (as produced by the external world of nature and the things man has made from natural resources). Illusion includes mystery: since it is beyond the merely subjective and the merely objective, it has a special object relationship endowed with many surplus values about whose legitimacy one cannot bicker in terms derived from either the subjective or the objective.

It should be plain at this point that much of what I have said squares rather well with the current preoccupation in philosophy with logic and language.[11] Linguistic philosophy has introduced the notion of language games; various human enterprises are couched in different grammars, vocabularies and syntaxes, each germane to an aspect of the complex world in which we live. There is a language of natural science, another language suitable for religion, still another one for the arts, etc. The language that refers to events in the external natural world is not the same as the language which deals with symbols, or certain classes of symbols. Thus, the illusionistic world has its own special language games, and children are trained to attain special facility in the use of the right language for the right situation or events. Since most of us have acquired facility in several of these languages and have some intuitive inkling of their respective differences, we should realize that *talking about the illusionistic world is sui generis.* There is a language of belief, and this is not the language of scientific experimentation, the language of dreams, the language of the marketplace, or the language of war.

Nevertheless, it is incumbent on any responsible person to bring his experiences of the autistic sphere, the realistic sphere, and the illusionistic sphere to bear upon each other. We cannot afford to live as three persons amnesic for each other, but must seek some integration of these three ranges of experience in order to be *one person*. Beliefs must be tested in the realistic world, and they must also be of some organizational value for our inner world. If our private fantasies take over and become dominant, our beliefs become only whimsical day-dreams or chimeras that threaten our peace, if not the peace of others. After all, Hitler and Stalin had beliefs for which the world had to pay a bloody price. If, on the other hand, our dedication to sensory reality takes over and becomes dominant, we are likely to become stuffy, unimaginative positivists who have nothing to say about the unseen, the arts, religion, and metaphysical accounts of our world.

The personal guidelines which devolve from this view of the transmission and instilling of cardinal beliefs is that beliefs must repeatedly go through various crucibles during one's lifetime, lest they deteriorate into atavisms or absurdities. Beliefs must be constantly updated and brought into line with what we have learned from the traffic with our private inner world, our common outer world, and our shared illusionistic world. None of these worlds can be kept at bay, all three storm at us with claims for our attention. Reality testing must proceed, the inner world must be listened to, and the illusionistic world must be practised with increasing sophistication. Faith and reason can only be separated at a high price.

It follows from these precepts that it is absurd to believe in, say, the literal inerrancy of Scripture when one also accepts the evidence that all portions of Scripture have been edited to address specific historical situations. It is absurd to compare the Genesis story with the theory of evolution as if they were partners in the same language game. It is autistic to hinge one's decisions on the signs of the Zodiac if one accepts the advances of modern astronomy over Babylonian astrology. It is utterly naive to overlook the religious hoaxes that have been perpetrated on the minds of men in the course of history. In the unwary, arguments about religion sometimes partake of the same dangerous irrationality that besets certain secular arguments: for instance, discussions about gun control. It is playing with fire to resist gun control legislation when it is known that guns have solely destructive purposes and that most murders occur among people who are related to each other.

Maybe the greatest whimsicality of all is to seek in beliefs absurdity for its own sake: Tertullian's all too often quoted *credo quia absurdum* cannot stand alone—it presupposes a large and articulate context of thoughtful propositions and was never meant to be a *carte blanche* for anyone's lustful bumbling in the arena of beliefs. And so the more considered proposition is a dialectic between faith and reason, which yields as its synthesis a reasoned and reasonable faith—not a static, but a dynamic one which meets the ever changing exigencies of human life. I think this goal requires not only the ability to enter with skill into the separate language games of the three spheres I have described, but the higher skill, the art if one wills, of moving knowingly and elegantly back and forth between one sphere and the other.

Notes

1. Dr. Pruyser was the Henry March Pfeiffer Professor in the Department of Education of The Menninger Foundation, Topeka, Kansas 66601. He was an Elder in the United Presbyterian Church.
2. This proposition and several other ones which follow in this paper are more fully stated in: P. W. Pruyser: *Between Belief and Unbelief*. New York: Harper & Row, 1974.
3. W. James: *The Will to Believe, and Other Essays in Popular Philosophy*. New York: Longmans, Green & Co., 1897, p. 9.
4. E. Erikson: *Childhood and Society*. 2nd ed. New York: W. W. Norton & Company, 1963, pp. 247–251.
5. W. James: *The Varieties of Religious Experience*. New York: Longmans, Green & Co., 1902, p. 51.
6. D. W. Winnicott: Transitional Objects and Transitional Phenomena. In: *Collected Papers*. London: Tavistock Publications, 1958, pp. 229–242.
7. D. W. Winnicott: *Playing and Reality*. New York: Basic Books, 1971.
8. E. H. Erikson, Ontogeny of Ritualization. In: *Psychoanalysis—A General Psychology: Essays in Honor of Heinz Hartmann*, ed. by

R. M. Loewenstein, L. M. Newman, M. Schur, and A. J. Solnit. New York: International Universities Press, 1966.

9. P. W. Pruyser: Lessons from Art Theory for the Psychology of Religion. *J. Sci. Study Religion, 15*(1), 1-14, 1976.
10. E. Cassirer: *An Essay on Man: an Introduction to a Philosophy of Human Culture*. New Haven: Yale University Press, 1944.
11. A. J./E. G., Ayer: *Language, Truth and Logic*. New York: Dover Publications, 1946.

J. T. Ramsey. *Religious Language*. London: SCM Press, Ltd., 1957.

L. Wittgenstein: *Philosophical Investigations*. Transl. by G. E. R. Anscombe. Oxford: Basil Blackwell & Mort, Ltd., 1955.

10

Forms and Functions of the Imagination in Religion

Religion, like art, deals with peculiar entities that are neither utilitarian things in the external world nor inexpressible private ideas in someone's head. Even when natural entities such as mountains, trees, or animals are objects of religious worship and devotion, their alleged divinity lifts them above the condition of being mere specimens of geology, botany, or zoology. Two technical terms allude to the special ontological and epistemological status of these peculiar entities of religion: transcendence and mystery.

Despite the intellectual aura of these terms, which makes them unsuitable for discussions with young children (and quite a few adults), experience with religious education shows that children themselves have no serious problem in recognizing, appropriating, and dealing with the peculiar entities to which religion refers (and defers). Cognitively and emotionally, children can live with gods and accept various manifestations of deity, no matter how transcendent or mysterious these entities or events are. Similarly, so-called primitive peoples appear to have been able to live with their god(s) and to accept various manifestations of the divine, around which they typically engaged in ritual. The notion of "object" appears quite fuzzy in children and in primitive man: It includes intangibles, chimeras, dream fragments, and other "fancies."

In later developmental phases, reflexive thought may take enough distance from these peculiar objects, and from people's

Reprinted with the permission of the *Bulletin of the Menninger Clinic*, 1985, *49*(4), pp. 353–370.

habitual dealings with them, to question their peculiarity per se: What kind of objects are these religious entities? Do gods exist? What am I doing when I pray? The focus shifts from the *objects* to the *ideas* of transcendence and mystery. Thus, what do "transcendence" and "mystery" mean?[2] What kind of cognition and recognition pertain to these terms and what kind of observations or experiences do they address?

In this paper, I combine two of my major intellectual preoccupations, namely, the nature of creativity and the nature of illusionistic thought, in order to describe and assess the child's response to religious teaching and his subsequent modifications of his earliest religious thoughts. I will lean on two previous publications, "An Essay on Creativity"[3] and *The Play of the Imagination*.[2]

Limit Situations

The concepts of transcendence and mystery are tools for coming to terms with limit or "borderline" situations.[4,5] When deeply experienced and reflected upon, these limit situations can lead to acknowledgment of a gap in being between the human subject and the divine object. The limit encountered in certain existential situations (such as birth, death, awesome events, conversion, feelings of guilt, and confrontation with exquisite goodness or evil) becomes variously defined as coming up against one's own limited power or authority or knowledge, restricted radius of action, narrow perception, failure of reasoning, inadequate inexpression, failure of nerve, and captivity. When people experience their dependency on powers beyond human control, they may find that a gap separates their frail existence from a mightier cosmic Being felt to be its own cause.[2]

From this recognition may arise the insight that limit situations produce a momentary shift in the customary cognitive subject–object relations: The experiencing subjects no longer cognitively dominate their object but find themselves *known by it, grasped by it, and confronted by it* as feeble, frail, groping, and bungling entities unable to lay claim to self-sufficiency. Otto[6] reconstructed the phenomenology of limit experiences in religion by specifying the forms in which contingency is experienced when encountering the Holy. Otto's phenomenology includes the momentary subject–

object reversal whereby the religious person acknowledges the prior existence, greater power, august presence, and overwhelming dynamic self-affirmation whereby the Holy poses itself and reduces a person to its object, which then undergoes an ambiguous state of awe and bliss. The crucial feature is the Holy's dynamism, unmatchable by anything human.[2]

When we are satisfied with such descriptions of limit experiences (which need not be dramatic incidents), can we venture on to a psychological interpretation of them? Can psychology contribute to the understanding of people's relation to the peculiar entities with which religion deals? I think it can, especially by using a developmental approach.

Childhood Discoveries

I have said that young children do not appear to have serious trouble entertaining and acting upon the notion of God. Like most other children, I was introduced to religious ideas and attitudes through stories told by adults and by copying observable adult religious behavior such as saying grace. Whether the family avails itself of the Bhagavad Gita, the Koran, or the Bible, the essential transmission of religion to children takes place through storytelling and ritual: without stories, no religion.[2,7,8] In the story, some aspect of the structure and dynamism of the universe is conveyed in the form of a happening, a narrative, en evolving plot. And along with religion, I was introduced to the arts at the same age.[9] The religious books were illustrated, the prayers were rhythmic (with special diction and voicing), the ritualized body postures aesthetically approached dance, some passages in the stories were quite poetic, and worship involved singing or listening to great music.

As a toddler, I played with blocks, putting them on top of or alongside each other not only to make certain lineups but also to pretend that the resulting patterns were towers or trains or houses. "I discovered that I could play at being an animal and that even serious-minded adults entertained the thought that animals could feel, speak, and act in quasi-human ways. There were many pictures in books to prove it."[10] I found gradually, and with delight, that certain shapes, such as a short upright line or a curved line, denote something special that is neither just a whimsical, subjective thought nor an ordinary thing but the letter "I" or "C," and that one of these letters (the "I") undergoes a metamorphosis of status and meaning when taken for the number "1." Upon learning to read, I discovered that some words could be read backward to produce other words: "God" becomes "dog." Grown-up people would affirm these discoveries, but with a proviso: "I" was only "one" when talking about numbers and never when dealing with letters; "God" could never be spelled backward in prayer! And so I got my first inklings of language games.

Moreover, as these novel worlds dawned on me as new opportunities, and as I began to practice the skills and thoughts and words appropriate to each, I found them mutually reinforcing. Between the inner world of my private fanciful images, as in dreams and reverie, and the patently outer world of perceptible things that fill space, a whole set of new worlds shaped up that contained neither mind-filling private thoughts nor space-filling things but entirely different entities in some way peculiar: They were mostly intangible, yet proved shareable, and they could be talked about in a certain language different from "this is a table" and "here is a tree.' When I said, "Our Father who art in heaven," no one called me stupid or crazy or unrealistic, and even I did not confuse the referent of this phrase with the referent of another nearly identical phrase according to which my natural father, who had died, was allegedly in heaven. In fact, only by leaping into a third language game, pertinent to joking and mockery, could I gigglingly utter the phrase while glancing at my father's photograph, supported by the laughter of my siblings, and instantly checked by my mother's dismay.[2]

> It will surprise no one when I summarize these reminiscences from early childhood by saying that I practiced the imagination; that I received much external stimulation in developing my imaginative leanings or talents; that I engaged in thought, speech, and acts with imaginary beings; and that I received much approval and help from adults in keeping traffic with the imaginable—as long as my thoughts, words, and acts proved shareable with other people or, better, touched a responsive chord in them.[11]

Transitional Objects and the Transitional Sphere

The title of this section apposes two concepts introduced by the British pediatrician and psychoanalyst Winnicott.[12] This observer of children noted that older infants develop a strong temporary attachment to some "thing" from their environment: a piece of blanket, a soft toy, a rag doll, or whatever. They keep it close to them in moments of duress, cuddle it when excited, finger it when dozing off, or stick it into their mouths when frustrated. The "thing," called a "transitional object," functions as a tangible contour that delineates the child's inner world from the outer world but also brings the two together. More astutely, Winnicott also called attention to the special cognitive and emotional attitude "family members assume toward the child and his transitional object. These family members do not dispute the child's special claim to his piece of blanket [or rag doll], but indulgently allow for his intimacy with it."[13] Wise mothers know that the transitional object cannot be taken rudely away from the child (e.g., to be laundered or put into the toy chest for neatness's sake); they also know that in moments of distress their emotional access to the child can be eased by being routed through the transitional object. In a word, the whole family knows, undoubtedly from their own childhood memories, that the transitional object is to the child not just a thing among other things in the world, but a quasi-sacred, ritual object that is to be handled with reverence and solemnity.[2] It is a transcendent, mysterious, symbolic object through which family members will seek contact with the child and engage the child in playing. The family deals with the transitional object just as ritualistically as does the child. A special pattern of stylized human interactions ensues that differs from ordinary reality testing. The whole network of these actions and interactions around the child's chosen symbol, which approaches the nature of a liturgy, is what Winnicott calls the transitional sphere.[2,3]

Two Worlds or Three?

A large body of developmental, psychological, and psychiatric writings describes the neonate's inner world as "autistic." "Drives, affects, longings, and kinesthetic sensations preponderate, constituting [what Freud, 1911/1958, called] the *primary process*."[14,15] It is the world of dreaming, suffused with extremely subjective, essentially solipsistic, and ineffable fantasies. In the world of the deranged adult, unchecked indulgence in the primary process accounts for psychiatric delusions and hallucinations. In the child's autistic world, everything is possible as long as it is imaginable—designed by the omnipotence of thought. Traces of this infantile omnipotence persist in adults: Anyone who does not like his current situation can daydream (fantasize) a better one.

As the mother's initial hyperadaptive attitude gives way to more normally adaptive or "realistic" ministrations, frustrations increase for the infant. Through these frustrations, the child becomes forcefully aware of the outer world as a mixed pattern of positive and negative stimuli with which he must come to terms. A distinction between me and not-me will slowly emerge, with increasing awareness of discernible external entities such as food, bathwater, people, and qualities such as lights, colors, sounds, and temperatures.

> Coming to terms with this outside objective world gradually elicits the *secondary process* which is a cognition based on reasoning, logic, objectivity, and reality testing, eventually to be expressed in words with firm denotation values and in consensually validated language. For years to come, the child will receive much guidance in practicing and perfecting this secondary process [according to culturally recognized stage-specific timetables].[15]

Thus, the psychological literature on development formally recognizes two worlds: the inner and the outer, the subjective and the objective, the autistic and the realistic. And according to much of that literature, the goal of growth and pedagogy is to give up the autistic world and embrace the realistic world, that is, reality works to curb the promptings of fantasy. The leitmotiv of development is that the secondary process shall overtake the primary process. Reason shall triumph over affect, order replace disorder, instincts be tamed, and thus man will become civilized.

Spurred on by my own childhood reminiscences and enlightened by Winnicott's concepts, I find that this two-world vision of traditional psychology amounts to a truncated statement of the options for growth and development. Beyond or between the autistic and the realistic worlds lies a third world (Pruyser, 1974, 1979, 1983) that has entities and events of its own, foreshadowed by Winnicott's transitional sphere with its transitional objects. It is the world of play, the world of the imagination, the world of illusion. I shall call it the illusionistic world,[2,3,16] and to give a provisional definition of terms, I quote from Freud:[17]

> These [religious ideas which profess to be dogmas] . . . are illusions, fulfillments of the oldest, strongest and most urgent wishes of mankind. The secret of their strength lies in the strength of those wishes. . . . An illusion is not the same thing as an error; nor is it necessarily an error. . . . In the case of delusions, we emphasize as essential their being in contradiction with reality. Illusions need not necessarily be false—that is to say, unrealizable or in contradiction to reality. (pp. 30–31)

There it is: Illusion is not hallucination or delusion but can deteriorate into them. "Illusion formation is . . . a unique process that derives from the imagination. It need not be captive to the autistic process and cannot be locked into the reality testing procedures prescribed by common sense, let alone what Woodger[18] calls the 'finger and thumb philosophy' of positivism."[19]

While Freud spoke of illusion in religion, Gombrich[20] devoted a large book to *Art and Illusion*. Art is not a representation of reality, but rather a thoroughgoing transformation of stimuli from the inner and outer worlds. As creations of the imagination, both religion and art have to be distinguished on the one hand from reality in the ordinary sense and on the other hand from solipsistic subjectivity. If too natural, too realistic, art vanishes into mere representation and religion into mere rationality (or fundamentalistic double-talk about an unseen world taken as literally as the sensory world). If too subjective, too autistic, art and religion will fail to get a hearing since they come too close to delusion and hallucination. Everything depends on using the imagination to keep its products linked with, but different from, the realities of the outer world and the common human stratum of the inner world. The culturally successful use of imagination must be coupled with adequate reality testing to circumvent deterioration into madness.

The Illusionistic World

In Table 1, taken from my essay on creativity,[3] I compare the three worlds previously outlined. I have put the illusionistic world between the autistic and the realistic worlds not only to suggest an ideational space for it but also to correct the entrenched genre of thought that imposes a forced—and I think false—choice between autism and realism.

TABLE 1

Autistic World	*Illusionistic World*	*Realistic World*
Untutored fantasy	Tutored fantasy	Sense perception
Omnipotent thinking	Adventurous thinking	Reality testing
Utter whimsicality	Orderly imagination	Hard, undeniable facts
Free associations	Inspired connections	Logical connections
Ineffable images	Verbalizable images	Look-and-see referents
Hallucinatory entities or events	Imaginative entities or events	Actual entities or events
Private needs	Cultural needs	Factual needs
Symptoms	Symbols	Signs, indices
Dreaming	Playing	Working
Sterility	Creativeness	Resourcefulness
Internal object (imago)	Transcendent object prefigured by the child's transitional object	External object

Illusionistic objects transcend those of the autistic and realistic worlds, albeit certain traces of internal and external objects may codetermine their form and content. They are not products of the whimsical private fantasy nor replicas or representations of sensory data. They evolve from a tutored fantasy rooted in the collective imagination of the human mind and its history. Much of the "relatedness" between people occurs through this collective imagination. Illusionistic objects and illusionistic thinking are *sui generis*, irreducible to the strictly private, ineffable, autistic, and essentially solipsistic mind, or the public, demonstrable, look-and-see entities of the realistic world that bombards the senses. Between autistic dreaming and realistic working lies the opportunity to play and to engage in symbolic transactions, shared with and supported by other civilized people. (I use the words *symbol* and *symbolic* in the sense given to them by Tillich,[21] namely, that they participate in the power to which they point.) Illusionistic thinking pertains to symbol systems such as religion and the arts and, as Polanyi[22] and Kuhn[23] have demonstrated, to the spirit of science. What else is a scientific "paradigm" but a playfully entertained contract inviting certain believers to engage in a game, abide by its rules, and be excited by the prospect of some intellectual "payoff"?

Illusion Processing in Religion

If Winnicott was correct in his programmatic statement that religion and the arts are developmentally rooted in the child's practicing with transitional objects in the transitional sphere, and if my construction of a "third world" of illusionistic objects is plausible, then religious development hinges on a set of functions that could be called *illusion processing*.[2,3] This processing is obviously an exercising of the imagination with the help of certain cultural resources and guided by certain tutors. Just as it leaves room for innovation and creativity, for personal variation of collectively held ideas, so also can it be stifled by pressure for slavish conformity to public models.

In regard to the latter situation, a strong caveat is in order, which takes into account a perversion of the illusionistic sphere occurring all too frequently: the staging of illusionistic ideas or entities as if they were realistic. Many religious debates are enmeshed in this fallacy. For instance, if the doctrine of inerrancy of scripture (which is properly an illusionistic proposition) is literalized and concretized in the manner of the realistic sphere, one is saddled with having to deny evidence for the theory of evolution. Along with relocating illusionistic propositions from their proper sphere into the realistic sphere, one also must switch from one language game to another, or else (as frequently happens in arguments of this kind) engage in double-talk that makes no sense at all. While the example just cited may be attributed to poor or undisciplined thinking and mental sloth, it is apparent that other perversions of illusionistic ideas are a product of institutionalization. For instance, arguments about poor fit between the "invisible church" and any "institutional church" are elicited by a playful conception of an ideal uneasily juxtaposed to that ideal's historical concretization in an organizational structure: with headquarters in Rome, Geneva, or Augsburg; with paid officers, buildings, libraries, moneys, and all kinds of political and fiscal entanglements with the state. In the process of institutionalization, the original illusionistic idea may eventually become unrecognizable, and playful attitudes, let alone innovative proclivities, may be overtaken by a grim pseudorealism that sanctions deviancy. The acme of perversion by institutionalization was the Inquisition.[2]

Barring such perversions, the constant threat of which requires unrelenting vigilance, how does or should or might the religious imagination develop? As everyone knows, the infant sooner or later gives up and replaces its original transitional object with new ones. But the practice of attachments to symbols goes on, continually allowing the growing person to experience their fascination, excitement, and solace. Though transitional objects are characteristically felt to exude warmth so that they are close to the heart, one may feel a degree of unresolved ambivalence toward them that may produce occasional outbursts of anger against them—which may at a later age amount to doubt about or disbelief in the very object of one's faith. But even apart from affective lability and ambivalence, the inevitable ambiguities of life are likely to always give the illusionistic sphere and its objects a somewhat delicate, if not precarious, status. Proof of this delicate quality of illusions (in religion, art, and science) lies in the historical fact that civilizations can decline and regress to barbarism, if not savagery. In that case, autism and realism prevail, one barely checked by the other.

Such historical collapses of a people's illusionistic sphere highlight an important feature of illusionism: the opportunity it offers for sublimation of erotic urges and the neutralization of aggression. Civilized persons modify their impulses by deflecting their aim, focusing them on well-chosen objects they can engage in harmless and possibly even constructive activities. Thus the imagination, especially the culturally tutored fantasy, fashions the symbols, stylizes the modes of dealing with symbols, and sets the rewards for engaging in symbolic activity. Through the trained imagination, the illusionistic sphere promotes that optimal fusion of erotic and aggressive energies whereby the former has the edge over the latter and transforms it into healthy and constructive activity—not just in one's head, as in a daydream, but also in the civil arena. As an example of such constructivity—nay, of creative innovation—I cite Martin Luther King's work, culminating in his glorious "I have a dream" speech.[3] That speech straddled both the world of ideas and the world of facts; it introduced a new paradigm[23] after showing the bankruptcy of an older one; it combined Yahwistic wrath with the benevolence of a God-in-Christ. But for all his patent creativity, what reliance King had on the great illusionistic traditions of the Bible, black preaching, and Gandhian nonviolence! Absorption in these traditions had become to him a sacred playing—with one sidewise glance at the brutal facts of the realistic world and another keen glance at the ever-present explosive turbulence of the autistic world.

If I may turn again to autobiography, I recall the great affection my brothers and I had for a transitional object that served us many years: an illustrated children's Bible. It was read to us in an atmosphere, staged daily after dinner, of motherly concern and warmth, complete with body contact as we huddled up to her, listening and looking at the pictures, punctuated by moments in which we boys took turns holding the book ourselves and reading passages aloud. The book stood ready day and night in a corner of the mantel, always visible, close to a large portrait of our deceased father. I mention this latter fact to allow for the likelihood that feelingful aspects of person (autistic) imagos became intermingled with the illusionistic personages in the biblical stories, with whom transitional or enduring identifications could be made.[2]

Another experience that had no little effect on my appropriation of religious ideas was the fortuitous circumstance that I attended a denominational school (through the ninth grade) that stood for much greater Calvinist orthodoxy than did my family. Thus, home and school presented me with two different religious and emotional worlds. The first was mellow, optimistic, and forgiving; the second strict, somber, and punitive—both equally taking recourse to scripture and the *Institutes of the Christian Religion*! There is nothing like such an upbringing to convince a young boy that religion is what you make it, that all of it is what I now call "illusionistic." Fortunately, home won over school, undoubtedly because of its deeper roots in my childhood practicing of the transitional sphere.[2] The hand of God, much talked about in school, was closer to my mother's tender-and-firm hand than to the threatening and often slapping extremities of my teachers. Small wonder, then, that I have always found the highlight of worship the benevolently outstretched hands of a fulsome pastoral blessing,[24] and that one of my dearest pictures is Rembrandt's etching of the father blessing the prodigal son upon his return home.

In my ongoing practicing of religion, it also began to dawn on me, in part because of the school's intellectual demands for rote memorization of psalms, catechism, and biblical passages as well as Palestinian geography and lore (with grades to be taken as seriously as those for reading, writing, and arithmetic), that learning religion is not unlike learning a craft. One must know a lot and must master certain procedures and skills. Religion makes demands on the intellect and on linguistic performance, in addition to its work on feelings. In my case, the religious imagination had to follow canons of excellence and live up to high aims. I had to read, study, and engage in intelligent debate to hone my skill in thought and argument. No effort should be spared to acquire religious savvy—we were told that man was, after all, only a dash lower than the angels![2]

In this precept, of course, lies the ever-present danger of arrogance. In psychodynamic terminology, religious education must address the autistic givens of primary narcissism and omnipotent thinking. I do remember vaguely that religious practices and instruction made me feel, at times, a bit small, for they admonished me to feel and act humbly—much as doing so went against the grain of my natural inclinations. Yet these experiences must have stuck, so that they prepared me for the emphatically affirmative response I was to make, many years later, when I came across the following statement by Sidney Mead:[25]

> no man is God. This is what I understand to be the functional meaning of "God" in human experience. Whatever "God" may be—if indeed being is applicable to "God"—a concept of the infinite seems to me necessary if we are to state the all-important fact about man: that he is finite. (p. 754)

Marvelous! The function of the infinite, the universe, or any god is not merely to be there, but to teach us *that man is not it.*[2] Voltaire, the skeptic, proceeded from an Enlightenment image of man as a rational and capable being; Schleiermacher believed that man needed to recapture a lost feeling of reverence. Mead, living in the twentieth century, recognized that man is naturally given to grandiosity, with dire results such as the Nazi holocaust and the atomic bombing of Hiroshima.

I must admit that, despite all these antecedent religious lessons, as a teenager I had a hard time making the mandatory "profession of faith" to formalize my membership in the Dutch Reformed Church. My philosophical bent, coupled with a degree of neurotic blocking on anything externally imposed, made me uneasy with "convictional language"[26] and confession. I partly despised, partly envied my classmates who seemed at ease as they rattled off answers to the examining committee's questions and went through the rituals of induction, which included receiving communion for the first time. Enlightened as I felt I was, I would not participate in a bloody "cannibalistic feast," least of all under pressure. Did not Christianity preach emancipation from legislated rituals of atonement? Many years later, two insights changed my mind on this issue. The first evolved from a series of earnest conversations with a clergyman which led me to realize the narcissism in my opposition to the communion ceremony: I had imagined myself omnipotently not only above regression but also beyond any need for even temporary regression, after I had grandly diagnosed other people's communion celebration as a primitive, regressive act. The second insight came when I attended an Easter communion service in Calvin's St. Peter's Church in Geneva where we were served *sparkling, white wine*! This occasion proved what I had long surmised, namely that the "blood and broken body" imagery and parlance of typical Protestant communion services had somehow gone awry, completely ignoring the other meaning of blood as "vital juice" and of bread as "staff of life." Such incidents exemplify the workings, for better or for worse, of the imagination.[2]

The symbolism of ritual can become skewed in destructive directions by all participating parties, not least the church itself. Ritual becomes dislodged from its playful functioning in the illusionistic sphere and displaced into the realistic one when the institution grimly legislates it as a necessary act. Precisely then it leaves nothing to the imagination but becomes instead only a token of realistically advocated conformity to somebody's Kafkaesque rules.

A Warning: Threats to the Imagination from Two Sides

At several places in this essay, I alluded to the precariousness of the illusionistic sphere and the delicacy of its objects. The imagination is constantly threatened from two sides: from the side of autism by hallucinatory entities or events, and from the side of realism by actual entities or events. Much of what follows is meant to alert pastors and religious educators to situations of danger encountered in their work with people.

As some of my autobiographical citations have shown, neurotic needs and defenses may encroach on the orderly imagination and tutored fantasy in illusion processing. As Winnicott[27] observed, these symptomatic intrusions from the side of the autistic sphere produce a morbid quality in some children's play: Oral and anal, sadistic and masochistic preoccupations make their playing compulsive, repetitive, and stereotyped, and cast a pall of grimness over their activities. This kind of playing is not joyous and imaginative, least of all creative. It stands in sharp contrast to the *happy* playing of a healthy child who "is able to feel *satisfied with the game*,"[28] without undue intrusion of excited id impulses. In Winnicott's opinion, happy playing depends on the child's *capacity to be alone* (p. 419).

This capacity to be alone is rooted in early childhood experiences "of *being alone, as an infant and small child, in the presence of mother*."[29] Winnicott was well aware of the paradoxical nature of his statement; it stems from the fact that the separation–individuation process occurs at the transition from one matrix to another. "In the first matrix, mother and child are mutually dependent, even symbiotic, and the child neither feels nor is regarded as an autonomous self."[30] In the subsequent matrix, the child practices separating from the mother, and his increasing independence, "aloneness," and autonomy round off to a felt and granted selfhood. What makes for this crucial "capacity to be alone"? Could it be the condition in which the "I" and the "me" form a synthetic unity?

Most theorists today would probably agree that the capacity to be alone means having within oneself a dynamic, trustworthy, reliant image of the benevolent mother, which not only sees one through in times when she must be physically absent but also functions as an auxiliary ego that enhances the child's mastery of impulses. Other clinicians accentuate different features of this growth dynamic, which is both intrapsychic and interpersonal.

> Erikson[31] sees "numinosity" in the greeting rituals between mother and infant, and stresses the quality of trust as an indispensable preparation for wholesome development. Schafer[32] speaks of the "loving and beloved superego" that benevolently guides the growth process.[2] (p. 175)

I believe that the vicissitudes of these internal and external object relations greatly influence children's induction into the illusionistic world and their chances for a wholesome practicing of its procedures and skills. Any "impingements" (Winnicott's term), from bad mothering and situational deprivations to mental or physical handicaps, thwart the formation of a good internal object and a trusting relation to the world outside, whether to persons, things, nature, or institutions. Such impingements generally stimulate the autistic fantasy, producing distortions in the appropriation of illusionistic entities and procedures: Gods become monsters, the self is held to be despicable or unworthy, curiosity becomes dangerous, thinking becomes beset by apprehensiveness, and playing becomes grim and repetitious. Rizzuto[33] describes the rather awkward representations of God held by some troubled adults and plausibly reconstructs their dynamic origins from the impingements that had occurred in their early lives.[2]

The imagination can also be threatened from the side of the realistic world. In fact, I think one may fairly say that a constant pressure from the realistic sphere works to curtail the novelty-producing, potentially creative imagination nurtured in the illusionistic sphere.

> From the angle of realism, illusions are dangerous, or at least frivolous. Yet single-minded dedication to reality forces the arts to be reproductive or representational, science to be utilitarian or technological, and religion to be the warp and weft of the social fabric that should not be disturbed.[34] In the clutches of the realistic sphere, symbols are turned into mere emblems or signs.[2] (p. 176)

And the cross becomes a piece of costume jewelry!

Realism has a distaste for the mysterious. Its objects should be tangible and unambiguously denotable: A rose is a rose is a rose. (Which reminds me that I once met a man wearing a rose in his lapel who stated that he put on a fresh one every day to witness to "the new life in Christ.") Without denying the virtues of common sense or minimizing the need for adequate reality testing, I must say that single-minded dedication to the realistic world leads all too easily to the intellectual narrowness of positivism and operationalism typified in Wittgenstein's[35] early phrase: "whereof one cannot speak thereof one must be silent" (p. 27). Or else, it leads to a "thingification" of ideas and propositions. In some cases of marked brain damage, the patient is reduced to concretism[36] due to failure of concept formation; more tellingly for our concern here, such a patient can no longer engage in "as if" thinking and lacks playfulness.

We cannot take the realistic world lightly if we want to survive. Realism is badly needed (as psychoanalysis has always held) to curb and counteract the dangerous impulsivity of the autistic world. These two worlds stand dialectically and dynamically related and mediated by the ego which derives its autonomy precisely from its double input of stimuli from the id and from the world.[37] The religious imagination can indeed go haywire, concocting incubi, witches, or unicorns. Given such demonstrations of the ever-present productivity of the whimsical, autistic fantasy and its occasional destructive impact on the social order—even on the rights and lives of citizens—realists are sometimes rightly fearful of the imagination.[2]

Moreover, we should acknowledge that perceptions of the realistic world—people, animals, plants, mountains, seas, and the firmament, as well as human artifacts such as buildings, tools, works of art, laboratoria, temples, and graves—are necessary stimuli for setting the process of imagination in motion and for providing it with some "stuff" to work on. Here we see the positive side of institutionalization: Without libraries we could hardly have theology; without churches we could not have corporate worship or liturgy. Without organized tradition we have no ritual, no sense even of origins and destinies. And without some assembled doctrines we could not have any illuminating reinterpretation of doctrines.

Realism has, however, a momentum that can lead to smothering the imagination. When realists are too fearful of the autistic fantasy going rampant, their fear may spread to the illusionistic sphere as well, with an end result such as forbidding the reading of fairy tales to children.[2] One only has to browse through Bettelheim's book *The Uses of Enchantment*[38] to learn the psychological and cultural deprivations such purism imposes. Indeed, an all too stark realism may relegate religion to the "fairy tale" category, thereby denigrating both.

But by "institutionalization" I mean not only ecclesiastical organization with its visible trappings; I include the invisible structuring of the mind that Kierkegaard[39] called "Christendom." Piously trained minds develop habits of thought and language that confuse illusionistic and realistic ideas. "Wittingly or unwittingly, a displacement occurs in which the products and the art of the imagination are pried loose from their playful ambiance in the illusionistic sphere and relocated in the realistic world where they are transformed into so-called plain truths and hard facts."[40] Entertainable religious propositions eventually become unarguable doctrines. Religious development becomes thwarted by doctrinaire teachers who insist on intellectual and behavioral conformity to enforced norms that leave nothing to the imagination. Thus, we are taught docility rather than venturesome explorations. And arguments for the existence of God and the correctness of certain church doctrines use the logic of natural phenomena and empirical verification, taking away all mystery from the religious object. (The churchly form of this displacement has been acidly stated by John R. Fry in his book *The Great Apostolic Blunder Machine*.[41] Along with this displacement, transcendence becomes scaled down to a mere intensification of the intergenerational power differences between teachers and pupils, parents and children, state and citizens.

In Christendom, pious people signal their religious "finds" rather than their struggles with religion. Their car bumpers carry stickers with "I found it" messages. Their commercially packaged tours to Israel are anachronistically labeled "visits to the Holy Land" as if they were pilgrimages. They pretend to know "what God says" and will tell you so, unasked. They present their convictions as churchly beliefs so self-evident that there is no room for doubt.

I think that this slippage from the illusionistic into the realistic sphere illustrates clearly and trenchantly the need for renewal. The slippage is so constant that attempts at renewal must be made with equal constancy and vigor on two fronts. To recapture a sense of mystery and transcendence, people must be called back from "thingish" and factual thought to imaginative thought, in which novelty of insight can be produced. The second front for efforts at renewal is, I suggest, ethical thought and action. The realistic sphere in which we dwell with an attitude of "that's the way things are" is always badly in need of infusions from the illusionistic sphere, which alone is capable of creating the ideals that may and should improve the conditions under which we live.

Notes

1. The author was Henry March Pfeiffer Professor, The Menninger Foundation, Box 829, Topeka, Kansas 66601.

2. Pruyser, P. W. *The play of the Imagination: Toward a Psychoanalysis of Culture*. New York: International Universities Press, 1983.
3. Pruyser, P. W. An essay on creativity. *Bulletin of the Menninger Clinic, 43*, 294–353, 1979.
4. Jaspers, K. *The Perennial Scope of Philosophy* (R. Manheim, Trans.). Hamden, CT: Shoe String Press. (Original work published 1949), 1968.
5. Tracy, D. *Blessed Rage for Order: The new Pluralism in Theology*. New York: Seabury Press, 1975.
6. Otto, R. *The Idea of the Holy: An Inquiry into the Non-rational Factor in the Idea of the Divine and Its Relation to the Rational* (2nd ed.; J. W. Harvey, Trans.). New York: Oxford University Press. (Original work published 1917), 1970.
7. Pruyser, P. W. *A Dynamic Psychology of Religion*. New York: Harper & Row, 1968.
8. Wiggins, J. B. (Ed.). *Religion as Story*. New York: Harper & Row, 1975.
9. Pruyser, P. W. Lessons from art theory for the psychology of religion. *Journal for the Scientific Study of Religion, 15*, 1–14, 1976.
10. Pruyser 1983, p. 159.
11. Pruyser 1983, pp. 160–161.
12. Winnicott, D. W. Transitional objects and transitional phenomena. In *Collected papers: Through Paediatrics to Psycho-Analysis* (pp. 229–242). New York: Basic Books. (Original work published 1951), 1958.
13. Pruyser 1979, p. 317.
14. Freud, S. (1911). Formulations on the two principles of mental functioning. *Standard Edition* (Vol. 12, pp. 218–226). London: Hogarth Press, 1958.
15. Pruyser 1979, p. 316.
16. Pruyser, P. W. *Between Belief and Unbelief*. New York: Harper & Row, 1974.
17. Freud, S. (1927). The future of an illusion. *Standard Edition* (Vol. 21, pp. 5–56). London: Hogarth Press, 1961.
18. Woodger, J. H. *Physics, Psychology, and Medicine: A Methodological Essay*. London: Cambridge University Press, 1956.
19. Pruyser 1983, p. 165.
20. Gombrich, E. H. J. *Art and Illusion: A Study in the Psychology of Pictorial Representation* (2nd ed.). London: Phaidon, 1962.
21. Tillich, P. *Systematic Theology*, Vol. 1: *Reason and Revelation*. Chicago: University of Chicago Press, 1952.
22. Polanyi, M. *Personal Knowledge: Towards a Post-critical Philosophy*. Chicago: University of Chicago Press, 1958.

23. Kuhn, T. S. *The Structure of Scientific Revolutions* (2nd ed.). Chicago: University of Chicago Press, 1970.
24. Pruyser, P. W. The master hand: Psychological notes on pastoral blessing. In W. B. Oglesby, Jr. (Ed.), *The New Shape of Pastoral Theology: Essays in Honor of Seward Hiltner* (pp. 352–365). Nashville: Abingdon Press, 1969.
25. Mead, S. E. In quest of America's religion. *The Christian Century, 87*, 752–756, 1970.
26. Zuurdeeg, W. F. *An Analytic Philosophy of Religion*. Nashville: Abingdon Press, 1958.
27. Winnicott, D. W. *Playing and Reality*. New York: Basic Books, 1971.
28. Winnicott, D. W. The capacity to be alone. *International Journal of Psychoanalysis, 39*, 416–420, 1958.
29. Winnicott 1958a, p. 417.
30. Pruyser 1983, p. 174.
31. Erikson, E. H. Ontogeny of ritualization. In R. M. Loewenstein, L. W. Newman, M. Schur, & A. J. Solnit (Eds.), *Psychoanalysis—A General Psychology: Essays in Honor of Heinz Hartmann* (pp. 601–621). New York: International Universities Press, 1966.
32. Schafer, R. The loving and beloved superego in Freud's structural theory. *Psychoanalytic Study of the Child, 15*, 163–188, 1960.
33. Rizzuto, A-M. *The Birth of the Living God: A Psychoanalytic Study*. Chicago: University of Chicago Press, 1979.
34. Durkheim, E. *The Elementary Forms of the Religious Life* (J. W. Swain, Trans.). London: George Allen & Unwin. (Original work published 1912), 1915.
35. Wittgenstein, L. *Tractatus Logico-Philosophicus* (F. P. Ramsey, Trans.). New York: Harcourt, Brace. (Original work published 1922), 1947.
36. Goldstein, K. *Human Nature in the Light of Psychopathology*. Cambridge: Harvard University Press, 1940.
37. Rapaport, D. The theory of ego autonomy: A generalization. In M. M. Gill (Ed.), *The Collected Papers of David Rapaport* (pp. 722–744). New York: Basic Books. (Reprinted from *Bulletin of the Menninger Clinic*, 1958, *22*, 13–35), 1967.
38. Bettelheim, B. *The Uses of Enchantment: The Meaning and Importance of Fairy Tales*. New York: Knopf, 1976.
39. Kierkegaard, S. A. *Attack upon Christendom, 1854–55* (W. Lowrie, Trans.). Princeton, NJ. Princeton University Press. (Original work published 1854–1855), 1944.
40. Pruyser 1983, p. 177.
41. Fry, J. R. *The Great Apostolic Blunder Machine*. New York: Harper & Row, 1978.

VI

CONCLUSION

11

Where Do We Go from Here? Scenarios for the Psychology of Religion

The first and obvious thing to say at this annual meeting of the American Psychological Association is that psychology has become so diversified and subspecialized that it makes ever less sense to continue to speak of psychology of religion as if it were one enterprise. There may be nearly as many psychologies of religion as there are APA divisions and branches of psychology—each being a special view of the thing purportedly studied: religion. For instance, there are several social-psychological views, several behavioral views, several cognitive views. There is a classical psychodynamic, an ego-psychological, a British objective-relations view. One can distinguish a clinical psychological view, a pastoral psychological view, a para-psychological view, an organizational behavior view, a life-course developmental view, a stress and crisis view and much more. Maybe there is even a military psychology of religion being pursued somewhere in the Pentagon!

The second obvious thing to say is a complement of the first one: the phenomena of religion, i.e., what is being studied by any of the psychologies of religion, are also so diverse and often so systematized in their diversity, that we should no longer speak of religion at large, but of specific religions, faith groups, denominations, sects, cults, or individuals, perhaps even further qualified by adjectives such as liberal, orthodox, fundamentalist, evangelical,

Reprinted with the permission of the *Journal for the Scientific Study of Religion*, 1987, *26*(2), pp. 173–182.

Hindu, Shiite, Sunni, capitalist, Marxist, anabaptist, militant, pietistic, established, in free-church tradition, or what not. For should we not expect significant and possibly irreconcilable differences in religious experience, cognitive outlook, life-style, social orientation, and value behavior between, say, religions that insist on an instantaneous conversion and those that prize loyalty to orderly and civil habits under staid liturgical control; or between groups whose young men are trained to be conscientious objectors and those who blithely send their sons to military academies to be trained for a God-and-country ideology; let alone between religiously well informed free-thinkers and religiously under-educated persons who avidly submit themselves to the wiles of Eastern or Western despotic cult leaders?

What I am describing here is diversity in the workings and forms of psychologies and of religions—in some cases such a pronounced diversity that a comprehensive psychology of religion is very difficult to attain. But there is also an attitudinal factor in some scholars who do not even strive toward comprehensiveness because they are ill at ease with pluralism as a philosophical principle and a political stance. Both of these grant diversity not only its right to exist and be manifest, but approach the diverse positions with tolerance, though not without judgment. Such tolerance is simply too much for some minds.

Motives and Aims in Psychologies of Religion

At any rate, given the diversity of psychologies and the almost bewildering multiformity of religious phenomena, it is small wonder that there are marked differences also in what appears to motivate scholars to engage in psychology of religion and in the aims that their works are to serve. Let me briefly articulate some motives and aims that no one can miss when surveying a sizeable portion of the accumulated literature. I spot at least the following positions:[3]

1. Some psychologies of religion seek to buttress religion or to defend it apologetically by trying to describe, if not prove, its psychological necessity or inevitability. While this can be done with sophistication, it is often done naively, for instance by trying to show that mental health or stable human relations rest on engage-

ments in religion, either the writer's preferred religion or just any religion or piety. There are numerous sub-scholarly tracts of this ilk, and because of the often half-literate popular conservatism that spawns a good part of them, they ironically deal more often with a vague attitude of genteel religiousness than with the specifics of a particular persuasion.

2. Some psychologies of religion seek to make subjective and private experiences objective and public by providing them with psychological understanding, fine description, or explanations. Works on mysticism tend to have this aim. They seek to articulate what is alleged to be ineffable and are, as Rudolf Otto once observed, sometimes unusually wordy in conveying the sacred silence of their subject matter. Some studies of mystical experience go further than describing and explaining and frankly advocate paranormal experiences—no matter how induced, to what end, and at what possible psychic cost.

3. Some psychologies of religion seize upon strange, rare, deviant, controversial, or sectarian practices, for instance glossolalia, ecstasy, or hallucinatory states, which are seen by others as abnormal or are generally disdained, so as to bring them within the range of normal or adaptive processes, making them not only understandable, but also acceptable and possibly even respectable. They form a complement to other studies of the same phenomena that set out to show how pathological they are.

4. Some of the other psychologies of religion clearly aim at exposing religion as a whole as an atavism or anachronism by focusing on its archaic origins, its continuous anachronistic practices, its primitive modes of thought and action, the thought control it fosters, or the unreason on which it is allegedly based. Metapsychological or metaphysical postures behind these endeavors include a by now somewhat dated hyper-positivism, hyperrationalism, and ill-conceived developmentalism.

5. In contrast to the previous endeavor, some psychologies of religion appear to have been written in order to expose with benign fascination the psychic roots of religion in archaic imagery of childish wishes or defense mechanisms, so as to maximize the continuities between ancient and modern man, or between child and adult. This kind of work is often embedded in, or in turn fosters, an encompassing, but probably quite syncretistic, general psychology or transhistorical world view.

6. A rarer form of psychology of religion seeks to apply, in playful tinkering fashion, the conceptual and operational apparatus of a particular psychology (e.g., clinical, experimental, social) to one or more of the many phenomena of religion, just to see where these would lead in understanding religion, with minimal prejudice from personal agendas. For some minds, this enterprise can be reinforced by the conviction that religion has long been a taboo subject for scientific investigation, and that the time has come to break this taboo. For other minds the very richness of religious phenomena, their subtlety, and their seeming intractability are challenging them to do this kind of investigating in an intellectually joyous spirit.

7. Often mixed with one of the other positions is an approach that pays respect to religion's historical persistence, its power, its impact on individuals and groups, and its richness of forms by bestowing great curiosity upon it, in a nonpartisan spirit, but with a no holds barred analysis.

My list is not a classification of works, but an inventory of apparent aims and motives that have produced the body of literature on psychology of religion. One writer can have several aims and motives at once, or change in the course of time from one to the other.

In addition to these aims and motives we should be aware of the possibility that in some intellectuals with critical analytical minds their engagement in psychology of religion is a substitute for, or a once-removed form of engagement in religious thought, or an intellectualized expression of loyalty to their religious origins or affiliation. Moreover, psychologists who prize introspection may find themselves constructing half-experimentally certain forms of intense involvement in religion that would provide grounds for psychological reflection, e.g., trying to speak in tongues or taking psychedelic drugs. Or in searching for psychological clarification they may engage in religious practices or strive for religious experiences, e.g., by meditating, fasting, or attending mass evangelizing meetings, legitimating their acts by their scholarly ambition. In a word, there are ample opportunities for mixed motives to operate in studying psychology of religion.

Given the diversities that I have sketched, it should not surprise anyone that scholars in the psychology of religion tend to form little cliques based on similarity in preferred psychological theory, method of study, professional setting, motive, and aim, and not infrequently on shared denominational or sectarian allegiances. Many scholars pay little attention to works produced outside their own clique, and broad cross-referencing leaves much to be desired in the bibliographies of books and articles. To put it more sharply, I find there is a great deal of parochialism which in its way undermines the viability of the phrase "psychology of religion."

Perspectival Integrity in the Study of Religion

In academic settings there is considerable variability and sometimes interdepartmental bickering about the proper auspices for courses in the psychology of religion. In some cases these courses are taught in psychology departments and by psychologists, in other cases in departments of religion by faculty members who may or may not be psychologists. In either case the offering of a course appears to be quite dependent on the fortuitous availability of a faculty member who has an interest in the subject—an interest which is not always a guarantee of adequate mastery of the subject. Further complications are produced by divinity schools and theological seminaries which usually have no formal psychology departments with the kind and degree of autonomy and spectrum of interests these departments would have in the graduate schools. And still, other complications occur when psychology of religion courses are taught in church-sponsored or sectarian colleges; in that case I worry about the level of grasp that can be expected from students who know very little psychology and are simply not old enough and are possibly too narrowly indoctrinated to know much about religion either. In that case the level of instruction and of assigned textbooks is likely to be commensurably low.

Among the several hidden assumptions that are apt to lie behind each arrangement, I would like to focus on some that have formal implications for the integrity of psychology of religion as a branch of psychology as well as for guaranteeing a minimal adequacy in representing the scope and depth of religion which is its subject matter.

Most organized scholarly domains are a distinct combination of one or more basic sciences, ancillary sciences, and applied sciences, and sometimes of techniques or skills, and any discipline is usually distinguishable from others by an evolved, unique language game. Using this formal schema and opposing from the start any complete fusion or blatantly syncretistic mixtures, I suggest that the disciplines of psychology and of religion can function vis-à-vis one another in the first place as ancillary sciences. Knowledge of humankind's ongoing engagement in religion and the world's literature about it can be helpful in the formation of learned and astute psychologists, if only because of the amount and variety of soul-searching that religion has traditionally fostered as well as the large margin of pathology it has always produced. Conversely, psychology's questions and findings about how minds work, how feelings affect cognition and how thoughts entail feelings, how behavior is motivated and shaped, etc. can hardly be ignored today by religionists with scholarly ambition and a sense of intellectual responsibility. But in either case, the ancillary discipline is to be kept in a subordinate position as a safeguard against identity confusion.

Moreover, the moment one accepts the rationale for such a mutually ancillary role at the scholarly level, questions of selectivity and specificity arise, derived from both the pluralistic situation I described earlier and the parochialism I noted. What kind of psychology is defensibly ancillary to what kind of religion, and vice versa? Though this question is rarely explicitly raised, it has in practice been answered in strikingly different ways, as my brief inventory of positions has already shown.

In addition to a mutually ancillary role, psychology and religion can function vis-à-vis each other at the applied science level and in relation to techniques and skills. Barring again syncretism and fusion, it can be said that clinical psychology and counseling practitioners can benefit from knowing how religious practitioners make their melioristic interventions in the lives of troubled people, and how religionists assess their charges' behavior, thoughts, feelings, or needs. Reciprocally, professional religionists can benefit from studying how applied psychologists make their assessments of people's needs and make their melioristic interventions. It must be said that the clinical pastoral education movement has done the latter kind of exploring with great eagerness and thoroughness, whereas psychologists have not shown much interest in the reciprocal exploration.

Does it follow, then, that perspectival integrity in either of the two disciplines is vouchsafed by the choice one makes between them at the basic science level, fortified by the language game one adopts along with that choice? I am inclined to say roundly, Yes to this question, were it not for a few added considerations. Surely a psychologist should be identified with psychology and its vocabulary and grammar, no matter what special topic he or she studies. And surely a religionist should be grounded in divinity studies and use its parlance no matter what interest may lead him or her to pursue psychology. But even so, there are complications on the horizon that may come to present problems.

The first complication is methodological and epistemological. What conceptual outlook, what categories, what theoretical framework should guide the psychologist studying religion? If one looks at the accumulated literature one will find that the vast majority of psychological studies of religion have been topically organized by the categories of religion itself, or by religious designations of religious experience. In other words, the subject matter has largely determined the points of focus and organization of the textbooks, such as conversion, mysticism, idea of God, types and stages of faith, prayer, worship, confession, the sick soul, etc. My own 1968 work *A Dynamic Psychology of Religion*[4] was the first one to break with this surrender to the dictates of religion, and to use instead a large collection of psychological processes as means to address, describe and evaluate the many phenomena of religion. The fact that this feature of my work has found few if any imitators suggests that the psychology of religion is still dominated by the religious scene, if not by overt or covert religiosity, and has insufficiently asserted its autonomy and integrity as a psychology.

I am well aware that the psychology of anything, say of art, literature, mass behavior, gender, work, play, or small groups, must take the natural articulations of its subject matter into account. But it has to place its subject matter in a perspective that is and remains psychological, or else it is no longer a psychology of the subject matter in question. In the case at hand, religion is metaphorically speaking to be looked at through psychological eyes or glasses, palpated by psychological fingers, listened to by psychological ears, and smelled by psychological noses. It is to be thought about in psychological terms. To do this kind of perspectival exploring with any degree of thoroughness one needs to be quite conversant with religion and be aware of its many fascinating phenomena, but without identifying oneself with its ontological and epistemological assertions. Especially when the psychologist has a denominational commitment and is a participant in the phenomena studied, he or she must be on guard against slipping from psychological into religious considerations.

I have now used a word, *commitment*, that presses for caution in some scholars and for boldness in others, based on how they rank the disciplines of psychology and religion in order of their respective comprehensiveness, truth character, ultimacy as foundational discipline, or teleological value. With which of the two disciplines or human enterprises is one most deeply identified, or which one does one take as vantage point while purporting to do a psychological study of religion? Is it possible to take both psychology and religion at once, in one act of combined thinking, as basic sciences? The fact is that there are not a few scholars and professionals today who have advanced degrees in both disciplines. And among those there are some who have come to their two academic degrees because they have perceived – rightly or wrongly – a certain affinity between the discipline of psychology and the discipline of religion, and in some cases wish to make soul mates between these two human enterprises.

I think that these situations require extraordinary vigilance and a great deal of self-control if the resultant work is to be a perspectivally intact psychology of religion. As Vitz has indicated,[5] some psychologies parade or are seen by their adherents as quasi-religions, and as James showed many years ago,[6] some religions parade as quasi-psychologies, especially those with a pronounced healing cult. It is but a few small steps to move from sensing some affinity to espousing syncretism or even advocating fusion. And as must have been clear from my presentation thus far, I think that neither psychology nor religion is served by such inadequate thought patterns. Nor, for that matter, is the catechumen, counselee, psychotherapy patient, novice in religious orders or aspiring believer served by such mixings. The Jesuit novice is not taken through the Ignatian Spiritual Exercises to become healthy or wise, but to become firm in his incarnational Christian faith; the mental patient with delusions of grandeur is not to be strengthened in his belief that he is a son of God, but led to accept the surpassing power of reality and the limitations of being human.

Suggestions for Needed Studies

Continuing the psychodynamic, ego-psychological, and introspective orientations that have characterized my previous work, but being open to a variety of study methods ranging from observing and interviewing to measuring, I would now like to make some suggestions for topical studies that could bring new fascination and depth to the psychology of religion.

Leaning on a classical reflection about projection made by Feuerbach and Freud and many others, I would like to see studies done on aspects of religious experience and attitudes in aging people and old folks. To put Feuerbach's and Freud's thesis in a nutshell, if personality development implies emancipation from childhood needs and an increasing awareness of one's own projections, one would expect that some people's notions of deity will shed their anthropomorphic features or will be replaced entirely by a more abstract principle of cosmic creativity, ethical value, or ultimate truth. In such people, religion of childhood may become an ethic of maturity as they take back their previous projections. Their religiousness may become atheistic in the sense that they no longer feel impelled to pay homage to a quasi-human God in worship and prayer. Such an atheism is not conflict-ridden, strident, or bellicose, and the person's previous more traditional religiousness is not necessarily disowned; in fact, the person may now have a benign, slightly bemused attitude towards fantasies and feelings, ritual acts, and various obligations in which he or she used to engage with the same sincerity that typifies the present abstinence from such observances. I have seen this special kind of emancipation happen in some of my aging friends.

Moreover, from introspective self-study I must affirm that something like this process has slowly and steadily been happening to me and from impressionistic observations of old people in hospitals, nursing homes, and hospices and from conversations with their attending caretakers, including chaplains, one learns that there appears to be a bipolar distribution of religiousness in the aged and dying: some becoming more intensely or articulately religious than they were before, and others becoming less involved than they were. Moreover, despite the adage that there are no unbelievers in fox holes, I have long been impressed by the frequent absence of any religious allusions, imagery, or feelings in many people's self-accounts of traumatic situations, their dreams around important events, and their responses to life crises—even in those persons who have a denominational affiliation, know religious language, and have had religious training—people whom one would expect to experience such events religiously.

What is one to make of these loose but trenchant impressions? Do some people "outgrow" religion after having embraced it? Is there a developmental or dialectic dynamic in religion itself that moves from more or less anthropomorphic theistic imagery to impersonal or atheistic conceptions? Have the accumulated data of the psychology of religion been skewed by disproportionate preoccupation with college students, children, and early life stages? Have we focused too much on people's images and conceptions of God and neglected to study their world views and ethos? These questions are enough to indicate that we are dealing with a complex but interesting issue that can be approached from many different sides.

A second study topic that I like to see addressed is based on the observation that many bright, well educated, and articulate persons who have reached rather high levels of intellectual, technical, professional, or artistic development appear to be singularly undeveloped in their religious ideas and beliefs. Some of these cases show a noticeable disparity in cognitive achievement levels and articulateness, with startlingly low competence in religion. These persons appear to maintain a stylized stupidity, primitivity, naivete, or dull-wittedness in religious matters, much as a country may maintain a nature preserve or National Park area in an otherwise developed or industrialized region. Anyone who has attempted to teach adult church school classes with a high proportion of college educated or professional members can make this interesting if shocking observation.

What can account for such disparity in which religion in church affiliated persons comes off worst? Is it a personal selectivity based on conflict with parental teachings, early religious indoctrination, or painful disenchantments? Is it lack of interest due to lack of received stimulation and guidance? Is it a perverse (but possibly quite widespread) form of piety that anxiously clings to the Biblical verse: . . . "Unless you turn and become like children you will never enter the kingdom of heaven" (Mt. 18:3 RSV)? Or is this situation the expression of a special quality that some critics have considered to be unique to religion itself, namely its indulgence of childish wishes and its readiness to gratify almost any primitive prompting—in other words, its failure to be a sublimation? Is religion, even among the educated and intellectually ambitious, a favorite and socially sanctioned area of stagnation, fixation, or regression? We need well-documented answers to these questions.

A third recommendation I wish to make has to do with typology. Much use has been made and continues to be made of two old war horses, one a typology of religious *experience*, the other a typology of religious *behavior*. I hardly need to say that the first one is William James's elaboration of Francis Newman's distinction between once-born and twice-born believers;[6] and the second is Gordon Allport's distinction between intrinsic and extrinsic religion.[7] Both happen to be bipolar typologies and have for good reasons been used so much that they may have drained attention away from other deserving ordering schemes.

Religious phenomena are so varied and many that surely several worthwhile distinctions can be made between them. For instance, the types of religious experience formulated in 1965 by Erwin Goodenough[8] have excellent face validity and in my opinion combine rather nicely a psychological with a church-historical and religious-studies perspective. Goodenough's sophisticated definitions and apt descriptions add up to the following typological list: (1) Legalism; (2) Supralegalism; (3) Orthodoxy; (4) Supraorthodoxy; (5) Aestheticism; (6) Symbolism and Sacramentalism; (7) The Church; (8) Conversion; and (9) Mysticism. To the best of my knowledge, Goodenough's typology has not found many users, which is puzzling because it is not only very articulate and well-defined, but also an ecumenical typology that reflects the author's knowledge of world religions. I hope that Goodenough's work will be rescued from its apparent oblivion and will become belatedly appreciated for the seminal work it is. After all, much of its ideational structure derives from two giants, Rudolf Otto and Sigmund Freud, whose concepts of the *mysterium tremendum* and of the dynamic unconscious respectively should serve the psychology of religion for at least another fifty years.

But as my previous statements on perspectival integrity imply, psychologists have the option and may indeed prefer to group their observations in terms of psychological variables operating in the religious life rather than in terms of how religion itself articulates its forms. Most of Goodenough's categories are classical terms in divinity studies rather than chapter headings in psychology textbooks. In distinction but not strong opposition to this approach I have become intrigued by the possible usefulness to the psychology of religion of Bernard Lonergan's finely honed analysis of cognitive processes and decision making in his book *Insight: A Study of Human Understanding.*[9] In a nutshell, Lonergan, a Jesuit theologian with a respectable grasp of psychology, has dug deeply into the part processes that operate in human knowing, including those aspects of knowing that overlap with faith. Lonergan's first act or level of consciousness consists in experiencing; his second act or level is a kind of probing or hypothesis forming about that experience which he calls understanding; and the third act consists of judgement. Judgment involves for Lonergan a critical review of the experiential and contextual data in combination with a critical evaluation of one's own thought processes in terms of their assumptions, proclivities, biases, etc.—in other words, with a critical view of oneself as knower of the experience. In this way, a person arrives at the meaning of an experience for himself or herself, while also being attuned to the objective referent of the experience. A fourth act or level of consciousness consists in a move from cognition to the conative and emotional or attitudinal functions: the making of decisions for action, commitment, and ethical stances and for doing so with the elan and passionate feeling that we typically encounter in the state of being in love.

These are only the bare bones, in my reconstruction, of Lonergan's very difficult but eye-opening text. It seems to me that the distinctions between the part processes of knowing, acting and loving thus described (by a thinker who is well aware of the power of unconscious thought) give us a set of benchmarks for types of religiosity, especially in terms of arrest at certain points of a noetic process that is meant to be unifying but in many people fails in this aim. We all know people who experience the world or themselves without being interested in understanding their experiences, let alone bring their understanding to the critical test of judgment. And we also know people who stop at judgment and fail to move from knowing to praxis, let alone to that bubbly and hearty form of praxis that deserves to be called loving.

I hope I am beginning to win you over to the view that there are many other fascinating psychological features of religion besides conversion and whether it is a gradual or an abrupt process, and the question whether anybody's religiosity is intrinsic or extrinsic. Religion is complex enough to deserve attention to other details, and psychology is capable enough to approach at least some of these as yet unattended details with its many conceptual tools.

In my own most recent work *The Play of the Imagination*,[10] I consider all great cultural domains such as literature, the arts, science, music, and religion as illusionistic in the special sense of being neither solipsistically autistic nor naturalistically real, but symbolic in a shareable, corporate way. One needs cognitive development and formal education to come to feel at home with what goes on in these vast cultural symbol systems. We need to be and usually are tutored to gain skills in such illusion processing. In this vein, I want to end up with two questions for you to ponder:

1. How do people process the illusionistic images and propositions of religion that their culture, denomination, or faith group hands down to them?

2. Can a typology of such processing be developed that honors both the integrity and capability of psychology and the intricacy of religion?

Notes

1. This article was first presented as an invited lecture at the annual convention of the American Psychological Association in Washington, D.C., August 1986. The author, a former president of the Society for the Scientific Study of Religion, was awarded the 1986 Bier Award by Division 36 of the APA in recognition of his work in the psychology of religion.
2. Paul W. Pruyser was Henry March Pfeiffer Professor Emeritus at The Menninger Foundation, Topeka, Kansas.
3. Some material from this section is derived from my article "Psychology of religion as an academic subject: Its challenge to scholarship and pedagogical impact." *Religion, Journal of Kansas School of Religion at the University of Kansas* 14 (2): 1–4, 1977.
4. Pruyser, P. W. *A Dynamic Psychology of Religion*. New York: Harper & Row, 1968.
5. Vitz, P. *Psychology as Religion: The Cult of Self-Worship*. Grand Rapids: W. B. Eerdmans, 1977.
6. James, W. *The Varieties of Religious Experience*. New York: Longmans, Green & Company, 1902, 1945.

7. Allport, G. W. *The Individual and His Religion*. New York: Macmillan, 1951.
8. Goodenough, E. R. *The Psychology of Religious Experiences*. New York: Basic Books, 1965.
9. Lonergan B. J. F. *Insight: A Study of Human Understanding*. San Francisco: Harper & Row, 1957.
10. ______. *The Play of the Imagination*. New York: International Universities Press, 1983.

12

The Pruyser Legacy for the Psychology of Religion

Just what is the legacy of Paul Pruyser? It is questionable whether he would have anything to do with this question. Quite likely he would not. He was, as his colleague Virginia T. Eicholtz, wrote in a special tribute issue of *The Bulletin of the Menninger Clinic*,[1] a person with strong opinions and intense loves and hates.

It is interesting, however, that Pruyser, himself, was into "legacies" and "tributes." He wrote an incisive essay on "Sigmund Freud and his Legacy: Psychoanalytic Psychology of Religion" in Glock and Hammond's *Scientific Study of Religion*.[2] Furthermore, throughout his career, he wrote many tributes to colleagues who had distinguished themselves in one way or another, or who had died. Therefore this evaluation of his contributions would seem to be in order.

The James Connection

On the publication of Pruyser's *A Dynamic Psychology of Religion*, *The Christian Century* suggested that, "With some qualifications one could say that Paul Pruyser's is the most significant single work in the field of the psychology of religion since the classic study of William James."[3] Unfortunately, Pruyser's volume is already out of print, whereas James' *The Varieties of Religious Experience* is still available.[4] Nevertheless, Pruyser's impact is ongoing, as can be seen in references to his writings in over half of the recent texts devoted to the psychology of religion.[4]

For a scholar who died so short a time ago (1987), who was

writing the day before he died, and whose last essays were published posthumously, this influence on his contemporaries is, indeed, noteworthy. Like James, Pruyser had been awarded honors by several learned societies; the American Psychological Association, the Society for the Scientific Study of Religion, and the American Association for Pastoral Counselors.

It can be said that Pruyser was in the James "descriptive" tradition; both were masters at describing, in vivid and convincing detail, the experience of being religious. The only other writer to approach this proficiency of graphic detail was Walter Houston Clark in his 1958 volume *The Psychology of Religion*.[5]

It could also be said that Pruyser outdid James, as well as Clark, in his commitment to describing the everyday religion of the average person. For all James' intent to discuss "whatever men do in relation to that which they consider divine," he, nevertheless, followed the custom of his day in emphasizing the extremes—conversion and saintliness, for example.

Pruyser's interest was more mundane and, at the same time, more inclusive. Unlike James, Pruyser came close to implying that all persons have, and use, their Gods, in spite of the fact that they may not acknowledge them. Consummate clinician that he was, he encouraged counselors to listen for "religion" even when the words that were spoken did not include any overt "God talk."

Pruyser also went beyond James in yet another way: he was concerned with the "motivation for," as well as the "outcomes of," religion. It was not that James ignored these issues, but he clearly chose to focus on the fruits, or results, of religion over its roots or origins in human motives.

Of course, the roots and fruits coexist along a continuum. The issue is one of relative emphasis. Pruyser was not unconcerned with religious outcomes. His discussion of the difference between "coping" and "defensive" uses of religion and his warnings about over-concreteness and over-etherealness in religion are but two example of this concern. The weight of his thinking, however, was focused on the origins and intrapsychic functions of religion. As he stated in the article "The seamy side of current religious beliefs," reprinted in this volume as chapter 3, religion is "a problem-solving effort *sui generis*" (p. 49).

This concern for what James would call "roots" was based in Pruyser's penchant for thinking of religion within the psychoanalytic model. Pruyser wrote *post*-Freud; James wrote *pre*-Freud. Although James and Freud were, in a sense, contemporaries, James did not appear to be influenced by Freud, whereas Pruyser grounded his basic model in Freudian concepts.

This thorough grounding of his work in the psychoanalytic approach could be considered Pruyser's greatest contribution. It may be presumptuous to single him out as the sole psychoanalytic psychologist of religion since the question of a psychology of religion has received so much attention over the last half-century. By 1978, Beit-Hallahmi[6] identified over 1500 publications on the subject. Nevertheless, through the respect he engendered among mainline psychologists, Pruyser did more than any other scholar to keep the psychoanalytic psychology of religion alive.

Pruyser contributed significantly to remedying the theoretical void which, as early as 1969, James Dittes[7] suggested was the major weakness of the psychology of religion. Although Spilka[8] reiterated this observation a decade later (1978), Pruyser's significant contribution must be acknowledged. With this evaluation of his contribution, it is to a more thorough critique of Pruyser's use of the psychoanalytic model that we now turn.

The Freud Connection

Two aspects of Freud's thinking were adopted and adapted by Pruyser. These were Freud's contention that religion arose out of persons' feelings of helplessness in the face of their limitations and Freud's use of the term "illusion" to characterize religious thinking.

The Motivation for Religion

According to Freud, the motivation for religion lay in persons' desires to make their helplessness "tolerable." In his essay on Freud's legacy, Pruyser[2] quoted Freud's contention that the gods "must exorcise the terrors of nature, they must reconcile men to the cruelty of Fate, particularly as it is shown in death, and they must compensate them for the sufferings and privations which a civilized life in common has imposed on them" (p. 262). These three themes (control over the uncontrollable, a promise of meaning beyond the passage of time and death, and compensation for the deprivation suffered in society) were all affirmed by Pruyser as motivating forces that would keep religion alive well into the twenty-first century. As he stated,[2] religion is "an immensely relevant, useful, powerful tool for ameliorating what man [*sic*] feels to be his lot in life" (p. 331).

In predicting the future of religion, Pruyser saw no abatement of these human needs, save in the control of nature. He had great faith in the advancement of science, as did Freud. In fact, it might be said that he had a somewhat overly optimistic trust in the ability of science to conquer the ravages of nature. Unfortunately, the ravages of nature and the misuse of scientific knowledge have continued to prove such reliance misplaced. Earthquakes, tornadoes, airplane crashes, boat sinkings, floods, ozone layer depletions, atomic bombs, wars, and strategic defense system developments go on unabated. The need for gaining rational control over the human application of scientific discoveries as well as the elements of nature would seem to be as current today as it was in past centuries. Pruyser would not disagree; he would simply remain disappointed.

Pruyser's agreement with Freud that humans would do better to resign themselves to these anxieties over control, fate, and fortune provoked his evaluation that much religion was immature. He never quite affirmed Freud's contention that religion is "mass neurosis," but he certainly came close. In his essay "A psychological view of religion in the 1970s" included in this volume (Chapter 1), Pruyser unequivocally contended that religion of the evangelical, conservative, and dogmatic kind is dysfunctional. He discounted any religion that became overly "concrete." He was uncomfortable with religion that became too specific about its object of devotion or the character of divine action. In "The seamy side of current religious beliefs" (Chapter 2, this volume), Pruyser listed nine criteria for neurotic religion. The list includes regressions that fixate people in archaic modes of thought, compromises that do not effectively neutralize aggression, distortions that distort the natural or cultural environment, expenditures of energy that are incommensurate with the satisfactions that result, and sacrifices of growth capacities and talents.

In regard to what Pruyser termed "defensive religion," several times in his writing he stated a preference for "eschatological" thinking rather than "apocalyptic" thinking. The latter, typified by such biblical writings as Daniel and Revelation, was based on the belief there were explicit times, places, and events in which God would act, whereas eschatological thinking referred to the ultimate, but mysterious, control of history by God in an as yet only dimly understood manner. For Pruyser, apocalyptic thinking is immature; it serves regressive needs. In contrast, he saw eschatological religious thinking as mature because it serves interpersonal coping needs.

In his final essays, Pruyser[9] applied this dictum to himself as he discussed "hope" (p. 463ff). Here he advocated a somewhat stoical resignation to fate and rejected the kind of meaning that is based on an explicit form of afterlife. Here again, he reaffirmed his preference for a type of religion that involved persons in efforts to attain social justice rather than preoccupations with determining explicit times and places where God was active. This preference for a socially involved religion indicates that, while Pruyser agreed with Freud that religion originates in humans' need to overcome helplessness, unlike Freud, he was convinced that it was possible for persons to outgrow immature religion's infantile foundations.

Pruyser offered no explanation of how this movement toward maturity could occur other than to suggest that religion could develop from autistic to realistic; from primary to secondary process thinking. He summed up this process with the term "intelligence." Intelligent religion, for Pruyser, is non-dogmatic, almost non-institutional, non-concrete, and socially conscious.

Although he saw mature religion as non-dogmatic, Pruyser was one psychologist of religion who called for paying serious attention to theology.[3,10] In the final analysis, however, he explained theological differences as a consequence of psychological dynamics. He followed many scientists from the 1700s to the present in expressing a disdain for much of the substantive content of traditional institutional religion. Although it is true that he was very popular with many leaders in organized religion during his career,[11] he, nevertheless, remained somewhat unimpressed and uninformed regarding the importance of various religious dogmas in social and emotional adjustment. His implicit "universalism" treated casually many beliefs that have been life-determining for the mental health of many persons. His distinction between mature religion and its immature forms was more a broad-sweep model than a sensitive consideration of the import of theological distinctives.

In this regard, it may be that Pruyser agreed with Freud's conclusion that religion was, in the final analysis, a "delusion," not simply an illusion as his book *The Future of an Illusion*[12] might imply. In spite of the fact that Oskar Pfister claimed that Freud was critical only of "bad" religion, Freud's opinions, expressed in such books as *Totem and Taboo*,[13] *Civilization and Its Discontents*,[14] and *Moses and Monotheism*,[15] reveal his true feelings—that the content of religion was pure projection, i.e. untrue.

By affirming a stoic acceptance of life's realities and emphasizing the centrality of social justice for mature religion, Pruyser may have come to a similar conclusion. Toward the end of his life, he spoke of no longer feeling comfortable participating in organized religion. Although Pruyser reportedly remained a Presbyterian elder, he nevertheless stated that worshipping with the same people week after week had become boring and that he much preferred being where groups were acting in behalf of the poor and oppressed. The article "Where do we go from here" (Chapter 10, this volume) evidences this point of view.

While such a concern for the poor and oppressed is commendable, it may nevertheless reflect Pruyser's sincere opinion that the content of religion was mere projection, i.e., delusional. At the very least, beliefs or content were not psychologically central.

Illusion in Religious Thinking

Although Pruyser may have considered religious "content" delusional, he felt that religious "thinking" is illusional. This is the second area in which Pruyser followed Freud. Freud contended that all thought that reached beyond concrete reality is illusional. Pruyser extended Freud's thinking by providing a psychodynamic model for these "illusionistic" processes. He disagreed with Freud concerning the legitimacy of this type of thinking. Pruyser believed that religious illusioning, like art and music, is a valid and inevitable part of life.

This difference between Freud and Pruyser on the status of religious illusions is a subtle and important one. Hood[16] has noted that psychologists with personal religious commitments tend to emphasize Freud's seeming neutrality toward illusions (p. 4). These religious psychologists have suggested that Freud believed in the necessity of illusions and that he simply felt that the illusion that science held the answers to human needs was a better illusion than religion.[17] However, Hood concluded that these religiously committed psychologists have failed to realize that Freud looked on science as reality based while religion, to him, was grounded in autistic wish-fulfillment. Ultimately, Freud felt that illusion, as a dynamic process, would be replaced by reality testing based on facts. Religion and science, according to Freud, were not the same. Religion was delusional and unnecessary for mature persons.

This is where Pruyser parted company with Freud. Although he, too, considered the content of religion ultimately delusional, he also considered illusions to be a necessary part of mature, as well as immature, psychological development. This places Pruyser in a different position from that held by Freud's early optimistic critic, Oskar Pfister[18] who spoke for all religiously committed psychologists in insisting that Freud felt that science was simply a better illusion than religion. Pruyser did not go that far. He saw religion as ultimately serving a different function from that served by science, and he agreed with Rizzutto[19] that "Reality and illusion are not contradictory terms" (p. 209).

The key to Pruyser's contention that "reality and illusion are not contradictory" lay in his understanding of aesthetics, particularly art. Here Pruyser is dependent on Winnicott,[20] who contended that the "illusory experience" was the basis for culture. And culture is the uniquely human essence of reality—be that the reality of society or of science. Freud wrote at a time when a positivistic philosophy of science did not comprehend the truth that all reality is based on apriori assumptions, which, in turn, are agreed upon by groups of persons. Winnicott, and Pruyser after him, were aware of what Berger and Luckman[21] termed the "social construction of reality."

Unfortunately, Pruyser's description of Winnicott's theory of illusory "transitional objects" reflected more a fascination with these ideas than an understanding of them. Because of his distrust of dogma and his optimistic trust in science, he may not have appreciated fully the profundity of Winnicott's contention that the compulsive need for teddy bears, blankets, or other idiosyncratic objects among infants was the child's first experience of the divine.

Winnicott's focus was put on the parent and the family, who reinforced and shared the illusion, whereas Pruyser's emphasis was on the infant's need for security. For this reason he did not emphasize the psychosocial reality that shared illusions, beginning in infancy, are the very stuff of culture. As Hood[13] states, " . . . for Winnicott, while culture has a material base, it is never simply material. It is shared SUBJECTIVE EXPERIENCE, a common mode of experiencing our humanity which is necessarily illusory in a sense that takes us well beyond Freud" (p. 16). Pruyser affirmed Winnicott's importance for his contention that religion and art are essential, but apparently he missed the central idea that illusions are the cultural fabric from which science, as well as religion, is formed.

Winnicott makes a distinction between "object relating" and "object use." In *A Dynamic Psychology of Religion*,[3] Pruyser apparently affirmed this point of view in contending that a person's experience of God was a prime example of object relations. However, he never went as far as Winnicott, who suggested that it is absolutely necessary to differentiate illusory objects from their essential natures. Winnicott[16] noted that it is essential to accept the paradox that "the baby creates the object, but the object was there waiting to be created" (p. 89). Hood[13] states the issue succinctly, "Unlike object RELATING, in which the object has no independent existence as indicated by the subject's omnipotent control over it, object USE entails no magical control: the object has independent existence. . . . The object's autonomous existence survives the subject's will and cannot be "wished away" (p. 18; emphasis added).

Pruyser would be confused with Winnicott's paradox concerning the independent existence of the object of faith because he basically believed that religious illusions were ultimately "unreal." This led him to the confusing position of promoting client diagnosis based on religious ideation in his *The Minister as Diagnostician*[7] but distancing himself from research designed to make operational the importance of dogmatic differences in psychological evaluations.

Ironically, it is in this research on differences in beliefs about the character of God and God's intent for human life that Pruyser's most lasting legacy may be found. The Religious Status Interview and the Religious Status Inventory are the results of a program of research that assesses persons along the dimensions that Pruyser suggested were important categories for ministers to use in religious diagnosis.[22] In his long-time association with the Menninger Foundation, Pruyser promoted the inclusion of serious religious diagnosis by chaplains in the case studies of psychiatric patients. He suggested in *The Minister as Diagnostician*[10] that such a diagnosis should be grounded in theology—which was the forte of ministerial functioning.

He proposed such categories as Awareness of God, Dependence on God, Awareness of God's Grace, Forgiveness, Involvement in Organized Religion, Individual and Social Ethics, Vocation, and Openness in Faith. These categories were overt dogmatic dimensions within the Judeo-Christian tradition. Terming these dimensions "functional theology," Malony[22] and his students have designed standardized measures that have proved valid in distinguishing persons along varying levels of emotional disturbance, aged persons who experience less life distress, church members judged more religiously mature by their pastors, and individuals who rated themselves as "more religious."

Just before his death, Pruyser indicated that he did not support this application of his ideas into psychometric measures. Yet, such standardized tests of "optimal religious functioning" may turn out to be among his most enduring legacies. Despite the fact that he was uncomfortable when theological beliefs were taken seriously, his contention that psychologists of religion should no longer avoid the validity question of the reality of God may prove to be a significant theme in the psychology of religion.

Pruyser may implicitly have been too closely aligned with Freud's belief that the substance of religion is, in the final analysis, delusion but he was also implicitly and intuitively distrustful of such an assertion. He probably believed more than he realized, as his affirmation of the ideas of Winnicott demonstrates. We are convinced that Pruyser struggled hard with the reality of God, but that his struggle was probably more with the nature of God than with the existence of God. In personal conversations, he expressed an attraction to the orthodox Judaic proscription against imposing any limitation on God—even in the pronunciation of God's name!

Summary and Conclusion

Paul W. Pruyser should be considered the most influential psychoanalytic psychologist of religion in the last quarter of the twentieth century. Collection of his published works, coupled with this evaluation of his legacy, is intended to make his contributions accessible to scholars and students alike.

We have noted that Pruyser could best be known as a "humanistic psychoanalytic thinker." By intent and coincidence, he aligned himself with one of the world's best known psychoanalytic centers, the Menninger Foundation. There he distinguished himself both as a thinker and writer. He collaborated with the best minds in that setting, including Karl Menninger himself. He was known as a perceptive clinician, an intuitive theorizer, a consummate critic, a tireless scholar, and a worthy colleague. He chose to invest much of his intellectual energy in the theme of this volume, the psychology of religion. As such his significance became known far and wide. Some even accused him of being a frustrated theologian in psychologist's clothing, an ascription he would likely not deny at the same time as he would affirm strongly his identity as a clinical psychologist.

Admired by many in both the scholarly and religious communities, Pruyser may best be remembered for the following:

- a unique blend of personal biography and intellectual curiosity
- a resistance to arbitrary authority and dogmatic institutionalization of religion
- a life-long concern for social justice and benevolence beginning in his participation in the Dutch underground and ending in his assertion that true religion was involved in helping persons
- a serious attempt to delineate the differences between defensive and coping religious styles
- a perceptive description of the nature of religious thinking as it can be found in such related endeavors as art and music
- a call for the psychology of religion to pay serious attention to the validity question of the existence of God and differences in religious belief
- an awareness of how religion functions in the developmental stages of life
- a willingness to accord a legitimate role for all members of the mental health team, including chaplains
- a critical extension of psychoanalytic thinking about religion beyond the negative evaluation of Freud

We count it a unique privilege to have been compatriots of Paul Pruyser, and we hope that his contributions will provoke further developments among scholars of psychology and religion.

Notes

1. Eicholtz V. T. In Memoriam: Paul W. Pruyser, Ph.D. (1916–1987) *Bulletin of the Menninger Clinic, 51*(5), 420, 1987.
2. Pruyser, P. W. Sigmund Freud and his legacy: Psychoanalytic psychology of religion. In C. Y. Glock and P. E. Hammond *Beyond the Classics: Essays in the Scientific Study of Religion*. New York: Harper, 1973, 243-290.
3. Pruyser P. W. *A Dynamic Psychology of Religion*. New York: Harper, 1968.
4. James, W. *The Varieties of Religious Experience*. London: Longmans, Green and Company, 1945.
5. Clark, W. H. *The Psychology of Religion*. New York: McMillan, 1958.
6. Beit-Hallahmi, B. *Psychoanalysis and religion: A bibliography*. Norwood, PA: Norwood Editions, 1978.
7. Dittes, J. E. The psychology of religion in G. Lindzey & E. Aronson, Editors, *The Handbook of Social Psychology*, (Ed. 2) New York: Addison Wesley, 602, 1969.
8. Spilka, B. The current state of the psychology of religion. *Bulletin of the Council for the Study of Religion*. *9*(4), 96–99, 1978.
9. Pruyser, P. W. Maintaining hope in adversity. *Bulletin of the Menninger Clinic, 51*, (5), 463–474, 1987.
10. Pruyser P. W. *The Minister as Diagnostician*, Philadelphia: Westminister Press, 1976.
11. The bibliography of the Writings of Pruyser in *The Bulletin of the Menninger Clinic* [1987, *51*(5), 481–489], contains references to the many consultations and articles contributed by Pruyser to institutional religion. It is reprinted at the end of this book.
12. Freud, S. *The standard edition of the complete psychological works of Sigmund Freud*. James Strachey, Editor. London: Hogarth Press (1927) *The future of illusion*, Volume 21.
13. Freud, S. *The standard edition of the complete psychological works of Sigmund Freud*. James Strachey, Editor. London: Hogarth Press (1913) *Totem and Taboo*, Volume 12.
14. Freud, S. *The standard edition of the complete psychological works of Sigmund Freud*. James Strachey, Editor. London: Hogarth Press (1930) *Civilization and its discontents*, Volume 21.
15. Freud, S. *The standard edition of the complete psychological works of Sigmund Freud*. James Strachey, Editor. London: Hogarth Press (1939) *Moses and monotheism*, Volume 23.
16. Hood, Ralph W., Jr. Religion and the reality principle: Religious truth and Freudian theory. Presentation at the Annual Meeting of the American Psychological Association, New Orleans, August, 1989.

17. Malony, H. N. *Understanding Your Faith: A Christian Psychologist Helps You Look at Your Religious Experiences*. Nashville, Tennessee: Abingdon Press, 1978.
18. Freud, S., Pfister, O. *Psychoanalysis and faith: The letters of Sigmund Freud and Oskar Pfister*. H. Meng, E. L. Freud, Eds, E. Mosbacher, Translator. New York: Basic Books, 1963.
19. Rizzutto, A. M. *The Birth of the Living God*. Chicago: University of Chicago Press, 1979.
20. Winnicott, D. W. *Playing and Reality*. New York: Basic Books, 1971.
21. Berger, P. L., Luckman, T. *The Social Construction of Reality*. New York: Doubleday Anchor, 1967.
22. Malony, H. N. The clinical measurement of optimal religious functioning. *Review of Religious Research, 30* (1), 3–17, 1988.

Bibliography of the Writings of Paul W. Pruyser, Ph.D.

The following bibliography of Dr. Pruyser's works in English is organized topically to reflect his major areas of interest; one will notice that some works could fit in more than one area, which demonstrates the breadth of Dr. Pruyser's thought. Within topics, the bibliography is organized by books, book chapters, journal articles, and edited works, all listed chronologically. The bibliography does not include book reviews.

Psychology of Religion

Books

A dynamic psychology of religion. New York: Harper & Row, 1968.

Between belief and unbelief. New York: Harper & Row, 1974.

The minister as diagnostician: Personal problems in pastoral perspective. Philadelphia: Westminster Press, 1976.

Book Chapters

Contributions to *Religion in the developing personality* (Proceedings of the Second Academy Symposium 1958, Academy of Religion and Mental Health). New York: New York University Press, 1960.

Foreword to *Pastoral care and clinical training in America* by Heije Faber (pp. 7–8). Arnhem: Van Loghum Slaterus, 1961.

Religious and spiritual values (with K. A. Menninger). In S. Doniger (Ed.), *Becoming the complete adult* (pp. 95–118). New York: Association Press, 1962.

A psychological commentary on the doctrine of man in Calvin. In *Proceedings of the tenth annual convention of the Christian Association for Psychological Studies* (pp. 3–12). Grand Rapids, MI: Christian Association for Psychological Studies, 1963.

Contributions to *Psychology and religion: A contemporary dialogue* (J. Havens, Ed.). Princeton, NJ: Van Nostrand, 1968.

The master hand: Psychological notes on pastoral blessing. In W. B. Oglesby, Jr. (Ed.), *The new shape of pastoral theology: Essays in honor of Seward Hiltner* (pp. 352–365). Nashville: Abingdon Press, 1969.

Thought organization in religion. In W. A. Sadler, Jr. (Ed.), *Personality and religion: The role of religion in personality development* (pp. 57–72). New York: Harper & Row, 1970.

Sigmund Freud and his legacy: Psychoanalytic psychology of religion. In C. Y. Glock & P. E. Hammond (Eds.), *Beyond the classics? Essays in the scientific study of religion* (pp. 243–290). New York: Harper & Row, 1973.

Problems of definition and conception in the psychological study of religious unbelief. In A. W. Eister (Ed.), *Changing perspectives in the scientific study of religion* (pp. 185–200). New York: Wiley-Interscience, 1974.

Church sponsored hospitals and church aims. In V. H. Neufeld (Ed.), *If we can love: The Mennonite mental health story* (pp. 315–320). Newton, KS: Faith and Life Press, 1983.

The diagnostic process in pastoral care. In A. W. R. Sipe & C. J. Rowe (Eds.), *Psychiatry, ministry and pastoral counseling* (rev. ed., pp. 103–116). Collegeville, MN: Liturgical Press, 1984.

Psychoanalysis and the sacred. In P. E. Hammond (Ed.), *The sacred in a secular age: Toward revision in the scientific study of religion* (pp. 257–267). Berkeley, CA: University of California Press, 1985.

A transformational understanding of humanity. In P. W. Pruyser (Ed.), *Changing views of the human condition* (pp. 1–11). Macon, GA: Mercer University Press, 1987.

The tutored imagination in religion. In P. W. Pruyser (Ed.), *Changing views of the human condition* (pp. 101–117). Macon, GA: Mercer University Press, 1987.

Epilogue. In P. W. Pruyser (Ed.), *Changing views of the human condition* (pp. 196–200). Macon, GA: Mercer University Press, 1987.

Five articles: Doubt and unbelief; health and illness; hope and despair; psychopathology and religion; religious evaluation and diagnosis. In H. N. Malony, R. Hunter, L. O. Mills, & J. Patton (Eds.), *Dictionary of pastoral care and counseling*. New York: Abingdon Press, 1990.

Journal Articles

Religion and psychiatry. *Menninger Quarterly, 11*(3), 2-5, 1957.

Toward a doctrine of man in psychiatry and theology. *Pastoral Psychology, 9*, 9-13, 1958. Reprinted in S. Doniger (Ed.), *The nature of man in theological and psychological perspective* (pp. 35-41). New York: Harper Brothers, 1962.

Some trends in the psychology of religion. *Journal of Religion, 40*, 113-129, 1960. Reprinted in O. Strunk, Jr. (Ed.), *The psychology of religion: Historical and interpretive teachings* (pp. 99-116). Nashville: Abingdon Press, 1971; and in H. N. Malony (Ed.), *Current perspectives in the psychology of religion* (pp. 53-73). Grand Rapids, MI: Eerdmans, 1977.

Religion and mental illness. *Pastoral Psychology, 12*(117), 52-53, 1961.

Nathan and David: A psychological footnote. *Pastoral Psychology, 13*(121), 14-18, 1962.

Pass on the good news. *Presbyterian Life, 15*(23), 5-9, 42, December 1, 1962.

Phenomenology and dynamics of hoping. *Journal for the Scientific Study of Religion, 3*, 86-96, 1963.

Erikson's *Young Man Luther:* A new chapter in the psychology of religion. *Journal for the Scientific Study of Religion, 2*, 238-242, 1963. Reprinted as "From Freud to Erikson: Developments in the psychology of religion" in R. A. Johnson (Ed.), *Psychohistory and religion: The case of* Young Man Luther (pp. 88-96). Philadelphia: Fortress Press, 1977.

Pastoral conversations. *Pastoral Psychology, 14*(133), 17-21, 1963.

The church in the mental hospital (with T. W. Klink). *Presbyterian Life, 17*(3), 15-16, 38-41, February 1, 1964.

Anxiety, guilt, and shame in the atonement. *Theology Today, 21*, 15-33, 1964.

Life and death of a symbol: A history of the Holy Ghost concept and its emblems. *McCormick Quarterly, 18* (Special supplement: Myth and modern man), 5-22, January, 1965.

The freedom to be oneself. *Pastoral Psychology, 16*(157), 18-25, 1965.

Religion and psychiatry: A polygon of relationships. *Journal of the American Medical Association, 195*, 197-202, 1966. Reprinted in D. W. Montgomery (Ed.), *Healing and wholeness* (pp. 61-74). Richmond, VA: John Knox Press, 1971.

Five edifying discourses on mental illness and health. *Pastoral Psychology, 17*(164), 9-18, 1966.

Joy. *Journal of Pastoral Care, 20*, 90-94, 1966.

Psychological examination: Augustine. *Journal for the Scientific Study of Religion, 5*, 284-289, 1966.

Anton T. Boisen and the psychology of religion. *Journal of Pastoral Care, 21*, 209–219, 1967.

Calvin's view of man: A psychological commentary. *Theology Today, 26* 51–68, 1969.

A psychological view of religion in the 1970s. *Bulletin of the Menninger Clinic, 35*, 77–97, 1971., Reprinted in *Pastoral Psychology, 23*(220), 21–26, 28–30, 32–36, 38, 1972.

Assessment of the patient's religious attitudes in the psychiatric case study. *Bulletin of the Menninger Clinic, 35*, 272–291, 1971.

The church, the Mennonites and the mentally ill. *Mennonite Brethren Herald, 11*(4), 2–4, 27, February 25, 1972.

The use and neglect of pastoral resources. *Pastoral Psychology, 23*, 5–17, 1972.

Permissiveness—Or how to curse without being accountable for the use of foul language [Editorial]. *Newsletter, Kansas District Branch, American Psychiatric Association*, p. 2, February, 1973.

Intrusiveness—The beleaguered individual [Editorial]. *Newsletter, Kansas District Branch, American Psychiatric Association*, p. 2, May, 1973.

The minister as diagnostician. *Perkins Journal* (Perkins School of Theology), *27*(2), 1–10, 1973.

Aging: Downward, upward, or forward? *Pastoral Psychology, 24*(229), 102–118, 1975.

Lessons from art theory for the psychology of religion. *Journal for the Scientific Study of Religion, 15*, 1–14, 1976.

Revisiting Erikson's contributions to the psychology of religion. *Psychohistory Review, 5*(3), 32–35, 1976.

Psychology of religion as an academic subject: Its challenge to scholarship and pedagogical impact. *Religion* (Journal of the Kansas School of Religion at the University of Kansas), *14*(2), 1–4, 1977.

The seamy side of current religious beliefs. *Bulletin of the Menninger Clinic, 41*, 329–348, 1977. Reprinted in *Pastoral Psychology, 26*, 150–167, 1978.

Psychoanalytic method in the study of religious meanings. *Psychohistory Review, 6*(4), 45–50, 1978.

Narcissism in contemporary religion. *Journal of Pastoral Care, 32*, 219–231, 1978.

Psychological roots and branches of belief. *Pastoral Psychology, 28*, 8–20, 1979.

The ambiguities of religion and pain control. *Theology Today, 38*, 5–15, 1981.

Religion in the psychiatric hospital: A reassessment. *Journal of Pastoral Care, 38*, 5–16, 1984.

Where do we go from here? Scenarios for the psychology of religion. *Journal for the Scientific Study of Religion, 26*, 173–181, 1987.

Edited Works

Bibliographical focus: Erikson's *Young Man Luther* [three papers]. *Journal for the Scientific Study of Religion, 2*, 238–252, 1963.

St. Augustine's confessions: Perspectives and inquiries [five papers]. *Journal for the Scientific Study of Religion, 5*, 130–152, 1965; *5*, 273–289, 1966.

Introduction to "Religious and psychological beliefs: Past and present encounters" [four papers]. *Bulletin of the Menninger Clinic, 49*, 287–288, 1985.

Changing view of the human condition. Macon, GA: Mercer University Press, 1987.

Philosophical Essays

Book Chapters

Morals, values, and mental health (by K. A. Menninger & P. W. Pruyser). In A. Deutsch & H. Fishman (Eds.), *Encyclopedia of mental health* (Vol. 4, pp. 1244–1255). New York: Franklin Watts, 1963.

Problems of will and willing: A selective historical survey. In J. N. Lapsley (Ed.), *The concept of willing: Outdated idea or essential key to man's future?* (pp. 23–50). Nashville: Abingdon Press, 1967.

Journal Articles

The idea of destiny. *Hibbert Journal, 57*, 380–385, 1959.

Phenomenology, existential psychology, and psychoanalytic ego psychology. *Christian Scholar, 44*, 56–73, 1961.

The practice of science and values: A psychologist's odyssey. *Bulletin of the Menninger Clinic, 37*, 133–148, 1973.

Comment on "Science and technology vs. ethics and morals." *Bulletin of the Menninger Clinic, 37*, 163–168, 1973.

Existential impact of professional exposure to life-threatening or terminal illness. *Bulletin of the Menninger Clinic, 48*, 357–367, 1984.

Maintaining hope in adversity. *Pastoral Psychology, 35*, 120–131, 1986. Reprinted in *Bulletin of the Menninger Clinic, 51*, 463–474, 1987.

The Diagnostic Process

Books

A manual for psychiatric case study (revised edition by K. A. Menninger with M. Mayman & P. W. Pruyser). New York: Grune & Stratton, 1962.

The psychological examination: A guide for clinicians. New York: International Universities Press, 1979.

Book Chapters

The urge to classify (by K. A. Menninger with M. Mayman & P. W. Pruyser). In R. A. Dentler (Ed.), *Major American social problems* (pp. 434–438). Chicago: Rand McNally, 1967. Reprinted from *The vital balance: The life process in mental health and illness.* New York: Viking Press, 1963.

The diagnostic process: Touchstone of medicine's values. In W. R. Rogers & D. Barnard (Eds.), *Nourishing the humanistic in medicine: Interactions with the social sciences* (pp. 245–261). Pittsburgh: University of Pittsburgh Press, 1979. Reprinted in F. Shectman & W. H. Smith (Eds.), *Diagnostic understanding and treatment planning: The elusive connection* (pp. 5–17). New York: Wiley, 1984.

Journal Articles

The beleaguered individual: Images of man in clinical practice. *Bulletin of the Menninger Clinic, 37,* 433–450, 1973.

Psychiatric space flights [Editorial]. *Newsletter, Kansas District Branch, American Psychiatric Association,* p. 2, August, 1974.

Language pitfalls in diagnostic thought and work (with K. A. Menninger). *Bulletin of the Menninger Clinic, 40,* 417–434, 1976. Reprinted in F. Shectman & W. H. Smith (Eds.), *Diagnostic understanding and treatment planning: The elusive connection* (pp. 55–68). New York: Wiley, 1984.

Neuropsychological assessment in a psychoanalytic setting: The mind-body problem in clinical practice (by J. G. Allen, L. Lewis, M. J. Peebles, & P. W. Pruyser). *Bulletin of the Menninger Clinic, 50,* 5–21, 1986.

Edited Works

Introduction to "Diagnosis and the difference it makes" [15 papers]. *Bulletin of the Menninger Clinic, 40,* 411–416, 1976.

Epilogue to "Diagnosis and the difference it makes" [15 papers]. *Bulletin of the Menninger Clinic, 40*, 602, 1976.
Diagnosis and the difference it makes. New York: Aronson, 1976.

Art, Literature, and Creativity

Book

The play of the imagination: Toward a psychoanalysis of culture. New York: International Universities Press, 1983.

Journal Articles

The vitally balanced alphabet. *TRP* (employee newsletter of the Menninger Foundation), *27*(11), 3, 1967.
The SSSR anniversary alphabet. *Journal for the Scientific Study of Religion, 14*, 103–106, 1975.
An essay on creativity. *Bulletin of the Menninger Clinic, 43*, 294–353, 1979.
Creativity in the life and work of Karl Menninger, M.D.: An interview. *Bulletin of the Menninger Clinic, 43*, 389–392, 1979.
Forms and functions of the imagination in religion. *Bulletin of the Menninger Clinic, 49*, 353–370, 1985.
Creativity in aging persons. *Bulletin of the Menninger Clinic, 51*, 425–435, 1987.
An authors' alphabet. *Bulletin of the Menninger Clinic, 51*, 500–504, 1987.

Personality Theory and Psychopathology

Book

The vital balance: The life process in mental health and illness (by K. A. Menninger with M. Mayman & P. W. Pruyser). New York: Viking Press, 1963.

Book Chapters

Anxiety: Affect or cognitive state? In S. Hiltner & K. Menninger (Eds.), *Constructive aspects of anxiety* (pp. 121–141). New York: Abingdon Press, 1963.

A historical review of the development of the concept of schizophrenia (by R. Cancro & P. W. Pruyser). In R. Cancro (Ed.), *The schizophrenic reactions: A critique of the concept, hospital treatment, and current research* (pp. 3–12). New York: Brunner/Mazel, 1970. Reprinted in *Bulletin of the Menninger Clinic, 34*, 61–70, 1970.

"A child is being beaten": Metapsychology as the whipping boy. In S. Smith (Ed.), *The human mind revisited: Essays in honor of Karl A. Menninger* (pp. 369–396). New York: International Universities Press, 1978.

Journal Articles

The unitary concept of mental illness (by K. A. Menninger, H. Ellenberger, P. W. Pruyser, & M. Mayman). *Bulletin of the Menninger Clinic, 22*, 4–12, 1958. Reprinted in *Pastoral Psychology, 10*(94), 13–19, 1959; and in W. S. Sahakian (Ed.), *Psychopathology today: Experimentation, theory and research* (pp. 85–90). Itasca, IL: F. E. Peacock, 1970.

Is mental health possible? *Bulletin of the Menninger Clinic, 22*, 58–66, 1958.

Development, maturation, and the problem of age-specificity. *McCormick Speaking, 13*(4), 19–25, 1960.

Fear. *Crossroads, 11*(2), 92–95, January-March, 1961.

Depression. *Crossroads, 11*(4), 78–80, July-September, 1961. Reprinted in *The Mennonite*, pp., 114–116, February 20, 1962.

Delineation of the problem. *McCormick Quarterly, 16* (Special supplement: The authoritarian personality and mass movements), 5–12, May, 1963.

Psychological aspects of working. *Reflection, 65*(3), 1–6, 1968.

What splits in "splitting"? A scrutiny of the concept of splitting in psychoanalysis and psychiatry. *Bulletin of the Menninger Clinic, 39*, 1–46, 1975.

Work: Curse or blessing? A psychoanalytic systematization. *Bulletin of the Menninger Clinic, 44*, 59–73, 1980.

Edited Works

Introduction to "The early development of affects and moods: An interdisciplinary conference" [five papers]. *Bulletin of the Menninger Clinic, 43*, 1–2, 1979.

Introduction to "Moral development and its failures" [seven papers and responses]. *Bulletin of the Menninger Clinic, 44*, 423, 1980.

Psychiatric Treatment

Journal Articles

The prescription of treatment (by K. A. Menninger, P. W. Pruyser, M. Mayman, & M. Houston). *Bulletin of the Menninger Clinic, 24*, 217-249, 1960.

Trends and issues in community psychiatry. *McCormick Quarterly, 21* (Special issue), 9-22, July, 1967.

Mental health in politics [Editorial]. *Newsletter, Kansas District Branch, American Psychiatric Association*, p. 2, August, 1972.

Edited Works

Preface to "The Menninger Hospital's Guide to the Order Sheet." *Bulletin of the Menninger Clinic, 46*, 3-11, 1982.

Introduction to "Psychoanalytic hospital psychiatry in the 1980s: Celebrating the 60th anniversary of the Menninger Foundation's adult hospital" [nine papers]. *Bulletin of the Menninger Clinic, 49*, 399, 1985.

Education

Book Chapter

The impact of the psychological disciplines on the training of clergy. In *New thrusts in clinical pastoral education* (Proceedings of the fall conference of the Association for Clinical Pastoral Education, October 1967, Kansas City, Missouri, pp. 29-41). Reprinted in *Pastoral Psychology, 19*(187), 21-32, 1968.

Journal Articles

Sex instruction for young people. *Pastoral Psychology, 12*(118), 47-49, 1961.

Existentialist notes on professional education. *Social Work, 8*, 82-87, 1963.

The psychological disciplines in theological education. *Concordia Theological Monthly, 34*, 472-478, 1963.

Freedom and authority in the school. *Independent School Bulletin, 25*, 16-20, 1966.

Difficulties in learning—A talk to teachers. *Bulletin of the Menninger Clinic, 30*, 71-84, 1966.

New professionals in mental health: A perspective. *Journal of the National Association of Private Psychiatric Hospitals, 21*(1), 21-25, 1970.

Now what? *Bulletin of the Menninger Clinic, 51*, 475-480, 1987.

Edited Works

Introduction to "Psychiatric education—At what cost?" *Bulletin of the Menninger Clinic, 35*, 429, 1971.

Biographical and Historical Essays

Journal Articles

An editorial tribute to Jeanetta Lyle Menninger. *Bulletin of the Menninger Clinic, 35*, 3-4, 1971.

Tribute [on the death of Thomas W. Klink]. *Journal of Pastoral Care, 25*, 45-46, 1971.

The man of the month: Kenneth R. Mitchell. *Pastoral Psychology, 23*(222), 4, 66, 1972.

An appreciation of Karl Menninger's books. *Bulletin of the Menninger Clinic, 37*, 401-404, 1973. Reprinted in *Menninger Perspective, 14*(1/2), 26-27, 1983.

In memoriam: Herman Gijsbert van der Waals, M.D. (1894-1974). *Bulletin of the Menninger Clinic, 38*, 187-188, 1974.

In memoriam: Margaret Mead, Ph.D. (1901-1978). *Bulletin of the Menninger Clinic, 43*, 264-266, 1979.

In memoriam: Gardner Murphy, Ph.D., D.Sc. (1895-1979). *Bulletin of the Menninger Clinic, 43*, 266-267, 1979.

Seward Hiltner's contributions to allied disciplines—Medicine and psychiatry. *Pastoral Psychology, 29*, 17-23, 1980.

Editor's note [on the death of Charles K. Hofling, M.D.]. *Bulletin of the Menninger Clinic, 44*, 325, 1980.

Religio Medici: Karl A. Menninger, Calvinism and the Presbyterian Church. *Journal of Presbyterian History, 59*, 59-72, 1981.

Pastoral theologian of the year: Donald W. Capps. *Pastoral Psychology, 30*, 3-5, 1981.

The epic of Gilgamesh (with J. T. Luke). *American Imago, 39*, 73-93, 1982.

Index